PRAISE FOR
HEROES AMONG US

"However any of us feel about the politics of the war in Iraq, we must always honor the men and women who have volunteered for this difficult, dangerous duty. Chuck Larson has given us an inspirational and memorable collection of the personal lives and heroics of these brave young Americans. These are stories to be remembered and cherished."
                                                                    —Tom Brokaw

"Here are the voices that need to be heard . . . those of the men and women on the ground in the war on terror. They are courageous, humane, and gripping. Above all, they are truthful. If you want to understand this war and understand those who are fighting it, you must read this book."
                                                                    —Sean Hannity

"*Heroes Among Us* reminds us that many of our troops want to be in this fight. They believe in the mission, they believe in their country, and they believe in each other."
                                                —Laura Ingraham,
                                                talk radio host and author

"This book is an extraordinary testimonial to both heroism and humanity. These accounts are powerful reminders of why Americans in uniform deserve our respect, our support, and our gratitude."
                                                        —Senator Joe Lieberman

"During my time in the military, what I found most inspiring as well as most humbling is the courage and bravery exemplified by our men and women on the front line. They define honor and sacrifice; our nation is forever indebted to their souls. The stories, chronicled with unflinching honesty, capture their experience. *Heroes Among Us* transcends politics and ideology and will inspire us all."   —General Richard Myers

"On September 11th, my son, Todd, and the other passengers and crew of United Flight 93 launched the first counterattack in our homeland. . . . On that day, 'Let's roll' became a rallying cry across our nation. This spirit lives on today through the men and women who continue the fight in Iraq and Afghanistan. Chuck's account of their stories helps us to document their valor for generations to come."
                                                                    —David Beamer

HEROES AMONG US

FIRSTHAND ACCOUNTS OF COMBAT
FROM AMERICA'S MOST DECORATED WARRIORS
IN IRAQ AND AFGHANISTAN

Edited and with an Introduction by
Major Chuck Larson

With a Foreword by
General Tommy Franks

and an Afterword by
Senator John McCain

NAL
CALIBER

NAL Caliber
Published by New American Library, a division of
Penguin Group (USA) Inc., 375 Hudson Street,
New York, New York 10014, USA
Penguin Group (Canada), 90 Eglinton Avenue East, Suite 700, Toronto,
Ontario M4P 2Y3, Canada (a division of Pearson Penguin Canada Inc.)
Penguin Books Ltd., 80 Strand, London WC2R 0RL, England
Penguin Ireland, 25 St. Stephen's Green, Dublin 2,
Ireland (a division of Penguin Books Ltd.)
Penguin Group (Australia), 250 Camberwell Road, Camberwell, Victoria 3124,
Australia (a division of Pearson Australia Group Pty. Ltd.)
Penguin Books India Pvt. Ltd., 11 Community Centre, Panchsheel Park,
New Delhi - 110 017, India
Penguin Group (NZ), 67 Apollo Drive, Rosedale, North Shore 0632,
New Zealand (a division of Pearson New Zealand Ltd.)
Penguin Books (South Africa) (Pty.) Ltd., 24 Sturdee Avenue,
Rosebank, Johannesburg 2196, South Africa

Penguin Books Ltd., Registered Offices:
80 Strand, London WC2R 0RL, England

Published by NAL Caliber, an imprint of New American Library, a division of Penguin Group (USA) Inc.
Previously published in an NAL Caliber hardcover edition.

First NAL Caliber Trade Paperback Printing, January 2009
10 9 8 7 6 5 4 3 2

Copyright © Major Chuck Larson, 2008
Foreword copyright © General Tommy Franks, 2008
Afterword copyright © Senator John McCain, 2008
All rights reserved

NAL CALIBER and the "C" logo are trademarks of Penguin Group (USA) Inc.

NAL Caliber Trade Paperback ISBN: 978-0-451-22584-9

The Library of Congress has cataloged the hardcover edition of this title as follows:

Heroes Among Us/edited and with an introd. by Chuck Larson.
p. cm.
Includes bibliographical references.
ISBN: 978-0-451-22334-0
1. Iraq War, 2003—Campaigns.   2. Iraq War, 2003—Personal narratives, American.   3. Afghan War,
2001—Campaigns.   4. Afghan War, 2001—Personal narratives, American.   I. Larson, Chuck.

DS79.76.F575 2008
956.7044'34092273—dc22   2007021179

Set in Adobe Garamond
Designed by Ginger Legato

Printed in the United States of America

For our fallen American warriors and their families,
who made the ultimate sacrifice in the global war on terrorism

ACKNOWLEDGMENTS

FIRST AND FOREMOST, I THANK all of the volunteers who serve in our military and particularly those who have deployed to Iraq and Afghanistan. I had the honor of serving with these dedicated Americans, and without them there would be no book.

I thank the Penguin Group (USA) for its strong support. I especially thank senior editor Mark Chait, who had the vision to see what this book could be and to ensure first-class results. I thank my agent, Flip Brophy, president of Sterling Lord Literistic, for all of her effort in bringing the manuscript to press. I thank my friend of twenty-plus years, Gary Reed, who worked with me from day one to develop the concept of the book and to help make it a reality. I thank my friend Tim Hickey, who invested hundreds of hours revising the manuscript and serving as my guide to the publishing industry. A special thanks to Deborah Colloton for her early assistance in shaping the book. To verify the technical military accuracy of the book, I had the professional assistance of Major Brett Thoms, Iowa National Guard; Major Brian Bresnahan, United States Marine Corps (ret.); Major James Gregory, U.S. Army Special Forces Command; and Staff Sergeant Andrew Amberg, United States Army Reserves. I also thank my sister, Carrie Graham, and my brother-in-law, Andrew Graham. They are both veterans of the army and were very helpful in reviewing the manuscript for military accuracy and making creative suggestions as the bood evolved. And thanks to Samantha Eubank for her help in collecting and selecting the photographs that appear in these pages.

I thank my parents, Ellen and Charles Sr., for their support and suggestions. Thanks to my wife, Jennifer, and my sons, Will and John-Henry, for their support and patience during the many phone calls and never-ending e-mails as I progressed through the interviews and editing. Most important, I thank Jen for her support and understanding while I spent a year in Iraq.

—— CONTENTS ——

Contents

Contents

Contents

Contents

—— A NOTE TO THE READER ——

IN CREATING HEROES AMONG US, I hoped to produce a book that would help all of us better understand the experiences of the men and women who volunteered to serve in Iraq and Afghanistan. I also wanted to highlight a few incredible acts of heroism so we might clearly understand and appreciate these soldiers' courage and sacrifice. To do this, I reviewed hundreds of military commendations for acts of valor in combat, and from those selected ones that captured a range of voices and experiences. I then interviewed the combatants and asked them to tell their stories as they remember them, and in their own words. While these accounts are unvarnished and unfiltered, they have been edited for readability and coherence.

I felt that firsthand accounts were imperative to the book's success. The soldiers' workmanlike attitude toward death, their inability to accept their own heroics, their superstitions, eerie sixth senses, premonitions, hunches, gut feelings, the "surreal" quality of events—these impressions cannot be conveyed by any method other than personal testimony.

Through its personal nature I believe the book also resists the pitfalls of overheated prose, of editorializing, of choosing sides. It does not defend or condemn the war; however, I do believe it supports the troops through its presentation of recognizable Americans putting their lives in peril for their country.

In two instances first-person accounts were not possible. For the chapters on Medal of Honor recipients Paul Smith and Jason Dunham, both killed in action, I reviewed official accounts of their combat, interviewed military personnel who were there alongside them, and talked with family members. From these sources I attempted to accurately portray both the individuals and the actions that led to their commendations.

More women are currently serving in the United States Armed Forces than at any other time in our nation's history. While they serve at all levels of engagement in Iraq and Afghanistan, to my knowledge only one has received the Silver Star. Attempts were made to interview her, but she declined.

—— FOREWORD ——

WHAT AN HONOR IT IS to salute those who have earned our nation's highest awards for valor. For almost four decades it's been my privilege to work with troops like those whose stories are told on the following pages. And I can tell you if you wear a Silver Star, Distinguished Service Cross, Navy Cross, or the Medal of Honor on your chest you have my respect. As you read the stories of Paul Smith and Jason Dunham, Brad Kasal and Luis Fonseca, Tony Pryor and all these remarkable patriots, I think you'll agree. Major Chuck Larson has captured in these men's own words the actions, the deeds that raised them from warriors to heroes.

All of us face curves in the road, but our troops face the life-and-death reality of roadside bombs, vehicle-borne explosives, and ambushes. Our young marines, sailors, soldiers, and airmen are very good at what they do. They do their jobs and they do their best to protect their battle buddies and innocent civilians. This book salutes their courage.

Working in a world of uncertainty in the sun-blasted deserts of Iraq or the frigid mountains of Afghanistan, these soldiers, sailors, airmen, and marines do their work with purpose and pride and without fanfare or grandstanding. They get the job done. They do it the right way. They deliver the goods. I admire them. I've always been proud of our country, but when I see how those wearing our nation's uniform handle themselves in the chaos and complexity of war, it makes me doubly proud.

From time to time, kind and well-meaning people call me a hero. I always tell them, "I'm no hero . . . but I know a lot of them." This book is about a few of those heroes. Men and women who overcame their well-justified fears and rose above the call of duty.

America stands today at an important crease in history. We are blessed by all that has gone before . . . freedom and a way of life that permits us to dream the American dream. But we are perched on a razor's edge between this legacy, this past, and a future where fanaticism and tyranny carry the day. The fate of freedom rests on the shoulders of American patriots like those you are about to meet. I wouldn't want it any other way.

—General Tommy Franks

HEROES AMONG US

—— INTRODUCTION ——

THIS BOOK IS ABOUT HEROES. It is about valor, honor, and sacrifice. But it is also about truth, and two facts emerge from the stories collected here: War is terrible, and war produces heroes. In fact, the worse the circumstances, the greater the heroics. The Americans honored in these pages come from all branches of the military and from all levels of specialization, from the career soldiers of Special Forces to the army and marine reservists called away from their regular civilian lives. As the wars continue, new acts of heroism are being performed every day. This book brings to light a fraction of these acts and recognizes a few representative individuals from among the many.

With the exception of the two Medal of Honor recipients, the soldiers profiled in this book have seen the face of battle and lived to tell their stories. But talking does not come easily for them; most granted interviews reluctantly. The main challenge of the interviews lay in getting these soldiers to overcome their modesty and to talk about themselves. Their experiences range widely, but they share a few themes: humility, love for fellow soldiers, and love of country. We asked these men to tell their stories as they remember them, and in their own words.

The word "hero" gets tossed around too easily. A major leaguer hits a home run in extra innings and he's dubbed a hero. A state senator votes the right way on issues of interest to educators and he's called a hero. I've played baseball and I've been a legislator, but it was only when I landed in Iraq that I knew I was in the company of heroes. This book is about them, the best of the best, the soldiers who are serving as the tip of the spear for our nation's defense.

I've met with them and have listened in awe to their stories. I've been inspired by their bravery, struck by their humanity, and I have marveled at their humility. Over a million and a half Americans have served in Iraq and Afghanistan in the past four years, and in every imaginable way they have sacrificed. Under the broiling sun they've put up with sand in their eyes, grit in their teeth, and rocks in their boots. They have endured long stretches away from their homes and their loved ones. But only about one in every twenty thousand have earned a Silver Star, Navy Cross, Air Force Cross, Distinguished Service Cross, or the Medal of Honor.

Our nation's Silver Star is inscribed with the words "For Gallantry in Action," and is awarded to those who conduct themselves with exceptional courage and marked distinction. The Silver Star is our nation's third-highest military medal.

The Distinguished Service Cross, our nation's second-highest military decoration, is cast in bronze and overlaid with an American eagle. Established in 1919, it's awarded by the U.S. Army to a person who distinguishes himself or herself by extraordinary heroism while engaged in action against an enemy of the United States.

The Navy Cross is awarded to a member of the United States Navy or Marine Corps for remarkable bravery, extraordinary heroism, and sacrifice in battle against an enemy of the United States. Equal to the Distinguished Service Cross, the Navy Cross features a sailing vessel centered on a cross. The U.S. Air Force awards the Air Force Cross, its own equivalent of the Navy Cross.

The Medal of Honor is our nation's oldest, highest, and rarest military honor. The medal is presented by the president of the United

States to those who risked their lives above and beyond the call of duty, performing deeds of consummate bravery and self-sacrifice.

It's hard getting these medals. It's even harder getting the recipients to talk about themselves. But it's easy getting them to talk about their fellow soldiers, sailors, airmen, and marines, the debt of gratitude they feel toward the leaders they respect and admire most, and their desire to be a part of a noble cause, a higher calling or a larger purpose.

They come from all walks of life, representing the entire spectrum of races and creeds. They come from America's biggest cities and from towns so small they don't show up on the map. They are as different as they can be, but what unites them is their patriotic love for America and their willingness to sacrifice for others. Everyone in this book was willing to lay down his life for his comrades. In fact, some of them did. Living or dead, wounded or well, back home again or still serving in Iraq or Afghanistan, they're all heroes in my book. Ronald Reagan said that there are heroes among us if we just take the time to look. Every time I see an American in uniform, I see a hero.

In 120 nations around the globe, a quarter of a million American men and women proudly wear our country's uniform and stand ready to defend freedom. More than half of them are in Iraq and Afghanistan. They are stationed in lands they have never before seen, fighting for people they have never met, and they do it in the name of freedom.

That's another word that gets bandied about too cavalierly: "freedom." Sometimes I think we use the word so often we forget what it truly means or how valiantly America has fought to achieve that cherished destination called freedom. I know we take our freedom for granted.

Freedom is our birthright. It isn't something that can be granted, and the desire for it can't be taken away. It's precious and priceless.

Human beings are hardwired to want to make our own choices, to shape our lives and craft our destinies. From the day of this nation's birth, we've been the freest nation on the face of the earth. The moment we accepted this gift from God, we gave ourselves the mission of spreading liberty to the four corners of the earth and to the seven seas. Freedom is our number-one export. Half of the world lives in freedom today, more than at any other point in history. But it's not good enough, is it? When everyone is free, it will change the world forever. As George Washington pointed out, "When it begins to take root, liberty is a plant of rapid growth."

I was in Iraq for a year, where I served as the Command Judge Advocate for the 372nd Engineer Group and the Task Force 185th Aviation Group. I advised the commanders of the two major units on all military legal issues. Although discipline and morale were very good, we had nearly forty-two hundred soldiers, marines, and airmen, and as such we confronted many of the same problems a small town of that size would face. I was fortunate to have Captain Doug Hottle serve as my trial counsel. Doug, a successful Pittsburgh attorney, was one of the sharpest lawyers I had ever worked with. Staff Sergeant Andy Amberg, a Dubuque, Iowa, native, was our trusted right hand in the office and helped ensure the success of all of our missions "outside the wire."

In addition to my JAG responsibilities, I also spearheaded our command's humanitarian mission. We built twelve new schools, three town halls, two new water-treatment facilities, and we reestablished a veterinary clinic. Each building project was developed by the newly created city council in our area. For the people of this community, this was their first taste of democracy. Although at times the task was challenging, Iraqis were quick to embrace democracy, improve their community, and represent all citizens.

As long as I live I'll never forget the Iraqi children. They are sweet, beautiful, and smart. When I visited their schools, I noticed how desperately low on school supplies they were. To fill this tremendous need, our command started Operation Iraqi Hope. I sent an e-mail to fifteen thousand Americans requesting pens and pencils, erasers and spiral notebooks. Americans have a spirit of generosity that stretches from coast to coast. We received more than one thousand packages from twenty-five states, totaling over $100,000 in supplies. The children's shy smiles turned to squeals of delight. Each and every crayon or piece of paper was treated as a treasure. In all, we distributed seventeen thousand school kits. It's those children's future we're fighting for.

Helicopters serve as the modern-day workhorses of the war. The movement of troops, equipment, and resupply occurred twenty-four hours a day, seven days a week. The demand on flight crews was great. As a result, our JAG office volunteered to be trained and to serve as door gunners on Black Hawk and Chinook helicopters. By day, Captain Hottle and I worked as army lawyers, and by night we flew door gunner missions across the country. Before returning to the United States, I had completed over fifty combat missions on a twin-rotored Chinook helicopter.

My father, Charles Larson Sr., and I had overlapping tours in Iraq. He was the Justice Attaché, serving as the U.S. Department of Justice's Senior Advisor to Ambassador John Negroponte. His mission was to help build the new independent Iraqi criminal justice system. As we know in America, the foundation of democracy is the rule of law; thus, it was a significant milestone when Iraq established the Judiciary as a separate branch of government with the rule of law as its polestar. His team also included U.S. marshals, who worked to enhance security for Iraqi judges, and prison experts, who "stood up" the Iraqi prison system, focusing on enforcement of human rights.

Because of my work with the aviation group, we were able to catch an occasional half-hour helicopter ride to meet at the embassy or where I served in Balad. Although we were light on gifts, my father and I were fortunate to spend Christmas 2004 together in Baghdad. In June of 2005, my father returned to his duties as the U.S. Attorney for the Northern District of Iowa.

When I was deployed to Iraq in February 2004, I was proud to go, but I was naïve about the Iraqi people. I assumed they were different from me. They were Muslim and I was Christian. I spoke English and they spoke Arabic. I was familiar with our customs and culture and theirs were alien to me. Deep down, I may have even thought of them as my "enemy," but I quickly learned that nothing could be further from the truth.

These are good, loving, and hospitable people. They're born entrepreneurs. Iraqi moms and dads are no different from American parents. They have great dreams for their sons and daughters and they care deeply about good schools. They pray for peace and they yearn for a better, safer, and freer life. There is the misconception that because the Iraqi people have lived under the thumb of tyranny for so long, the concept of freedom is alien to them, or, worse, irrelevant. But Iraqis are freedom-loving people and they put their lives on the line every day for democracy.

When leaving Baghdad, after my tour of duty was up, I looked across the skyline of that magnificent city and nearly every rooftop had a satellite dish. To me, that symbolized their hunger for information and their deep desire for connection to the larger world. Information is the great liberator of the Iraqi people.

It's easy to forget how far Iraq has come, but it's important that we remember. Nearly five years ago Saddam Hussein and his psychopathic sons Uday and Qusay lived like modern-day Egyptian pharaohs while the vast majority of Iraqis lived in abject poverty and unrelenting fear. Nearly every Iraqi I talked to had a Saddam Hussein story. Each experience included chilling tales of arbitrary arrests, mass graves, rape rooms or torture chambers. One Iraqi worker

I spoke with showed me where government officials had burned five holes in his leg with a soldering iron as punishment for being five minutes late for work. My translator had three cousins and an uncle executed by the Hussein regime, victims of the mass arrests and killings that took place in the mainly Shiite town of Dujail. Is it any wonder that terror gripped the people of Iraq? Life was luxurious for a favored few, but the vast majority of the people lived in poverty, torment, and fear. Perched in one of his gilded palaces, Saddam Hussein was unfazed by their misery and unmoved by their suffering. If this man wasn't evil, no one is.

Iraq has one of the highest infant-mortality rates in the world. Tuberculosis is rampant. In many areas people get their water directly from the bacteria-contaminated Tigris River. While Saddam Hussein lived among more than ninety marble-encased palaces, Iraqi children often attended windowless, run-down schools made of mud, brick, and thatch. Teachers earned $3 per month. Today, they earn $280.

Democracies don't wage war against one another. If you want to be inspired, watch what people do with their newfound freedom. It's the power of an unchained human spirit and it's a sight to behold. Since time immemorial, the forces of good and evil have waged war against one another. From the concentration camps of Poland to the killing fields of Cambodia to the jungles of Uganda and the deserts of Sudan, the forces of evil have been cruel and ferocious killers.

Yet freedom is inevitable, unstoppable, and irreversible. The God who gave us the ability to dream and the capacity to love gave us freedom. When peace replaces war, and liberty replaces tyranny, the world will be a better place to live. In other words, in the battle between good and evil, despotism and democracy, bet on freedom every time.

—Major Chuck Larson
Des Moines, Iowa, 2008

"OUR NATION HONORS HER SONS AND
DAUGHTERS WHO ANSWERED THE CALL
TO DEFEND A COUNTRY THEY NEVER
KNEW AND A PEOPLE THEY NEVER MET."

—KOREAN WAR VETERANS MEMORIAL

FACE-TO-FACE IN THE DARK

★

Anthony Pryor, Master Sergeant, U.S. Army
Fifth Special Forces Group
Toledo, Oregon
Silver Star; Kandahar, Afghanistan; 23 January 2002

It was frigid cold and the air was thin at eight thousand feet in the mountains north of Kandahar, Afghanistan, when Tony Pryor and his fellow Green Berets entered an al-Qaeda compound looking for key leaders, maps, intelligence, and communications equipment. Pryor found himself alone in a twenty-five-by-twenty-five-foot room; it was pitch-black, and he was attacked from behind with a wooden beam that broke his collarbone and dislocated his shoulder.

ANTHONY PRYOR

Originally I'm from a small town near the ocean, Toledo, Oregon. It's God's country if God has webbed feet. Nine months of rain. I spent a lot of time in the woods as a kid, hunting, trapping, fishing and all that. The first movie I saw was *The Green Berets*, with John Wayne. I was a good student, straight A's in high school, but I didn't want to sit in a college classroom. I was tired of that. I was ready for something different. I got out of high school, spent some time in the woods, in the sawmills, commercial fishing. That was getting a little old. I was looking for some excitement so I joined the army. I believe army life agreed with me and I went about as far as I could go. I did everything I wanted to do and I went to every army school that I wanted to go to, and some I didn't care to go to.

Haiti, Somalia, Eritrea, Djibouti, UAE, Qatar, Bahrain, Saudi Arabia, Egypt, Kenya, Kuwait. All those were places I never would have seen if I had stayed at home and majored in who-knows-what. I'm not trying to glamorize army life, because the places that soldiers go aren't the nice places. Particularly because of the Christian-Muslim separation, soldiers are hidden like a third cousin. Soldiers stay in bad places like prisons so that they are out of sight. Other countries may need our help but they don't want anyone else to know we're there.

The army teaches you self-reliance and teamwork, and one contradicts the other. You learn to be independent, and that means achieving through your own ability and skills and having confidence in what you can do individually. Teamwork means achieving through a synergistic effort. One guy can do 20 percent. Three guys can do 100 percent, because you have more security, more guns in the fight, more eyes on the target, you have more trust. The army taught me to understand myself, my own strengths and weaknesses. Everybody has them, and when I go out on the range, I work on the things I'm not good at. Identifying weaknesses and working on them yourself, that's a big deal. I never want to be the one who lets my team or my country down. Second place in this business is a body bag. As a leader, I don't want my guys in the bags. That isn't something that sits right with me, because I care about my men more than they'll ever know.

Our Fifth Group's responsibility was the Horn of Africa and the Middle East. Our group was a bunch of type-A personalities and they were there to fight. That's what we trained for every minute. If we weren't fighting, we were cleaning up after a fight or planning the next one.

Our living conditions in Afghanistan were rough. We lived in the mountains at ten thousand feet. We slept in our clothes on the ground around a small fire. We got a bottle of water and an MRE [meals ready to eat] a day. We were relying on the kindness of strangers and we didn't get a lot of it. Our team's character was aggressive and professional. Al-Qaeda started it with the Twin Towers. We didn't hit them first. Like the Japanese attack on Pearl Harbor, 9/11 was another day that will live in infamy. When America is attacked first, when we're on the defensive first, we stay the course. We beat the Taliban in the middle of winter. We're in the right.

With me, what you see is what you get. I'm direct. I won't sugarcoat it. If you're going to be thickheaded, you'd better be thickskinned. I never follow behind my men. I led my men from the front and I'm glad I did. God puts you in situations you can handle, and this was one I could handle. I'm not sure if other guys could have. I have a lot of respect for my men and my men have a lot of respect for me. We're brothers forever.

Some of this may be classified so I won't say the number of the raid. This was in Afghanistan in January 2002 and it was a raid on a suspected al-Qaeda stronghold during Operation Enduring Freedom.

It was our fourth combat mission of the war, a sensitive site exploitation of two compounds suspected of harboring Taliban and al-Qaeda terrorists in the mountains. There were women and children within the compounds so aerial bombardment was not an option. Our mission was to search for key leadership, communications equipment, weapons caches, maps, and other intelligence.

It was a split-company operation and the other guys went in before us. They walked ten to fifteen kilometers at ten thousand feet altitude in ten-degree weather under cover of darkness to get near the target. They got there undetected, which is a big plus. We came in with two gun trucks. We brought bigger guns, and, you know, big guns are good. We landed, linked up on the ground, and got our guns up. We drove right through the middle of their town in the middle of the night. It was frigid. We saw goats and heard dogs barking and fires burning, but no people. Not a soul stuck his head out. As we got near the target, I did all of my last-minute checks. I had my pistol, my frags [fragmentary grenades], my knife. I could find my charges. Here was my flash bang. I counted my men. Making sure everything was good. There was a lot going through my head and a lot going on.

As we got up near the target, the AC-130 gunship reported that the enemy was moving around the roof of the compound. We were trying to drive up to it but we ran out of road. The road got so bad we couldn't get in that way, so we dismounted and we got right close to the target. The guys on the hill, the other half of the split squad, made the initial charge and they lit the way. Here we were out in the open, running, and one bad guy went squirting off to our right flank and Scotty, my A-Cell leader, ran over and rolled him up and handcuffed him and handed him off.

I got to the corner of the compound and I called out, "Jimmy, gimme a banger" [a flash-bang grenade designed to disorient the enemy]. Jimmy shoved a banger in, and when he chugged the banger it was like we hit a hornets' nest with a baseball bat. Everybody just started opening up on us from everywhere. There were muzzle flashes coming from every frickin' direction. There was a guy about four or five meters away, so close I could look him in the eye, and I stitched him. I put four in him. Anyway, that guy died.

There was another guy shooting at us. I was reaching to get a banger and a guy came at me from out of the door that I was fixing to enter. I just threw the banger out into the center and away from my guys. I started to pick up heavier volume of fire, but I wasn't seeing it with my night-vision goggles [NVGs]. I was getting it out of my actual vision.

A guy came at me out of a doorway that was covered by a blanket. I couldn't see who it was. I couldn't tell whether he had a gun. I just started beating the crap out of him. I was hammer fisting him down. I wasn't going to just shoot the blanket because it could have been a kid. I figured, nice time is over and we need to get out of this and get some cover now because this is getting real crappy and it's right out in the open. When the guy fell, we saw he was a man with an AK-47. Jimmy stitched him up and I went in the room. I thought Jimmy was right behind me. But his long gun went down and he was transitioning to his pistol. He was engaging a different threat. I went into the next room and ended up there alone. The enemies were sticking their guns out the window, trying to kill our other guys, who were entering the house like ducks in a row. I went down the line, from left to right, and started whacking them. There was so much going on outside they didn't realize that I'd come in. They didn't have any electricity, no NVGs, and it was really dark. I shot those guys.

I was getting pretty deep into this magazine and I needed to change mags real quick. While I was doing that I could feel someone coming up behind me. I thought it was one of my guys, but it wasn't.

This enemy guy whopped me on the shoulder with something, maybe it was a wooden beam, and crumpled me down. I got hit so hard that I saw white lights, floaters. *Bam*, I got hit and went down to one knee. The guy jumped on my back and tore off my NVGs. He was kneeing me in the back and started to get his stinking little fingers clawing in my eyeballs. I reached up with my right hand—he was a pretty big boy with a beard and a ponytail—and I got him by the back of his head and flipped him over. When I did, my elbow hit the ground and put my dislocated shoulder back in its socket. Now we were face-to-face in the dark.

The thing that really paid off for me was having done a lot of hand-to-hand-combat training in gear. I fought a lot of guys with my full gear on. A lot of people will do combat training slick, without gear. But you gotta fight with your kit on to make it more realistic. It's a totally different animal when you have a rifle, pistol, shotgun, frags, bangs, smokes, and eighty-five pounds of "lightweight" gear on. You can't get away with all those amazing kung fu moves. Those aren't in your arsenal.

We were face-to-face and my left arm was raging and I thought, *Man, it's you or me, dude, and it ain't gonna be me. I want it more than you do. You're not going to kill me. I got a life at home. My comrades got a life at home. And we're coming home.* If this guy got past me, he could have shot my guys in the back.

I went to biting on him. I could smell his sour breath. He was pulling around all over my gear and I was worried about him pulling a grenade pin or pulling one of my breaching charges and blowing us both up. This had to end. I couldn't reach my rifle, pistol, or shotgun. My left arm wasn't working so well. I pulled him by the hair close to my body with my left hand, and with my right hand I "shot-putted" his head. I broke his neck. I finished him off with a 9mm pistol.

I holstered up and got my rifle and started looking for my NVGs.

Then I heard the sound of an AK-47 going off and then the sound of metal bullets hitting concrete. I couldn't find my NVGs so I broke a rule and went to white light. One of the guys that I shot decided he wasn't dead yet. He was getting up with a long gun, and I felt on the floor for my magazine and stuck it in there, racked up, and I beat him to the reload. I put two in him in a hurry and he went to the ground. I went back to trying to find my NVGs, but I couldn't find them.

The first guy I fought hand to hand must have unplugged my communications system. I couldn't get ahold of my A-Cell and B-Cell leaders. I thought for a moment, *My guys aren't answering, maybe we lost.*

I gathered up rifles and all the ammo. I was starting to come out the door. I didn't want to come out with an AK, because if my guys saw that, they might think I was the enemy. I couldn't tell what was what because I didn't have my NVGs. I got to the door and yelled, "Is there an Eagle out here?" And Johnny yelled back, "Yeah, who is it?" I said, "Bucket." That was my nickname, because the guys said I had a bucket-shaped head. "I ain't got my goggles, give me a white light flash." He did and I went over to him while yelling, "Tony coming in! Tony coming in! Tony coming in!"

Johnny got my communications hooked back up. A lot of that stuff you can't reach yourself. And I got ahold of Scotty, Jimmy, Donny, and Brady and I knew everything was going to be good. There was still some shooting going on, battles within battles, on the ring and the east side. The guys back there were doing so much damned shooting I thought one of our guys had to have been shot or killed. But we were all okay.

Around the wood fire at base camp, I went around and I had to touch each one of my guys. That was good for them and good for me. Everyone looked like they'd aged ten years.

Being in charge isn't all good because you really worry. These guys put their trust in me to do the right things to keep them alive. I didn't want to disappoint my guys and I don't think I did. There were twenty-one enemy killed, no Americans killed or seriously wounded. It was a frickin' miracle. They were a bunch of good, hard-fighting dudes. Everything was stacked in our favor. It was meant to happen.

We captured quite a few POWs. They had guns but they weren't shooting at us, so they are alive and well. They didn't want to fight and we didn't fire. Our guys did what they were supposed to do. I'm proud of them. They did a good job in that war. The whole company had KIAs and WIAs but they kept rolling on. They kept doing what they were supposed to be doing. There are so many guys in that company who are heroes to me.

Some things you're going to have remorse over and regret them. I think that's a positive thing, because that lets you know you're still okay. When it's game time, lock and load and let's roll. Let's get it on. But when it's all over, pulling kids out of buildings, you feel good about that. Handing things out to people, you feel good about that.

I'd like to say I'm older and beat up and I got a lot of things that hurt. I would like to change some things I didn't do in my personal life with my family. The first twenty-four years are for God and country. The next twenty-plus years have to be for the wife and kid. Life means a lot. And when you come close to losing it a few times, it becomes considerably more precious. Two thousand–plus Americans have gotten killed in Iraq and I'm sorry they had to get killed. That's a terrible loss. That was somebody's son, daughter, mom, dad, wife or husband. Somewhere, somebody really loved that person.

War is a bad thing; it's an ugly business and people are going to die. It's a terrible thing for us to have to do. But hopefully our kids won't have to cope with it. Maybe people should at least keep us in their prayers.

★

Tony Pryor is a Green Beret and has been with the Special Forces for fourteen years. A mighty bull of a man at five feet eleven and 235 pounds, Tony bench-presses more than twice his weight. He went into combat wearing the medallion of St. Michael, the patron saint of soldiers, duct-taped to his dog tags.

He suffered serious but non-life-threatening injuries on January 22, 2002, and earned the Silver Star on June 12, 2003. He keeps a chunk of his collarbone in a jar. He forbids toy guns in his home.

Since this interview Tony Pryor has returned to Afghanistan, once again working with his men in combat—what Tony describes as Shangri-la.

THREE DECISIONS TO DIE

★

Brad Kasal, First Sergeant, U.S. Marine Corps

Afton, Iowa

Navy Cross; Fallujah, Iraq; 13 November 2004

Brad Kasal has spent twenty-two of his forty years in the Marine Corps. He brings a wrestler's tenacity and a middle linebacker's instincts to the battlefield. He saved the life of a fellow marine in Operation Phantom Fury, America's assault on the insurgent stronghold of Fallujah called Queens. "On that day," he says, "I did what I had to do because it was the right thing to do." Kasal (pronounced "Castle") was recently promoted to sergeant major and was awarded our nation's second-highest medal, the Navy Cross.

LUCIAN READ

By eighth grade I knew I would join the marines. It's what I had wanted to do forever. If I'm going to do something, I'm going to do whatever's the hardest. Boot camp was in San Diego. It wasn't that challenging physically because I'd wrestled and played football at East Union High School and I was in pretty good shape. Mentally, it was more challenging because I was away from home, and the marine lifestyle was so rigid.

The first day was a shock. The senior drill instructor was a very good man who was stern but fair. He took care of us well. The junior drill instructors spent the most time with us training and teaching. One guy didn't teach us anything. He just yelled at us.

I was the high shooter on the range. High PFT [physical fitness test] score. I was doing well. I knew how to shoot already from hunting pheasant back home in Iowa with an old hand-me-down twenty-gauge shotgun. The Marine Corps really helped me realize my potential as a leader. I have the ability to motivate young marines.

Since I joined the marines when I was seventeen years old in 1984, I've served in too many countries to name. Somalia, Djibouti, Afghanistan, the Philippines, West Africa . . . ten deployments in all. Our first deployment in Iraq lasted five months. Then on May 23, 2003, we went home.

In June 2004 I volunteered to stay on and go back. I was supposed to get orders to go somewhere else but I wanted to go back to Iraq. I've been in the infantry for twenty years and I have experience. I volunteered to go back because it was my duty and I believe in what we're doing over there. I've done other combat tours, but in my twenty years in the military, this is the most important. I believe in the mission.

We were in constant, almost daily action. We went to the outskirts of Fallujah, which was a hotbed, and we were always hitting the area, looking for the enemy, always engaging, very active. Search and destroy the enemy. These were foreign fighters and they were there to kill Americans. They didn't care if local children got killed. They were fanatics, well trained, very determined, and equipped with night-vision goggles. They were from Syria, Egypt, Afghanistan, Chechnya, and Jordan.

For three months all our activities were focused on the south side of Fallujah. It was a deception operation because when the heart of Fallujah was attacked, it was attacked from the north.

I was wounded in August 2004 in one of those operations. I was hit by shrapnel in the neck and shoulder. I gutted it out. I kept going, like a lot of marines do.

We were going strong, day in and day out, until the night of November 12, when we got our first decent night's sleep in a long time. We woke up in the morning and it was cool and eerie. There was a sewerlike smell in the air. We started out at dawn. Our orders were to clear every building, house, and street. We fanned out to try to clear that portion of the city we called Queens.

Around ten thirty a.m., I saw Sergeant Pruitt, one of my former marines in Kilo Company, walking down the street in the opposite direction from me. He was bleeding from the arm and leg and not carrying a weapon. He staggered aimlessly in a daze.

I ran out, grabbed him, and pulled him between two buildings for cover. I asked him what happened and he said three other marines had been inside this two-story stucco-and-brick house a couple of houses ahead of us. The four of them had gone into this house and all hell broke loose. All of them were wounded. Three marines were still inside. He said it was like the shootout at the O.K. Corral. He didn't know how severe their wounds were or what their status was. He did know they were still inside that house with the bad guys.

My first thought was, *Marines down inside the building with fanatical insurgents who would behead them or torture them or shoot them right on the spot.* Time was of the essence and I immediately grabbed whatever marines I could find. Four of us headed toward that house.

I ran into Corporal Mitchell, a squad leader from Kilo Company, and he was doing the same thing I was, gathering up marines. Since it was his squad, I didn't want to overstep him, even though I was senior and held a higher rank. I just said, "You take over and I'll help out because you need bodies."

We went to the side of the building and set up a stack to make an entrance into the building. We went in through the front door. I was the third person in. Inside the room I immediately noticed two dead guys, insurgents, on the ground, and another one in an adjacent room. I saw the "friendlies" who were wounded, bleeding in the middle of the floor. I walked in and there was a stairwell to the right, then three adjacent rooms, two straight ahead and one small room off to the left corner. Our marines fanned out and everybody went to those two rooms. We forgot about the third small room to the left corner. I yelled to the marines, "Hey, did anybody clear that room? Did anybody clear that room?"

No one answered. No one knew. I grabbed PFC Nicoll because he's a fearless marine I would always trust. I saw that it was a danger area and I said, "Hey, come with me, we've got to clear this room."

As I moved up to the room, I thought about our rear. I yelled to two marines, "Cover our rear and make sure you cover that ladder well." They set up and I went into that small room. I started "pieing" the doorway, which means to clear a little bit of the room at a time so you can see more and more of it without exposing yourself completely. To my left, less than two feet away, close enough that I could've shaken hands with him, was an enemy soldier with an AK-47 pointed right at me. I saw him and he saw me. I shouted, "Bad guy!" His AK-47 was inches from me. He screamed something in Arabic and I jerked back. He fired off a burst. A round skipped right in front of my chest and hit the side of the wall next to me. He just kept firing. I took my M16, stuck it over the top of his AK-47, put my barrel literally in his chest and kept firing until he went down. I shot eight or ten rounds into his chest at point-blank range before he fell. He was high on cocaine and other drugs, which was commonplace. This way they could withstand pain and sleep deprivation. They could take multiple hits without feeling the pain and could keep fighting.

He finally went down, and then, as he hit the floor, I put two more into his forehead just to make sure. I said to Nicoll, "That was a close one." I brought my weapon back up because I couldn't see deeper into that room. It was dark. No lights. No windows.

Just as I did that, I started worrying about our rear again because I didn't hear my marines back there who were supposed to be covering it. I didn't want to look back because I was responsible for providing security to the front. I yelled back to the young marines, "Hey, make sure you're watching our backs."

Just as I got done saying that, out of the blue from behind me and above, all hell broke loose, with AKs opening up on me and Nicoll, hitting us from behind. I never saw it coming. It felt like someone was hitting me with a hammer on my right leg. My legs buckled out from underneath me and I collapsed to the ground. Rounds were hitting all around me. I heard Nicoll go down. He was grimacing in pain so I knew he'd been hit. I looked down at my leg and it was shattered, totally pointing in the opposite direction of my body. I crawled on my stomach to get behind the wall, to get into the room and get some cover.

As I was crawling, I became aware of Nicoll, still stuck out there and getting shot at. I crawled back out to pull him to safety. As I did, the insurgents started shooting back at me again. Rounds were hitting all around and eventually one hit me in the buttocks area. I just kept going. I kept crawling until I reached Nicoll. I grabbed him by the back of the body armor and dragged him across the floor while I was on my side, dragging first myself and then pulling him with my arms, until we got around the door. Then I threw him over the top of me so I could get him on the far side. Now there was a wall between us and the enemy, but they were in the very next room.

I looked at his wounds and I looked at mine. We were both bleeding severely. I started treating Nicoll's wounds. Blood was spurting out of my leg and it was nearly cut in half. My first thought was this: *We have two field bandages between us and we have multiple wounds.* I had gunshot wounds to my lower extremities, lower back, and butt. He had gunshot wounds to his belly and legs. I made the decision right there to treat his wounds. I made three decisions that day to die. Not that I wanted to, but it was either both of us die or one of us die. That was my thought process. I put one dressing on his leg as a tourniquet to stop his leg from bleeding. I took the other one and I tried to take off his body armor so I could treat his belly wound. But with me lying on my side because I was shot up and him lying on his back, it was hard for me to get his gear off.

We were in this little three-by-five-foot room; the dead guy that I had shot was at my feet. It was that cramped. My shattered leg was just lying there like a limp piece of sausage. As I tried to get Nicoll's armor off to treat his wound, I kept thinking that the enemy on the other side wasn't going to settle with us being in here. I also worried about friendly fire. I took my M16 and laid it in the doorway so that if any friendlies came in, they'd see that and maybe pause before shooting up the room. I pulled my 9mm pistol and used that as defense. Then I went back to trying to treat Nicoll's wounds. I was bleeding pretty severely but, like I said, I made the decision to give up my bandage and use it to treat his wounds while I continued to bleed out. If I had put one on him and one on me, we'd both die. My adrenaline was flowing too high for me to black out. I kept yelling at Nicoll to keep him conscious, even though it meant that the enemy knew we were still alive.

I was worried that the enemy would try to skip rounds around the room or throw a grenade. No sooner did I start to think that than I heard a thud to my right, the sound of metal hitting concrete. I rolled over and saw a green pineapple grenade, its pin pulled, landing just beyond arm's reach. I didn't have time to roll over to my right and try to swat it back to the other room. The only thing I had time to do was roll over and protect Nicoll with my body. I covered him up in a bear hug. People say it's heroic, but I thought I was going to die anyway, so why should both of us die?

The blast went off and hit me all over the lower back, arms, and legs. I felt the sharpness and the pain like severe bee stings. My ears were ringing and I was pretty dazed, all the other things that come with a blast. It rang my bell pretty good. I shook my head and tried to clear the concussion. As soon as I did, I rolled back over and tried to treat Nicoll's wounds, while keeping out an eye and an ear in case the enemy came in the doorway to finish us off.

I heard some movement outside the door, so I took my 9mm and brought it up. It was Corporal Mitchell, the original squad leader. As he ran toward our room, the bad guys started shooting at him. He took some shrapnel ricocheting from the AK-47. He was stuck in the corner of the doorway. Then he was able to get into the room with us. He asked how we were doing. I told him not to worry about me. I said, "Just take care of Nicoll. I put a tourniquet on his leg but I couldn't get it real good so you'll have to redo it, and he's got a hit somewhere in his chest or belly but I can't get his gear off to see where it is. I'll cover the doorway, you take care of him." I was still pretty alert.

I was lying on my side with my feet propped up on the dead insurgent. The whole time we were in the room, the dead insurgent was still twitching. That's how high on drugs he was. His nervous system was still going and his eyes were rolling around in his head. In fact, Corporal Mitchell thought he was still alive and stabbed him with his bayonet. But he was dead.

I guarded the doorway while Mitchell gave first aid to Nicoll. When Nicoll was stabilized, we tried to figure out a way to get out of there. Then some more marines came and set up in the doorway. They lay on their backs and shot up into the skylight where the enemy was, suppressing them while two young marines came into the room to carry us out. They'd left their weapons behind to carry us, and those guys are the real heroes in my book. We had to go through the kill zone to get out. I put my arms around their shoulders and kept my 9mm in my right hand ready to shoot. They were able to keep the enemy suppressed enough that I didn't have to use my weapon.

They pulled me across the room and out the front door, dropped me on the steps, and the marines from the outside grabbed me and pulled me into a Humvee with the rest of the wounded. We headed out of the city and went to the battalion aid station. The total time Nicoll and I were in that room was over sixty minutes. I refused all medical attention so Nicoll could get it. I refused all morphine because I wanted to keep a clear head. I never lost consciousness, although I lost 60 percent of my blood. I'll be honest, a couple of times I didn't think I was going to make it out. I thought I'd never see my family again because I was going to bleed to death. People think that it was a medical miracle, but it was either stay awake or die. The only thing keeping us alive was me staying awake and conscious to guard that door. I did what any marine would do. At the battalion aid station, they gave me a couple of shots of morphine, put a splint on my leg, cut off all my gear, bandaged me up, put on a tourniquet. Then a helicopter flew me to a naval field hospital at Camp TQ, where they took me right into surgery.

That was my first of many surgeries. I've had twenty surgeries and lots of rehab. I'm walking now with a limp and a lot of pain. I'm using a cane, and it's getting there but there will be a lot of pain and rehab yet to come. I'll never get my leg back to where it used to be. I'll never be 100 percent. Everything was shattered from about an inch below my knee to just above my ankle. The fact that I'm still alive is stunning to most people. I was shot seven times and took forty-six shrapnel wounds and lost 60 percent of my blood. It's a miracle to most people, but I'm a Kasal and we're tough.

The sixty-six-day hospital stay was the worst, but if there was any hospital in the country I would choose to be at, Bethesda Naval Hospital would be the one. The nurses, doctors, and staff were phenomenal. The worst part was being away from my marines for Thanksgiving, Christmas, and New Year's. It's a bond that's hard to explain. They're like a second family to me.

President Bush came to visit. There was a big aura about him when he walked into the room. You could tell he was the president of the United States. The main thing I remember was that he showed good leadership, he showed sincerity, and he showed compassion. At the time, I had a roommate who was a junior marine, but my bed was closest to the door when President Bush entered. He came in, and instead of going to my bed, he said, "I'll talk with you next, First Sergeant." He went to the junior marine first, as he should. Then he came to me next. Not a lot of people would have known to do that. I could hear the sincerity in his voice and see it in his eyes. Also, he didn't have a big media circus. It was just a photographer and a close personal friend. That was it. No media. No security. No nothing.

I'm going to will myself back to health. Just out of sheer willpower, I'll come back stronger. Retirement will wait. I want to serve in the Marine Corps for another couple of years. If anything, I love the Marine Corps more. I want to go out as I came in: healthy and in uniform, with pride.

★

The day before Brad Kasal was promoted to sergeant major and awarded the Navy Cross, his father, with whom Brad shared a close relationship, passed away. Brad has since returned to Iowa, where he serves as the sergeant major of the marine recruiting station.

He is now walking without a cane and beginning to run again. "It wasn't pretty, but I was able to do it," he said. His goal is to get strong enough to return to the infantry and go back to Iraq. "We started it; we need to finish it. I believe in what we're doing. I'd go back in a heartbeat."

THE PERSON BESIDE YOU

★

Timothy Nein, Staff Sergeant, U.S. Army

617th Military Police Company

Henryville, Indiana

DISTINGUISHED SERVICE CROSS; BAGHDAD, IRAQ; MARCH 2005

Southeast of Baghdad, twenty-six supply vehicles were ambushed by fifty insurgents armed with AK-47s, RPK rifles, rocket-propelled grenades, and hand grenades. Shadowing the convoy of mostly eighteen-wheelers were the 617th MPs in three armored Humvees. The squad leader, Staff Sergeant Nein, and his soldiers outflanked the enemy, cut off their escape route, fought off the enemy's massive firepower, plunged into a canal to take on the last insurgents, and disrupted the enemy ambush. Twenty-seven insurgents were killed, six wounded, one captured, and none escaped.

TIMOTHY NEIN

I'm thirty-seven years old and I've always lived in Clark County, Indiana. In civilian life I was with International Paper Company for over fifteen years, working in the free press department, making the plates that went on the presses. The last couple of years we went digital and I worked with computers.

I've been in the Kentucky Army National Guard since I joined in November 1996. I'm with the 223rd Military Police Company, which is about twenty miles south of where I live, across the border in Kentucky. I completed my basic training in June 1997 and I was an honor graduate. I've been deployed to Bosnia, Panama, and Ecuador. I got called up to go to Iraq when the war started.

I was a squad leader in charge of nine other soldiers of the 223rd, and I guess you could say there was a little apprehension. But I was excited because this is what we'd trained for and it was time to do our job for real. I remember being in Kuwait in 2003, getting ready to cross the border into Iraq, and I heard the alarm go off. There had been an enemy launch. We could see the incoming missile. We were all lined up in our suits, watching this scud flying through the air. While we were watching it, getting our gas masks on and all, we saw it blow up. The scariest thing to me was taking cover inside the tents or the foxholes, thinking this could be chemical warfare. You can hide from a bullet, but gas is something else. If your equipment isn't working right, you're going to die. If you don't do what you're trained to do, if you don't get it right the first time, you're in trouble. I can remember thinking, *What have I gotten myself into?*

After that, it was a matter of reacting and of doing the things we were trained to do. We got shot at here and there. We'd see roadside bombs and car bombs. The enemy wasn't really superorganized. It was hit-and-miss stuff. They'd shoot at us and run. On every second or third night, we'd get mortar fire, and my job was to try to catch the guys who were sending it. With our listening posts and technology, we'd try to triangulate where the mortar was coming from, plot the grid, trace it back to its source, and then head to that area to try to catch the guys. Usually they would have moved on. Because they were locals, they knew the area, so they had the jump on us. Sometimes we'd see a vehicle off in the distance trying to flee the area, but it was dark, about two or three a.m., and the vehicle was just far enough away that we couldn't be 100 percent certain whether they were the bad guys or not. We didn't want to engage a civilian. We didn't want to take any chances.

My first tour of Iraq lasted just over nine months. Then we rotated back to the States. I worked for International Paper the next couple of months while also helping other Army National Guard units train up. A couple of other units were about to rotate into Iraq from the state of Kentucky. I volunteered on several different occasions to help them get ready. I spent about three months total in 2004 helping to train up other units, particularly the 617th Military Police unit. I got to thinking about something: I knew what mission was coming up and I knew they were going to be in pretty much the same area, around the Baghdad International Airport. I thought that if I volunteered, my knowledge and experience in Iraq could be a great asset to the unit. I explained that to our unit, the 223rd, and we all volunteered to go into the 617th to help them. My wife was actually against it but she said she would support me in whatever decision I made.

To be honest with you, I felt a little guilty about having left Iraq before the year was up. We'd been there nine months and we lost one soldier. That soldier was from my company and he'd been killed in a mortar attack. We never caught the guys who did it, and I felt guilty about it. Since we were there just nine months and other units were staying for a full year, I felt like someone else was doing my job. As a man, as a soldier, I didn't like somebody else having to do my job.

This was the best squad I ever had. I couldn't ask for a better bunch. They were always confident and willing to learn and train. Everyone had great morale. I can honestly say I never heard any member of my squad say, "Boy, I'm sorry to be here" or "Boy, I want to go home." They all wanted to support not just me but each other. This squad was bonded together.

We had two white females, Sergeant Leigh Ann Hester and Specialist Ashley Pullen. We had Sergeant Jason Mike, who is African-American and Korean. Sergeant Joe Rivera, whose father is Puerto Rican and whose mom is Korean. Specialist Jesse Ordunez is a Mexican American. Specialist Casey Cooper, Specialist William Haynes II, Sergeant Dustin Morris and I are white men. It's probably the most diverse squad that I've ever been in and possibly the most diverse squad the army's ever had. We all worked together as a team and we never fought. We would joke around here and there but we'd always end up laughing. It never occurred to me that one of the guys might not like the other one because he was black, Korean, Puerto Rican, Mexican, or a woman.

We were south of Baghdad and shadowing supply trucks. We ran this route every couple of weeks, and we'd change up so the enemy wouldn't know our tactics and routines. We had the enemy figured out. They were making the same mistakes, always doing the same things. They would come in from the south, attack the convoys, and get away in cars. They would never stay and fight and we could never catch them.

Around March 17 we decided we were really going to hit this route hard. We weren't going to take any breaks. We were going to watch all the spots that might get hit and we were going to find these guys. We developed a tactic of shadowing the convoys that came through. We would get behind them as they moved through our patrol sector and we would follow behind them until they left our sector. If they made contact with the enemy or a truck broke down or a vehicle got hit by an IED, we would stop and do what we needed to do. We did some really good reconnaissance and we checked out all the roads, the little towns, so we could pursue the enemy without getting sucked into another ambush.

On the seventeenth we hit the route hard and we stopped for a second to drink some water. A convoy went by. The route had been real quiet and we were surprised, because we thought we'd see some action. I guess about noon we grabbed a sandwich and took off to link up. We could hear an ambush going on. I listened to the radio to get a grid and I thought, *Hey, that's exactly where we were just sitting. No, that can't be right.* But I checked it again and it was.

We jumped in our vehicles and took off down there. Out of about thirty vehicles in the convoy, sixteen had been shot up and four or five of the drivers had been killed. That was something we'd never seen.

On the eighteenth, at about ten o'clock at night, my sergeant said, "Look, I don't know about you guys, but I really feel bad about this. We just took a break and people died because of that. I know you can't be everywhere at one time, but tomorrow I don't want to do that. These are our last days on the route. We know what to do. What do you all think about getting the guys together and saying that we aren't going to stop for anything. Unless we have to stop and urinate, we're not stopping."

March 20 rolled around. We woke up that morning and triple- and quadruple-checked all our equipment to make sure everything was good. Everybody was anticipating, really hoping that these guys might come out to ambush and attack us.

The patrol had been slow all morning. All of a sudden, around ten thirty or eleven a.m., I noticed a truck in front of me, one of the semis, going right and then left. I thought maybe they made contact.

I was in the lead vehicle and Sergeant Dustin Morris was driving. Specialist Casey Cooper was on the .50-caliber machine gun on the turret, and he was stomping and yelling down that he could hear gunfire. I told Sergeant Morris to drive over to the northbound lane so that we could pass the convoy. At the same time, I radioed up to the relay station to get a medevac and get information to the other units. I told them what was going on, requested air support, and we gave them a grid. Thirty seconds later, Sergeant Morris saw an opening in the convoy and we crossed over to the south side of the road. My gunners immediately turned their weapons systems onto the enemy. Originally, I saw just ten guys. They were in an orchard about two hundred yards from us. Immediately, we took a mess of fire. It was unreal how much fire started pounding our vehicle. I could hear the bullets hit the door. I looked down at the door and thought that at any time these rounds were going to come straight through and hit me.

We kept pushing. My gunners up with the .50-cal were drumming away. I looked in the mirror and the trucks behind me looked like they were just fine. We were in the orchard field and I yelled at Morris that I knew there was a road that ran parallel. I thought if we turned right, we could outflank the insurgents who were shooting at us. We'd be able to cut them off.

We got to the corner, and as soon as we turned we got hit with an RPG. It just smacked us. My first thought was of Cooper. He was lying facedown on my right and I thought he was dead. I grabbed him and he didn't respond, so I climbed over the top of him. The way it turned out, he had been knocked out for a minute, and then he got back in the fight.

I looked up expecting to see a couple of enemy cars, but I saw seven of them, all lined up with their doors and trunks wide open.

My heart just sank. I wasn't scared. I wasn't nervous. But I realized if there were seven cars and all four doors were open, I was looking at about twenty-eight enemies. There were ten of us. They had us outnumbered about three to one. Little did I know that there were thirty-five of them in this field, and just to the other side of a large canal there were fifteen more.

I had committed us to it and we had to go ahead and attack this ambush. I told Morris to go two hundred yards down the road and stop. My intention was to get all three of our vehicles lined up about hundred yards apart. I remember looking out the window to count people and I could see bullets hitting us on the side of the vehicle. Dirt flew up all around us. I remember the whole windshield was covered in oil. We were in a lot of trouble. There were three times as many bad guys out there, we were two hundred yards off the road, and I had a vehicle that might not keep running.

I saw a guy behind a tree about a hundred yards away turning around with an RPG. I jumped out of the vehicle and ran straight over to the berm about twenty meters away. I shot at him twice through the scrub bush that was around him. I waited for him to peek out again and I shot him in the head.

I could never hear the firing of guns around me. I knew they were going off but they didn't seem loud. All I could hear was Cooper yelling at me that there was a guy behind us, engaging us from the large canal. I left my cover from behind the berm and ran over. Sergeants Hester and Morris saw me, and they dismounted and ran next to me, engaging different targets on either side of the berm. Specialist Pullen dismounted on her side, the noncontact side, and she probably went through a magazine, engaging. Then she'd go back and give radio updates. That was how we did it. We'd practiced that if the fight really got intense, she'd man the radio while I either directed the fire or was directly engaged in it.

Cooper was yelling at me that he needed to engage somebody behind the berm with a grenade. Each team leader had two grenades and I had three. I ran over to the vehicle and asked him where the enemy was and he pointed. I threw the grenade up over the twenty-foot berm. It exploded. I took about five steps back and took off running as hard as I could to climb over the berm. I figured if the grenade didn't kill him, I was going to, because he would have been behind us. I got over the berm but I couldn't see him anymore. I figured he'd rolled over dead into the canal.

I came back down from the top of the berm and Specialist Pullen told me that Sergeant Rivera had been hit. I could see him and another soldier lying on the ground, rolling back and forth. At this point I thought two of my guys had been shot. I could see Specialist Mike shooting. I didn't know it at the time, but he had an M249 automatic weapon laid up on the back of the Humvee and was firing down on the canal's main trench line. There were about twenty enemy guys in there and he was trying to take them out.

Specialist Haynes was still shooting the .50-cal. About that time I turned and went back to Sergeants Hester and Morris and Specialist Ordunez. Ordunez yelled that we were taking fire from a house. I told him to light it up. He used his Mark 19 grenade launcher, let loose, put in ten to fifteen rounds, and devastated it. It was unbelievable to see. I went back on line with Sergeant Hester and Sergeant Morris, and they were engaging some more guys out in the field who were hiding behind the berms. Others were in the main canal system, trying to escape our machine-gun fire. I looked at Sergeants Hester and Morris and told them Mike was probably hit and that we needed to get into the canal system and start fighting these guys because we were taking so much fire from down there. Either Morris or Hester shot one guy. Sergeant Hester and I rolled into the canal and we were just a foot apart, trying to make our way, trying to hug the wall as tight as we could. I was in front of her and she would shoot over my right shoulder. Her barrel was inches from my head. I didn't hear her gun go off but I could feel the percussion of it hit my cheek. I could hear her talk just fine but everything else was blocked out.

I had two grenades left and we were trying to make our way down the canal. There was a guy about twenty or thirty yards away and I have no idea to this day how he never hit us. He stood there and sprayed from the hip. I could see bullets kicking up in front of me and the dirt was flying everywhere. I was on one knee with my rifle and I was shooting at this guy. I can remember seeing the actual bullets hit him square in the chest and he just kept shooting. Hester and I would move a couple of feet forward, squat low, and shoot. She prepared a grenade and shot one. I told her to shoot her 203 but we could never get it low enough. It would come out of the tube too high and land out in the field, close to the guys that were in the canal, but it would blast over their heads. Finally we killed him.

There's something else that went on in the canal. I remember two guys shooting at us and two other guys shooting up at Sergeant Rivera's truck. All of them turned on us. I just don't have a clue how they didn't hit us. I don't want to compare it to one of those old westerns where the people are standing in the middle of the street shooting at each other, but that's the way it was, only we were in a canal. We looked straight at each other and there was nothing between us and them. Those four guys in the canal had grenades. If they had thrown them at us, we would have died. If they had just stayed focused, I'm sure they would have shot us. I can't believe that one of us didn't get shot in the face or something. I can still hear the bullets whizzing past. We killed those four guys.

I worried that the Special Forces guys arriving to help might mistake us for the enemy. I looked up at one of the guys and gave him a cease-fire hand signal just to let him know that I was a friendly. It's an open hand facing out, waving it vertically up and down. He acknowledged me, waved back.

Sergeant Hester and I exited the canal system, and Sergeant Morris met up with us. Sergeant Hester ran past me. I wasn't running and I wasn't walking; I was what we call "range walking." I didn't want to pass anything up. I was more worried about security. I was looking around, trying to assess everything. Sergeant Morris was doing combat lifesaving skills and preparing for a medevac.

Specialist Mike directed everyone. He wasn't only trying to aid them; he was trying to supervise to make sure people were doing everything they could for the three wounded. When I came out of the canal, I saw that Specialist Haynes, our gunner, was covered with blood. I yelled to him, "Are you okay?" and he said, "Yeah." I asked him if he could still fight and he said he could. He'd been shot through the left hand but he stayed up on the .50-cal machine gun.

The firefight was over and I went down through the canal. I just couldn't believe how many people were out there. There were bodies everywhere. Even when I got back, I don't think I ever realized what went on. Maybe it's not even clear today. My platoon sergeant showed up later and he walked through and counted all the bodies out there and said, "Do you realize how many people were out there?" I didn't have a clue. I think the total was that twenty-seven enemy died. We captured six, and then later we captured a seventh one who was alive but hiding out in the field acting like he was dead.

I can say that I don't know 100 percent what went on that day. I know that if someone had asked me in the morning, "Do you want to be on the side with thirty-five or do you want to be on the team with ten?" I'd have picked the team with thirty-five. When it all boils down, it isn't anyone being a superman or being really brave. It's just the fact that people did what they were trained to do and they did it to make sure that the person beside them was going to live. By the grace of God I wasn't hurt.

I'm doing all right. If they asked me to go back tomorrow, it would just absolutely destroy my wife, but I'd do it. If they told me they needed me tomorrow, I would go. We're doing the right thing. I believe 100 percent in the mission. It's not going to be an overnight thing. Everyday Iraqi people are really no different than we are. Human beings are human beings and it doesn't matter if you are Caucasian, African-American, Asian. Iraqis want to prosper. They want to work, raise families. They want their kids to be safe. I cannot imagine what they've gone through. I told my wife this: If somebody said there was an IED in my county, I'd pack up my family and move.

The Iraqis are literally living in a world where twenty or thirty yards outside their house, there may be an unexploded round hidden in the ground. Their kids may be walking past IEDs on the way to school. This is the world they live in.

I tell a lot of kids, especially the ones who are about ten years old, that by the time they are twenty, Iraq is going to be a lot better. And I can almost guarantee that by the time they're thirty, Iraq will be a safe and prosperous country that they won't have to worry about.

★

Two members of the 617th Military Police earned the Silver Star: Leigh Ann Hester and Specialist Jason Mike. Leigh Ann Hester is the first woman to receive the Silver Star since World War II. Specialist Casey Cooper, Specialist William Haynes, and Specialist Ashley Pullen each received a Bronze Star with Valor. Two other members of the Kentucky National Guard unit, Sergeant Dustin Morris and Specialist Jesse Ordunez, received an Army Commendation Medal with valor device.

Tim Nein is currently living in his hometown of Henryville, Indiana, with his wife and two young sons. He continues to serve on active duty with the Kentucky National Guard.

GROUND TRUTH

★

James Coffman, Colonel, U.S. Army

Great Barrington, Massachusetts

Distinguished Service Cross; Mosul, Iraq; 14 November 2004

Serving as an advisor to the Iraqi Special Police Commandos, Colonel James Coffman found himself in the thick of a firefight in Mosul, battling for his life and the lives of his Iraqi comrades. When insurgents attacked several police stations on November 14, 2004, Colonel Coffman moved in to help and was ambushed by rocket-propelled grenades and small-arms fire. One hour into a four-hour battle, he was wounded in his shooting hand, his left, and his rifle was rendered useless. Coffman picked up an AK-47 and kept shooting with his right hand, rallying his Iraqi soldiers and driving off the enemy. "When the bad guys started advancing," recalls Coffman, "I was

JAMES COFFMAN

essentially the only guy in the area shooting. I thought I might not be able to beat them off, but I had a bunch of wounded guys behind me, and whatever it took to keep those guys from getting to us was what I was going to do." For his bravery Coffman was awarded the Distinguished Service Cross, the army's second-highest award, at a ceremony in Baghdad.

We live in a rich country full of opportunity people can seize on. In my own experience, I come from a very poor background but I worked hard and with a few opportunities I was able to make something of myself. I think that's one of the strengths of the United States. We tend to be a fairly compassionate people, and we want to make the world a better place. This is particularly true in the military. I think part of the military culture is compassionate toward the conditions of people around the world. There's an instinctive trend toward humanitarianism that can be seen in soldiers from the private to a general officer. There's a collective sense of wanting to make things better.

I had the opportunity to spend about two years in Iraq. In October of 2003 Ambassador Bremer went to Secretary Rumsfeld and said that he wanted some senior military assistants embedded in the Coalition Provisional Authority. They were looking for a military assistant with my background. I became his eyes and ears and "ground truth" for things going on in Iraq. I arrived in Baghdad in December 2003 and had fairly unfettered access, not only to Ambassador Bremer but also to the goings-on in the field. I was all over Iraq, in a number of flashpoints. We weren't in Humvees or armored cars. It was very low profile, low signature. We worked with the Iraqi leadership, the Iraqi minister of the Interior, the senior deputy minister of the Interior, and the police within the ministry.

On June 28, 2004, sovereignty was returned to Iraq and my tour of duty was over. I returned home a week later. I was called back to Iraq in September. The Iraqi army was just beginning to gel. It was in its infancy. There was a lot of high violence in Iraq, particularly in the Shiite area south of Baghdad. No counterinsurgency force was available in Iraq so the minister of the Interior created "special police commandos" to deal with the violence. I told Lieutenant General David Petraeus that this was an organization worth supporting and I became an advisor to them. I was asked to stay a little bit longer: my two weeks turned into another year over there. Lieutenant General Petraeus gave me the freedom to go anywhere in the country that I needed to go, to see whatever it was I needed to see, and to give him the ground truth of how the Iraqi security forces were doing. I had a chance to see things at a very tactical level. Also, because of where I was and because of my Coalition Provisional Authority experience working directly with Ambassador Bremer, I saw firsthand the decisions at the strategic level. It was a bit like being a reporter with a gun.

I didn't spend nearly as much time with the American soldiers as I did with the Iraqi soldiers, but I'll give you my observations on both and I'll start with the Americans. The American soldiers over there are very compassionate. They see the suffering of people. They want to improve conditions and they want to help them. At the same time there is outrage at the acts of terrorism, in particular its effects on the innocent. The soldiers are, I would say, very heartbroken by the results of those terrorist acts, because the American soldiers tend to move into an area and get close to people. Soldiers are human, and it's hard not to be moved by the death, maiming, or wounding of innocent civilians. At the same time, they're working in an uncertain environment and they don't speak the language well. They may not be aware of all the innuendos or subtleties. American soldiers have a vast reservoir of heroic compassion and the heartfelt endeavor to improve the Iraqi condition; this is in opposition to the soldiers' tougher side. I saw many instances of the Iraqi people being truly thankful for the assistance and privately saying how glad they were that Americans were there providing stability.

I found the Iraqis to be a warm and friendly people on the whole. They want the same things that the people of the United States want. They want a better life for their children, economic opportunities, and to improve their conditions. They want to do well in life. Part of this is in response to the lack of opportunities during thirty-five years under a very tough regime. I saw many instances of very heroic action, almost romantically so. At the same time I saw them with all the frailties that human beings around the world have. But again, they are soldiers and I can tell you that their level of skill and the individual training were very high in many instances.

The units that were well trained and had good leadership experienced surprisingly few bad deeds. Those units that were less well trained and had poor leadership may have allowed individuals to do some bad things. The Iraqi soldiers know what's at stake. For them there's no "rotation date." Their hope for a better future is on the line. They know what they need to do and they know they have to get rid of the insurgents and the criminal element to allow Iraq to thrive.

The Iraqis are proud people. They have good reason to be. Iraq has been at the center of the Middle East culture for several thousand years. It is a wealthy country in terms of human capital, water, natural resources, oil, and arable soil. I found the Iraqi people to be incredibly clever. They are very commerce-oriented, born entrepreneurs. It seems that every Iraqi you meet has a little business on the side. You see all this vast potential that they want to realize. They want to better themselves, and they are thwarted by the insurgency. It's fairly well documented that much of the insurgency's support comes from outside Iraq. You can't characterize it as a single group. There are multiple insurgencies and motivations for the different factions. There are the Baathists, the born fighters. There is also a large criminal element running an economic enterprise.

But yes, absolutely, things are heading in the right direction. It would be naïve to say, or uninformed to say, that bad things don't happen. In the West we are conditioned to getting things done quickly. But the truth of the matter is it's much more difficult than that, and the Iraqis are as impatient as anybody. I spent two years there through some very turbulent times and was involved in some combat operations. I remain optimistic. I see progress. I see things changing for the better. There are some ups and downs but the trend line, the general movement, is all positive. There are more cars in Baghdad now than there were two years ago, and more access to the news for the local population. They have more opportunities than they did in the spring of 2003. They want to get on with it.

In November 2004, the U.S. and Iraqi forces were building up to go into Fallujah. It was obvious there was going to be a major operation there. A number of insurgents left Fallujah and came to Mosul, where they threatened the police stations. The city was in crisis. We decided that the Iraqi Special Police Commandos would establish five strategic points in the city to start to bring stability back to Mosul.

On the morning of November 14, 2004, the Iraqi commandos and I were going to occupy several police stations. About ten thirty that morning, we were informed that the northernmost station was under fairly heavy attack in a particularly dangerous area of the city. We were far south but we organized a Quick Reaction Force of about ten vehicles to relieve the pressure on this police station. As we neared the police station we began receiving small-arms fire from a eucalyptus grove. We returned fire and moved on. We got within about hundred yards of the police station and we came under very heavy fire. I'm not sure if we were hit with RPGs or IEDs, but we stopped and got out of the vehicles because they made us more vulnerable.

We were under a heavy concentration of fire. One of our commandos got hit in the neck and the bullet came out his right cheek. I tried to administer first aid to him. We didn't have any medical equipment with us. I pulled his body armor off and I took my knife to cut strips out of his T-shirt to use as a compression bandage on him. I got one of the other commandos to apply the compress.

When you are in a firefight, it seems like all the bullets are coming at you. Some of the soldiers were scared, which is of course normal, and I tried to rally them to fire. They had a tendency to put their weapons over a wall and fire without looking. I went around to each of the soldiers and looked them in the eye, told them they'd be okay. Then I positioned them on the wall so we'd have a better defense. I called the Stryker Brigade headquarters to tell them what our situation was and that we needed some air support to break up this attack. We continued to return fire and tried to suppress the enemy that was across the street from us. We started taking more casualties and we had to treat the wounded. One soldier took a round through his leg. I think it hit his femoral artery. He was bleeding heavily so I ripped shirts to use as a compress on the wound and put a tourniquet on it. As things turned out, he bled out and died.

About an hour into the battle, we were running low on ammunition and our men down below started throwing magazines up to us. An Iraqi, Captain Abbas, who was right next to me, dashed out into the open under fire to grab those magazines. I saw these kinds of heroic acts and it really upsets me when I hear people say, "Well, the Iraqis won't fight; you know they're cowards." I saw plenty of heroism. The captain got hit and we pulled him back, and then I got hit in my left hand, my shooting hand. The bullet went through the back of my hand, through the fleshy part of my thumb, and into the stock of my M4, which rendered it inoperable. I picked up an AK-47 and emptied the magazine into the building from which we were receiving fire. By this time we had quite a few casualties so there were plenty of unused weapons around and I used those. But we were getting low on ammunition and we had enemy guys rushing at us a couple of times.

At that point I called for air strikes. They had fixed-wing aircraft that could have dropped five-hundred-pound bombs, but I was concerned about the damage that could be done to civilians in the area. I was in a moral dilemma because we didn't have much ammunition.

We were about three hours into the battle at that point. We started taking RPGs and one hit the façade of our building and it collapsed down on us. I thought, *This is it*. It rang my chimes pretty good. I had four rounds left and there were six insurgents rushing our position. Things were a little tense. I was a little bit concerned about whether or not we were going to make it through this. The enemy was determined to overrun our position. We'd run out of loaded magazines and were using individual rounds.

Amazingly, an Iraqi Quick Reaction Force arrived just as the insurgents reached about twenty yards from us. They were engaged by the Quick Reaction Force and broke off their rush against our position. We were saved from being overrun, but the fight was not over yet.

That was about three and a half hours into the battle. We had heavy casualties: thirteen dead and forty-eight wounded. We were trying to collect the wounded at that point. There was a second Quick Reaction Force, a Stryker company, under heavy fire themselves, but they were moving up the road toward us. We linked up with them and they were an excellent company. We were still under attack so we put a Hellfire missile into that building. That's when things started to calm down. We were over four hours into the battle.

I refused to be evacuated until we accomplished our mission: secure the police station. We did secure the police station, and then I let a medic bandage up my hand a bit. I made sure that all my guys were out first before I agreed to be medevaced. The Strykers medevaced me to an aid station with all the other Iraqi wounded, whom I thanked for all their bravery. Eventually, I was sent to the hospital in

Mosul, but I refused to remain overnight and left to rejoin the Special Police Commando unit at their base. The next day, I was medevaced to Baghdad after I refused to go to Germany for medical treatment. I had shattered quite a few of the joints but I was able to heal after surgery at the Baghdad MASH. I don't have some of the fine motor skills left—I can't snap my fingers—but that's okay.

I don't have any nightmares or anything like that. I do think about it. In terms of combat, I saw some of the best come out of people. People risked their lives for me, and I was willing to risk mine for them. We'd had other operations prior to that, but there is a certain bonding experience between soldiers in combat, and it doesn't matter that we didn't have the same cultural background and didn't share the same language. I can get very incensed when I hear people afterward talk about the Iraqi soldiers, saying they're cowards. I saw firsthand just the opposite was true.

I was completely surprised by receiving the Distinguished Service Cross. It's humbling. I did what was expected of any soldier in those circumstances. I didn't think that I was particularly heroic. I fought to the best of my ability. I read some of the accounts of people who received the Silver Star and I thought, *Wow, they did a hell of a lot more than I did.* They should be getting the Distinguished Service Cross and not me. I probably shouldn't have been in that situation with no communication and everything else that went horribly wrong. Mostly, when people win their medals it's because something went terribly bad.

It was the Stryker Brigade Quick Reaction Force that came to save us that showed real courage. That takes a lot of guts. They knew how desperate our situation was and they were willing to come in and fight for us. I've got to tell you, there were a lot of heroics in Iraq from common soldiers that I don't think are recognized enough.

I guess I was surprised I was able to get through it. No matter how well you are trained, you always wish you were trained better. I think I learned the importance of training and experience, being able to maintain your sense and confidence in a very difficult situation. Looking back at it, I was surprised that I was able to do some of the things that I did. Most of it was instinctive. I remember thinking, *Where did that come from?* Autopilot takes over, and you do what you were trained to do. It's second nature. I don't know how much I learned about myself that day, but it confirmed to me what being a soldier is about.

I wrote to Lieutenant General Petraeus the day after it happened, when they were talking about medevacing me out. I wrote in the e-mail, "Yesterday I gave my blood for my country and for the Iraqi people. And I want to stay here, stay in the fight. Please do what you can to keep me from being evacuated." I felt like I had paid to stay, so to speak. There was a lot more to be done. I didn't want to leave. I would have felt like I was abandoning the soldiers. I could not just leave. It was probably far better for me from a mental-health standpoint to stay. With my hand in a cast, I was ready to carry on. From here on out, I'll continue to do what soldiers do: follow their orders.

★

James Coffman remained in Iraq, continuing his work with the Iraqi Special Police Commandos until September 2005. He has since returned to the United States and remains on active duty, currently stationed at the Pentagon.

IT WAS ME OR THEM, AND IT WASN'T GOING TO BE ME

★

Eric Stebner, Sergeant, U.S. Army
Pingree and Ellendale, North Dakota
SILVER STAR; AFGHANISTAN; 4 MARCH 2002

On a barren, frozen mountaintop that was later called Roberts Ridge, carrying eighty pounds of gear each, Eric Stebner and his four-man team climbed two thousand feet in snow three feet deep to rescue fellow soldiers who were under fire from al-Qaeda. It was an eighteen-hour battle for which Eric Stebner earned the Silver Star.

ERIC STEBNER

I grew up in North Dakota and I played outside every chance I got. My dad managed a grain elevator and my mom was a nurse who worked at the hospital. When I was in the fifth grade, one of my best friend's older brothers, who was in the Second Ranger Battalion, came home and showed me all his gear. Ever since then, that was what I wanted to do, join the army. I went to Fort Benning, Georgia, for basic training. It really wasn't a big change. I just accepted it and did what needed to be done. The hardest part was having my whole life taken away from me for thirteen weeks. I was on nobody's time but theirs.

Four years later, I was back at Fort Benning attending Airborne and Ranger School. I think everybody handles it differently; there's no set way of getting through it. There was a Florida phase where we walked through the swamp, totally exhausted and sleep-deprived, and soldiers would just fall asleep and fall over. It was tough but there wasn't a time when I was tempted to quit. This was something I wanted to do and I didn't want to accept anything different. To ask me specifically what I did to get through it or how I did it, I couldn't tell you. I guess it has to do with how I was raised and how I take life. I really don't know.

As far as being deployed to Afghanistan or Iraq, everybody was pretty pumped up. We had a heads-up before we left; we put two and two together. The Third Ranger Battalion ended up going before us and we all worried that we'd missed our chance. Little did we know that there would be deployment after deployment after deployment. We were training all the time and there wasn't any lackadaisical attitude about it. It was always full-charge ahead. We expected to be in combat and we trained for it. Our group was filled with very different individuals. There was a twenty-eight-year-old guy who had been a high school arts teacher. Some kids had parents who were doctors. Some were lawyers who turned down offers in order to be Rangers. Some of the guys were natural physical specimens and athletes. Some were entry-level privates. Everybody who was there wanted to be there. There wasn't anybody who complained or brought the team down. They were all willing to do their part. As a leader, I tried to teach guys at a basic level and let them go from there. I don't sit over someone and bark and scream or yell how to load a magazine or tie their shoes. I teach them the basics and let them apply themselves and expand from there.

If you put Afghanistan in the United States, it would be just one huge national park. Lots of mountains and vast empty spaces. When we first got to Bagram Air Force Base in Afghanistan, we stayed in tents. We had power but no heaters. We'd "spin up" a lot. That's what we called it: spin up, gear up, get ready, go down to the airfields, get ready to launch. It was just a drill to keep us alert. We had some contact with everyday Afghans but not a lot. Sometimes the kids would just sit there and watch us all day. We could throw a football around and that was something new to them. They have kind of a closed life, I guess.

We knew Operation Anaconda was kicking off but we didn't really know the scope of it or which units would be involved. We heard about the resistance they were getting and how they were having a hard time and taking a lot of casualties. It really frustrated us. "Why aren't we in there?" we asked. On the night of March 3, 2002, a call came in. We were all sleeping in our tents and they woke everybody up and we said, "Yeah, sure. We're just going to get spun up and go down to the airfield and come back again." Basically, everybody just got up, got ready, put our kits on and got ready to go.

We started hearing pieces of information. We heard a guy had fallen off an aircraft and they had eyes on him. We were going in as a Quick Reaction Force to pick him up. With a QRF, you never know the exact area or grid where you're going or exactly what you'll be doing. I just wore my desert uniform with a T-shirt, gloves, and desert jungle boots. I didn't wear my heavy cold-weather boots, because in an earlier deployment I worked in the Khowst area and the weather was pretty warm there and I was in the wrong kind of boots for two weeks and was miserable.

We took off in a Chinook helicopter and we heard that we were going to Gardez. They were still tracking the downed soldier. We circled the mountains and then we touched down. We sat there for quite a while and it was pretty cold. It just dragged on; it was a long time and we really didn't know what was happening. Then finally we took off. We learned at that point there had been four KIAs and that we were going to be in a hot landing zone [LZ]. I knew the people that were up there. I had a roommate up there, Sergeant Brad Crose, and he was one of my best friends. I got a feeling that something had happened to Brad; I don't know why. I didn't know what. I couldn't tell anybody else but something just told me that something had happened to him. I thought that I was not going to let any more of that happen. The thought going through my mind was that it was going to be me or them, and it wasn't going to be me.

As the Chinook approached the landing zone, we were told that the enemy was going to be to our front about two hundred meters. If you think about two hundred meters, that's well within effective range of a weapon system, which let us know what it was going to be like coming in. We landed, everybody exited, and we sat there for a second. There was a little high ground to my right so I walked over there to try to get any vantage point I could and to spread out our perimeter. The snow was deep but I kept pushing. This was a hot LZ but there weren't any shots being fired. It was quite calm and the only thing we could hear was the wind blowing. About that time, an aircraft did a gun run, pretty close, and we looked up and realized we had been dropped off two thousand feet below where we were supposed to go. It was a forty-to-seventy-degree slope and we were receiving sporadic enemy fire. It was an exhausting two-and-a-half-hour climb up the side of the mountain, and we were wheezing and slipping and weighted down with gear. I wanted to get there. I had roommates up there who were having problems and I wanted to get to them and say, "Hey, I'm here to help you out." There were four kills and I wanted to get there and start evening things out, doing what I could to get back at the enemy.

We finally linked up and got eyes on Chalk One, the first Chinook that had been shot down. They didn't see us at first. I was on point. We linked up with two people on an outcropping there and I asked them, "Hey, is this clear down here?" They told me it wasn't. We went through and cleared it. There were some weird things I saw, like an American MRE that was broken open and stripped down and then taped together. We'd do that to make them smaller and lighter and it blew my mind to see them there. At that point I asked one of the guys who was killed in action. He told me that I didn't want to know. I felt I already knew it was Brad. He told me that it was, and I knew I needed to do whatever they needed to make the situation better, complete the mission. It was time to clear out the bunkers, and we organized our little assault teams and came up with a plan for how we were going to do it.

We could see the smoke trails of the RPGs coming right at us. The RPGs don't fire in a straight line. Those things have been dragged around the mountains for years. They came at us skipping off rocks and we were wondering, *Is this thing going to hit me?*

We went across, assaulted the bunkers, and cleared out all of them. I guess that's when I would have been one of the first ones to go in and find Neil Roberts's body. I remember I was assaulting across and I saw the bottom of his boot with the little yellow marking of the Vibram sole. We kept clearing out in all directions and then we went down and started evacuating the casualties. The enemy had been a mix of everything. Some were determined fighters. Some would fight if they had an edge and otherwise take off. As far as their nationality, it was a little mix of everything.

We started organizing eight litter teams to carry out the casualties. That was the first time I saw the KIAs. We started moving casualties up the hill and we were drawing sporadic gunfire, AK and RPGs. Every time I'd go out to move a casualty, I'd draw enemy fire. But I had this thought in my head that they hadn't hit me yet and they weren't going to. We never had a real good streamline of people carrying out the evacuation because we'd have to change up crews to give people a break. The guys at the helicopter were saying, "Hurry up, hurry up!" We were moving as fast as we could. My nose was bleeding and I was coughing up blood because there was no air to breathe. I don't care if you're an Olympic star or a physical specimen, put yourself at twelve thousand feet and it's like you're sucking air through a straw. Frostbitten feet and severe headaches. The snow was melting and the footing was bad. We were moving casualties and the medics were taking care of the wounded. One of the bodies I helped carry was Brad's. And some of the people treating the wounded got wounded and became casualties themselves. I wasn't wounded. One of the hardest targets to hit is a moving target.

We didn't have any definite time when the aircraft was going to be there to get us out. We were told we were going to have to wait until nightfall. We didn't want to stay spread out; we collapsed down a little bit. It was weird: we could look down in the valley and see Operation Anaconda going on below us. We could see the fighting going from side to side. Up where we were, the firefight had pretty much died down. We'd overrun the area. When the relief came, we loaded up all the casualties and KIAs and took off.

Some people are drastically changed by a situation like that and some aren't. I try to use everything I learned as a stepping-stone and I try to basically keep the memories of those guys alive. I never really sit back and reflect on what I pulled out of that situation or what I learned. Basically, I think I wouldn't have changed anything I did; I wouldn't have done anything different. Even if I had cold-weather boots on, my feet would have been wet and cold anyway. I do keep a rolled-up dry pair of socks in my kit in a pouch. A fresh pair of socks feels like a million bucks.

It's up to the people of Afghanistan to determine what kind of a future they will have. I'm not into politics. I'll go there again and do what I need to do if those are my orders. What drives people to make them do what they do in certain situations and at certain times, I can't really tell you. Whatever type of person they are, whatever history they have, how they were raised, it all comes together during moments of crisis. It starts when you are a little kid. Why did I do the things I did up on that mountain? I don't know. I just did. A lot of people can't understand why we do what we do. They go to bed at night and don't realize what's going on. I hope people appreciate it more now. It would have been nicer to have received a lesser award and come home with the entire team.

I'd like to dedicate this chapter to my dad, Dennis, my little girl, Natalie, and my best friend, Brad Crose.

★

Eric Stebner continues to serve our nation as a Ranger platoon sergeant and has since redeployed to the combat zone. He plans to stay in the army.

THIRTY MINUTES TO ANYWHERE

★

Nathan Self, Captain, U.S. Army

Army Rangers

China Springs, Texas

Silver Star; Afghanistan; 4 March 2002

During his first two months in Afghanistan, Captain Nathan Self and his elite platoon hadn't seen any action. Now it was day three of Operation Anaconda in the cold, barren, and enemy-ridden Shahikot Valley in eastern Afghanistan. Attempting to rescue downed soldiers at the top of the 10,200-foot mountain Takur Ghar, the black Chinook rescue helicopter Nathan Self and his unit were in was hit. Four were killed instantly. The seventeen-hour battle that ensued was a shoot-out with a highly trained entrenched enemy only fifty meters away.

U.S. ARMY

I was born in Waco and grew up in China Springs, Texas. My father skipped around jobs for a while so we moved around the state. My mother went to work in the human resources department at a local hospital and she's still doing that. I went to a fairly small high school and had the opportunity to be involved in everything. Most of the kids who played on the football team moved on to the basketball team and then to the baseball team when the seasons changed. I was one of those. My future wife and I were both in the band. I didn't get involved in student government until my senior year, and I was vice president of the student council. I graduated second in my class, but there were just fifty-six of us. The youth group at church was important to me, too. I attended a couple of Bible studies on the side and a lot of my time was spent in church.

I became very interested in life at West Point and the challenges and opportunities beyond. I never wanted to go to a state school. I was comfortable with a small class size. I also wanted to go somewhere very challenging. When I went for a visit, it all seemed to feel right. From the outside looking in, the place is great and beautiful. It seemed to be an honorable place. It definitely has a draw to it.

I started in the summer. By the end of the first day they'd shaved our heads, put us in uniforms, taught us how to march, put us in our respective units, and had us marching in a parade for whatever parents had stuck around. We took our oath at the parade.

Within the first few minutes I was asking myself, *What am I doing here?* I remember standing in an archway under one of the barracks with my hands behind my back in the parade-rest position, staring at a wall for a couple of hours. People were walking by. Every second seemed like an eternity.

I was able to adapt pretty quickly. I felt my strengths were in the areas of leadership and group dynamics. I felt duty-bound to try to do the hard jobs. I felt some of my weaknesses were in the area of organization and time management. I wouldn't say I was a perfectionist, but it might take me a long time to finish a task because I wanted to do it a certain way.

Julie and I had been dating for six years and we got married two weeks after I graduated from the academy. We spent a couple of months on leave. I went to Fort Benning, Georgia, for infantry training and she went back to Baylor University because she still had a year of school left. Then I went to some other basic courses for infantry officers and Ranger School.

I found out I could do more than I expected in some areas and less than I thought I could do in others. There are times when you can overcome seemingly insurmountable odds and there are other times when you have to recognize your weaknesses and rely on other people. You can't do everything on your own because there will be times when you're too exhausted, too spent, sleep deprived, inexperienced, or just aren't on your game, and you have to be able to trust others to steer the boat for you. Up until that time, I thought that it was someone else's job to lead. Now, for the first time, I felt it was something I could do myself.

Army Rangers have an extreme passion for excellence. Their approach has always been absolutely realistic in terms of war and real-world tensions. The first unit I served in was in Germany. Then I went to Kosovo. We were responsible for just about anything you can think of for ten villages. We commandeered an abandoned house, put thirty-five guys in it, and lived on the outskirts of a Serbian town. There was a lot of urban patrolling. We conducted a couple of operations on insurgent camps up in the mountains.

We deployed for Afghanistan in December 2001. We weren't the first group of Rangers to go, and before we got there the Taliban was finished as an operating entity. It was fractured and the chase was on for high-value people. I wasn't allowed to tell anyone except Julie that I was leaving. My family didn't know. We deployed the day after Christmas, definitely not one of my best days. Our son, Caleb, was just two months old when I left, so it wasn't easy. We got to Afghanistan on New Year's Eve; my platoon was a Quick Reaction Force made up of Navy SEALs, Army Rangers, and Special Operations pilots. Our mission was to kill or capture high-value targets in Afghanistan, both al-Qaeda and Taliban. If there was a target that popped up quickly, we were always ready. We slept with our clothes on and our gear ready. Within thirty minutes we could fly anywhere in Afghanistan to do something.

The 101st Airborne, 10th Mountain Division was working with friendly Afghan forces in southeastern Afghanistan to kill and capture a big pocket of al-Qaeda who had fled from Tora Bora and regrouped in the Shahikot Valley in the Takur Ghar mountains. That operation kicked off in March and our group was on high-alert status as a Quick Reaction Force.

One of the insertion field teams went bad. A six-man team was going to try to land on top of the mountain. That's not normally the way you want to do things because it's pretty dangerous. It's a key piece of terrain and it can be assumed the enemy may be there. And they were. They shot them up as they were landing. They lost a man; he actually fell out of the back of the helicopter onto the top of a mountain. His name was Navy Petty Officer First Class Neil Roberts. All the pilot could do was land the helicopter someplace else, drop off most of the crew, strip down more of the gear, and take the original team back to try to retrieve Roberts. Once they got there, they came under heavy fire again. Now instead of one person injured, there were six of them.

We were listening to the radio at Bagram Air Force Base and I knew we would probably have to go and secure the helicopter until they could either destroy it or extract if from the battlefield. We began to get ready. When you're serving as a Quick Reaction Force, you take advantage of any chance you have to plan. The way it mostly goes, though, you don't have the time. A Quick Reaction Force is never going to know everything that's going on. If they did, then they wouldn't be quick. In this case, if we'd taken the time to plan everything out, the people who needed us most would have been in much worse shape. We were an hour's flight away. I had my map ready to go with the grid. Using the imagery our intelligence officer printed out, everything was focused on the area where the helicopter was, which happened to be eight kilometers away from the insertion point where Roberts had fallen out. We were not prepared to land on top of the mountain. But as we got closer, the radio reports became more urgent. We were going to have to land somewhere and figure out what was going on from there. We knew the landing zone was probably what we called hot. Finally, we were given a grid on the top of the mountain.

We came in to land and it was almost daylight. We were probably about twenty to thirty feet off the ground and we came under fire: RPGs, machine guns, and small-arms fire. It came from the front and both sides. They fired an RPG into the cockpit and into the engines and that disabled the helicopter. Basically, we landed pretty hard because we'd lost power. I learned later that the pilot kept it from rolling by maintaining controls until the rotors slowed down.

As soon as we hit the ground, the helicopter was completely riddled with gunfire and RPGs. The men in the cockpit were getting all shot up. The helicopter was just getting pounded. I was up really close to the front, near the cockpit, and all the people around me were either wounded or killed. As the Rangers started to run off the aircraft, the enemy had one particular gun firing right across the ramp. Two Rangers were killed coming off the ramp. A burst of gunfire went right over my head when I went down the ramp. Then I moved another Ranger who was with me around to the side and out of the line of fire. When he moved to the right side of the helicopter, we realized the enemy was there, too.

There was a clear sky; it was a bright morning even though the sun wasn't up yet, and we were ankle- to knee-deep in snow, depending on where we were standing. The bullets flying past made a clicking sound. The thin air smelled like cedar, fuel, gunpowder, metal, blood, sweat, and for some reason strawberries. I saw it all happening but it didn't seem real. It seemed like a bad movie. We were on the top of a ten-thousand-foot mountain. There were a few little depressions, boulders and outcroppings of rocks to provide a little cover. The enemy was firing down on us from the two o'clock position. They were about seventy meters away and they had a machine gun, and one man kept firing RPGs at us. There were just five or six of us fighting and everybody else was wounded. I'd say there were about fifteen enemy soldiers. They were poised in a landing zone ambush with some heavy firepower. They hit us when we couldn't fight back. They exploited a weakness. It wasn't until we got out of the helicopter that we were able to get some fire on them. I took shrapnel to the leg but it wasn't affecting me much.

We had three options: assault straight ahead, stay put, or retreat.

We tried to assault but the enemy was well protected by logs, leaves, and branches. We had just four soldiers and we were moving uphill in knee-deep snow. We didn't have enough firepower to assault. One of the air force guys on the radio with me was able to make contact with some F-15s. They offered bombs and some cannons. The F-15s started to strafe the enemy positions just seventy-five meters in front of us. It was high drama. We were watching these guys rip off rounds from a half mile away, and then a split second later there were explosions all around us. It's definitely interesting. They were good and we didn't get hit. I knew it was having some suppressive effect on the enemy but they were still menacing us. It was my decision to call in the air strikes and I did it because I wanted to intimidate the enemy. I tried to keep them from having any ideas about trying to outflank us or attack our position. I decided to drop bombs. When the target is that close, they generally ask for the initials of the guy in charge on the ground. I was passing my initials over the radio because they were dropping the stuff within fifty meters of us. They started on the other side of the mountain and walked the bombs closer to us from the other side. They got them closer and closer and the last one probably landed seventy-five to one hundred meters off the peak. That was close enough.

We knew reinforcements were on the way. There were about ten guys who had to climb two thousand feet, and that meant they were about three hours away. It was a cat-and-mouse game with the enemy. They kept trying to assault us. After a while, we started taking mortar fire that bracketed our position. We were ready to make some sort of decision about taking the one working helicopter and getting our people out. We found out there were Predators, unmanned aerial vehicles, over our heads and they had Hellfire laser-guided missiles. Those bombs are small and accurate, so we decided to employ those on the bunker position. The first one was way off the mark, I think purposely so. We only had two missiles so I asked them to put the second one right on the bunker, and that's where it hit, right on.

We took the ten Rangers who'd climbed up to meet us and we fought through the enemy positions. That's when we found Neil Roberts's body. Immediately we started moving casualties to the top of the mountain, which was a safer location. Within ten or fifteen minutes, the enemy launched a counterattack from my rear, but we fought it off.

When we got down, we looked at all the enemy bodies to see what we were dealing with. There were Uzbeks, Arabs, Chechens, and Taliban. These were people who had come to Afghanistan to fight. It was the end of February, they were at ten thousand feet, and they were wearing plastic shoes, like shower shoes. They were living up there in a combat zone because they knew the fight was there and they were there for the fight.

A lot of good men were killed or wounded on that mountain. Of the ten Rangers on board my aircraft, only one wasn't killed or wounded or had his equipment disabled. My wounds were somewhat superficial: shrapnel wounds from mid-waist down my right side. It bled for quite a while but not through my clothing. I was real sore for a while, but within a couple of weeks I was able to run. I had a dime-size hole in my leg, and there's still some shrapnel there that makes it a little tender. I don't really understand why I got the medals.

I think about what happened every day. Not once a day but all the time. I think there are probably things going on inside of me that I haven't figured out yet. I'm not active in the army anymore, and sometimes I feel like I'm not living up to the duty I've been called to do. The guy directly to my right was killed and we were touching shoulder to shoulder. The door gunner to my left was killed. Everybody around me was getting hit. It was an amazing experience. God spared me for a reason. The Rangers who died, they're the ones who really put everything into perspective.

★

Nathan Self has returned to private life in Texas, where he lives with his wife and family.

HOT PASSES

★

Christopher Russell, Captain, U.S. Air Force
335th Fighter Squadron
Colorado Springs, Colorado
SILVER STAR; AFGHANISTAN; 4 MARCH 2002

On a ten-thousand-foot mountaintop called Takur Ghar, a downed helicopter crew was receiving intense fire from a well-trained, well-hidden enemy that was just two hundred fifty feet away. With the enemy too close for bombs, the two F-15E Strike Eagles used 20mm cannon fire with pinpoint precision to save their fellow Americans. For his actions providing emergency close-air support, Captain Chris Russell earned the Silver Star.

CHRISTOPHER RUSSELL

I was an air force brat. My dad is a retired air force colonel, so we moved around quite a bit in the '70s. I was born in Sacramento, California; we moved to Shaw Air Force Base in South Carolina, then to Austin, Texas, for a couple of years while he was flying F-4s. Then we moved to Germany and spent about three years overseas. We moved to San Jose, California, where my dad completed his master's at Stanford University and then got a job at the Air Force Academy teaching aeronautical engineering. We ended up in Colorado around 1980. I was in the second grade and we stayed there until 1995, when I graduated from Colorado State University.

I remember the exact moment when I decided to join the air force. It was 1978, I was five years old, and we were living in Germany. My brother and I jumped in a truck on the air force base, and my dad was flying an F-4 that day. One of the pilots in his squadron took us up to the control tower to watch Dad take off, and they were doing maximum-performance takeoffs. They suck up the gear and flaps above the runway, accelerate to four hundred knots, and then pull the nose straight up and disappear into the weather. As soon as I heard the roar of those engines, I was hooked. My grandpa is a retired colonel, so is my dad. My brother is a squadron commander, and now I'm in the air force, too. My parents never forced me into the military. I just thought, *Wow, this is what I want to do.* It's what I always wanted to do.

After high school I went to Colorado State University and went through their ROTC program. I attended military and leadership classes one or two times a week. I learned to march, I trained, and on Thursdays I wore the uniform all day. Between sophomore and junior years, I attended my official basic training in San Antonio, Texas. I learned to make my bed, shoot guns, and I got yelled at a lot.

No one likes getting yelled at, but it didn't bother me much. It was fine. Growing up in a military family, I knew what to expect. The point of it is to put pressure on you and see how you react. Do you get flustered and give up, or can you power through that and actually reach your goal? At the end of those four weeks of basic training, I felt I was able to take control of a situation and lead somebody through it. It may not have been the perfect answer, but at least I was willing to think things through, take action, and get things rolling.

When I graduated from college, I discovered I didn't have the eyes to be a pilot. I wanted to become a navigator but a lot of the airplanes that required navigators were shutting down, replacing navigators with GPS. Instead, I went off to Los Angeles and worked the business side of the air force, in acquisitions. I did that for two years. Then when a navigator slot opened, I got picked up and went to navigator training. That was April 1997 in Pensacola, Florida. It was a joint navigation school with the navy and the marines and a few international allies, like Saudi Arabia, Italy, and Germany. I spent two years there and then I spent three months in Columbus, Mississippi, going through introduction to fighter fundamentals flying the T-38. Then I went to North Carolina to do the same thing with the F-15E. The first eight flights in navigator school are basically pilot training courses. We sat in the front seat and went out and learned everything that a new pilot would learn. We took off and landed, did spins, rolls, and stalls. Then we jumped in the backseat and started doing some navigating—either medium-altitude or low-altitude, at five hundred feet or one thousand feet above the ground. They wanted to see if we could handle that. The military's training is comprehensive; they don't miss a trick.

I was excited about Operation Anaconda in Afghanistan because I'd been training for that moment my entire military career. Everybody remembers his first deployment, gearing up, making the pond crossing over the Atlantic. It's something I'll never forget. There was excitement but also apprehension. We could sit at our desks talking about all the things we'd do when a missile is shot up at us, but having the experience is a totally different thing. Some guys, the first time they've got a missile coming at them, will just watch it with awe and say, "Wow, that was fast." It disappears before you know it.

We were deployed in January 2002, but we didn't see any action the first two months. On March 4, we took off early, before sunrise. We proceeded about three hours to Afghanistan. We did an airborne refueling while en route. Forty-five minutes after the sun came up we got our first call to support some ground troops at Whaleback Mountain. This mountain stood out from the desert floor and it really looked like a humpback whale.

I was one of two F-15s in the air. Our call sign was Twister 5-2 and my pilot was Captain Kirk "Panzer" Rieckhoff. I was the Weapons System Operator [WSO] in the backseat. The flight lead was Major Chris "Junior" Short and his WSO was Lieutenant Colonel Jim "Meat" Fairchild. They were Twister 5-1. As the WSO, our job was to find the target with our targeting pod while the pilot flew to a particular altitude at a particular airspeed. What happens is, we release the weapon—in this case, five-hundred-pound laser-guided bombs—and then in twenty seconds we turn the laser on the targets and there's a laser finder at the front of the bomb that guides it to the target.

On Whaleback Mountain, Twister 5-1 was cleared to release a single bomb and he did. It was a good hit. Then we were cleared to release four more bombs and we did that on our next pass. That was my first combat drop. I'm certain that was Captain Rieckhoff's first drop. It was pretty exciting because the ground controller said, "Nice bombs." We were off and rolling. At this point we were flying at fifteen thousand to twenty thousand feet and at about five hundred to six hundred miles per hour, just a little faster than you fly on American Airlines.

Our job was to deliver ordnance onto the target, which could be buildings, bridges, airplanes, soft targets, hard targets, or bunkers. Our job was to find the targets, talk to the guys on the ground, and confirm the target. The pilot flew to the release point, we released the weapon, and the backseater's job was to guide the weapon into the target. It's a huge responsibility and the guys are well trained to do that. In this situation, we were dropping the bombs on the enemy's mortar positions.

Between the two of us, we released five bombs, and then we got redirected to contact MAKO 3-0. They were one of the Special Forces teams on the ground looking for Petty Officer Roberts's body. They were on the move and receiving enemy fire. We checked in with them and we could hear heavy breathing. They were on the run. They reported to us that there were two injured and one killed in action. At that moment, the day and our priorities certainly changed. We were the only fighter jets in that particular vicinity so we knew we were going to be involved somehow.

Our guns are designed for air-to-air targets. They have been employed before in the air-to-ground mode, but at that time it was not something that was usual for the Strike Eagle. Our adrenaline certainly shot up at that point. My heart was pounding. There was a kind of silence in the cockpit because this was such a unique situation. We tried to remain calm, and when we talked to the guys on the ground via radio, we really tried to sound calm so they trusted that we knew how to do our jobs.

As far as providing emergency close-air support, it was not something we had on our doctrine statement. It wasn't something we trained to do on a day-to-day basis. The better-suited aircraft for that detail is the A-10, based on the way their gun is positioned on their aircraft. They'd been doing it a lot longer. But I felt we could do the job. Luckily, our flight lead, Junior Short, was a previous A-10 guy, so we couldn't have been in better hands than his.

After we talked to MAKO 3-0, our plane proceeded to the tanker.

We'd coordinated for the tanker to come to us from about one hundred nautical miles to our south. We went off and filled up on gas. At that point, we still didn't know there was a downed helicopter on the mountain. All we knew was that MAKO 3-0 was on the run, drawing enemy fire, had one guy killed and several wounded. Twister 5-1 released a bomb in the vicinity of the target. The bomb didn't hit the position they were talking about. Twister 5-1 was low on gas so they went to the tanker while we came back and started talking to MAKO 3-0. He talked us onto the point that he wanted to bomb and I cued it up on the targeting pod, and when we flew over it, I saw that it was a Chinook helicopter. We could see the helicopter on top of the mountain but we had no idea there was fighting going on on the ground.

Finally we were told to clear the airspace because the B-52s were coming in to lay down some bombs. It was difficult for us to do because these guys on the ground were obviously under duress; they were taking enemy fire, and one of their guys had already been killed. We resisted a little bit but we were told the B-52s would be in soon to drop some bombs.

The B-52s never received clearance to drop. After forty-five minutes we were directed back to Takur Ghar to make contact with SLICK 0-1, the guys on the ground where the helicopter went down. When they told us where they were, we knew exactly what they were talking about because we'd put eyes on it previously. They gave us the coordinates and we could tell immediately they were under enemy fire. We could hear it in the background. We got a quick "talk on," we got the orientation of the helicopter, where it was down, where the enemy was firing, and we knew that the enemy and the friendlies were just seventy-five meters away from each other.

Our Chinook helicopter had been shot down by an enemy RPG, and they hit hard, a crash landing on top of the hill. Three or four of our guys had been shot and killed almost immediately. They settled in and tried to find cover behind the rocks and snow. They were hunkered down, but obviously these were very difficult conditions. The Taliban was better guarded in their trees and they had the high ground on the hill with bunkers for protection. From the air, we could see the helicopter and the clump of trees the enemy was hiding in, but we couldn't see the bodies of the Taliban soldiers running around. We told our guys on the ground what ordnance we had on board since the enemy was only seventy-five meters away from our soldiers. A five-hundred- or two-thousand-pound bomb could have wiped everybody out. After a few minutes, our guys requested that we use the guns and only the guns.

Wow, pure adrenaline. My pilot and I had never deployed the air-to-ground gun before in combat or even in a live-fire exercise. But we were prepared to do it. The way we set it up, one aircraft was going to be cleared to employ the gun and the other aircraft was going to remain high; we call it high-and-dry, looking for any surface-to-air threats being shot at the guy that's rolling in. Twister 5-1 was cleared to strike. He rolled in and was going down to shoot. The enemy and the friendlies were so close to each other that SLICK 0-1 couldn't tell if the F-15 guns were pointing at him or at the enemy in the trees. That's how close it was. That attack axis or angle wasn't going to work. The guys on the ground called out, "Abort, abort," just as they were rolling down. They came off dry and they did another circling pass. On the second one, they were cleared hot and they strafed the trees, they nailed the trees, and after Twister 5-1 made a safe escape, the call came in: "Good guns, I can smell the pine tree!"

I was screaming in the cockpit, banging the canopy; we were that excited. I think the guys on the ground were pretty excited, too. That shut the Taliban down for a little bit and we continued this method. Twister 5-1 made two more hot passes. At that time, we were low on gas, approaching "bingo." Twister 5-1 directed us to go to the tanker, which was only five or ten minutes away. We filled up the tank half-way and returned to the battle.

We started what we called a yo-yo operation. We'd have one guy circling to the tanker and the other guy over the target providing air support for the ground troops. We were either employing our guns or dropping bombs or just providing noise to keep the enemy at bay. We were taking turns. After we came off the tanker, we'd go back to the target and set up for our first passes. Then we'd do five hot passes with our guns, empty our guns until we were absolutely Winchester: no more bullets.

At that time, the F-16s checked in and we showed up just in time for Major Short to give them a world-class fighter-to-fighter talk on exactly where to look to put their eyeballs on the target. He had everything doped out in about thirty seconds. It was really quick. We were told that our replacements were here and that we could return home. We fought to get back to the target area. We still had a couple of bombs on board and we thought we could help. But we were told to go home.

The F-16s employed a couple of five-hundred-pound bombs near that clump of trees and were successful. I believe they strafed as well. They did some awesome work. Then we finally got clearance to go back into the target area and release our five-hundred-pound bombs. We dropped the first bomb about four hundred feet away from the target area, and then for the subsequent bombs we marched them up the hill, getting closer and closer to the enemy without endangering our guys. When I released the first bomb, I prayed that the bombs would go where I had the crosshairs. I was confident I had the crosshairs in a safe place, but I just wanted to make sure that the guidance system on the bomb worked properly. They're 98 percent reliable. We didn't want this to be in that 2 percent of the time when things went wrong. I released my bomb and the guys on the ground said it was a good bomb, but they wanted the next one closer. We cut the distance in half and we hit our mark. Everything went according to plan.

As far as self-preservation goes, it honestly didn't even enter my mind. If it had, I would have flushed it out. Those guys on the ground were getting shot at and some of the guys they worked with had been killed. All I wanted to do was help the guys on the ground. They were in a much worse situation than we were up in F-15s. We never saw any shoulder-mounted surface-to-air missiles directed toward us, but after we got back one of the air terminal controllers said that the enemy was pointing their RPGs up at us and shooting and they were going off around our jets. They just didn't tell us about it, and I'm glad they didn't. It was probably good that we didn't know.

The total flight time that day was 12.3 hours. I believe we did six to eight refueling missions. It was a pretty long flight. At the point we returned home, we didn't know whether our guys on the ground were okay or not. We got debriefed by Intel for a couple of hours, and they told us to get some sleep and get ready for the next mission. I don't think any of us slept that night. It was tough to have a hot meal and to sleep in our warm beds because we were wondering whether our guys on the mountain had survived. Later on, I met Sergeant Kevin Vance and learned about the loss of Petty Officer Neil Roberts, the Navy SEAL who fell out of the helicopter, and John Chapman and Jason Cunningham. Those guys on the ground, they're the true heroes.

★

Chris Russell is now a major, serving as the Assistant Director of Operations for the 334th Fighter Squadron in North Carolina. He has been with the United States Air Force for twelve years and plans to stay, teaching younger airmen the lessons he has learned.

A VERY SERIOUS BUSINESS

★

Mark Mitchell, Major, U.S. Army

Fifth Special Forces Group

Milwaukee, Wisconsin

Distinguished Service Cross; Mazar-e-Sharif,

Afghanistan; 25–28 November 2001

When five hundred Taliban prisoners armed themselves from a secret weapons cache at Qala-i-Janghi fortress in Afghanistan, it was the job of Mark Mitchell and his commandos to rescue their Northern Alliance comrades, retake control of the prison by directing air strikes, reclaim the body of fallen CIA agent Mike Spann, and stop the rioting prisoners from opening up a new offensive that might allow Mazar-e-Sharif to fall into enemy hands.

MARK MITCHELL

Even as a child, I was drawn to the army. I saw it as an exciting career where I would have the opportunity to travel and give something back to our country. My parents always felt I was mature beyond my years. My mother used to kid around, saying, "You worry about things that you shouldn't worry about. You're going to have an ulcer by the time you're thirty!"

I went to Marquette University High School in Milwaukee. It was a Jesuit, Catholic, all-boys school. The Latin motto of the school meant "For the Greater Glory of God." The obligation of service to a greater cause was ingrained in the students from the very beginning. I worked at a Milwaukee County hospital as a volunteer, both in the emergency room and psychiatric ward. It was all a part of what we were expected to do—to serve and give back some of the blessings that God had bestowed on us. Of the 250 graduates in my class, five or six of us went into the military. I received a four-year ROTC scholarship and chose to attend Marquette University, which was another three miles downtown, closer to the lake. My undergraduate degree was in biomedical engineering, and at one point I thought about going to medical school. Had I taken a second course in organic chemistry, which I abhorred, I would have had all my medical school prerequisites, and years later I strongly considered leaving the service to do just that.

As a young officer, I had the benefit of serving with some great leaders, and I also implicitly understood what good leaders do. They teach, coach, and mentor their people. They set a good example. They always keep an even keel. In the military they have a derogatory term for a commander who loses his cool: a "screamer." I can't say they're completely ineffective but they are inefficient. They expend a lot of energy belittling and antagonizing their subordinates. My approach was to be a good example to my men, to know all there is to know about my area of expertise, to be an expert in my profession, to respect my soldiers as individuals and treat them with respect and compassion, and to maintain a sense of humor; don't strive for popularity, aim for respect. Even when unpleasant things need to be done, lead the way. Being a leader in the army is a growth process and you learn something new every day.

When Saddam Hussein invaded Kuwait in August 1990, I was serving in the First Brigade of the Twenty-fourth Infantry Division, one of the first units to deploy to Saudi Arabia for Operation Desert Shield. I recall arriving in Saudi Arabia in the middle of the night, and I remember walking off the airplane and thinking, *God, it's hot.* Because we were one of the first units on the ground, the situation was pretty chaotic but also exciting. This is what I had been training to do and this was where I wanted to be. I was there for eight months, through Operation Desert Storm, and it was an incredible experience. We literally lived in the desert for almost the entire time, and, in great contrast to life in the age of the Internet and e-mail, I talked to my fiancée, Mary Ann—now my wife of fifteen-plus years—maybe two or three times that entire period. We communicated almost exclusively by mail—usually with a six-to-eight-week delay.

My brigade was involved in one of the largest battles of the war—the battle of the Rumaylah oil fields—and utterly devastated units of the vaunted Republican Guards. As an army we were unstoppable. I looked at American soldiers on the battlefield displaying compassion and a humane attitude, taking care of the prisoners we'd captured. These enemy soldiers had been abandoned by their own chain of command. Their officers had fled and threatened the Iraqi soldiers with execution if they followed. My fellow American soldiers showed great mercy: in victory we were magnanimous on the battlefield.

Even though days before they had been our enemy, now that they were defeated we treated them with dignity and respect and cared for them as best we could. We treated them better than their own government did.

In late February 1991, I remember very vividly listening to President Bush [the forty-first president] give an address announcing the cease-fire. We had been alerted by our chain of command that the war had ended and that at 0700 the next morning we'd cease offensive operations. I had this rush of emotions. I just broke down. I was overjoyed that I'd survived and I was going to be going home. I still remember flying home on a charter aircraft, and they kept playing Whitney Houston singing the national anthem at the Super Bowl. We'd missed the Super Bowl, but every time they played that song, I broke down. I found myself in tears. I don't know how to explain it except as a deep love of country, gratitude, and pride, not just in being in the army but being an American.

Ten or so years later, I was still in the army, and in early November 2001 I found myself in a remote valley in northern Afghanistan. We had infiltrated Afghanistan under cover of darkness, and as the sun rose that first morning it was almost surreal. We were deep behind enemy lines, only weeks after 9/11, and there was this sense of amazement about being there but also a strong sense of apprehension. There were eight of us and we were unreachable by anything other than helicopter. The nearest U.S. helicopter was at least a four-hour flight away. We were isolated, in many ways at the mercy of our Afghan hosts, and unable to predict with great surety what was going to happen next.

As a Special Forces officer, to be on the ground in Afghanistan, especially after 9/11, hunting al-Qaeda and fighting the Taliban, it was supremely exciting. But we knew that things could go terribly wrong in a hurry there. I knew I could die there and that it was possible they would never recover my body. All of us at one point had seen pictures of Russian soldiers and officers who'd been captured by the Afghan mujahideen and how they were treated. It wasn't pretty and this wasn't an exercise; this was a real event. This was a very serious business, and at any minute we could have found ourselves fighting for our lives. Thinking back on our Special Forces training, however, I remembered what I learned at the culmination exercise of the Special Forces Qualification Course. It was set in a fictional country called Pineland; we were working with guerrilla forces to overthrow the despotic government. In Afghanistan I found myself turning to my sergeant major and laughing because we both had the same sense of déjà vu. I had done all of this before in training and we were as well prepared as anyone could be for this situation.

What happened in late November 2001, well, it's a complex event, so let me give some context. There was a city in northeastern Afghanistan named Kunduz. Numerous reports indicated that the Taliban and al-Qaeda forces were gathering in Kunduz, after fleeing in advance of the U.S. and Northern Alliance forces. At that point, there were only about sixty U.S. soldiers in all of northern Afghanistan, and the rest were all Northern Alliance. There were unconfirmed reports that up to fifteen thousand Taliban, al-Qaeda, and, possibly, Pakistani soldiers had gathered in Kunduz. It was shaping up to be a huge siege. The Northern Alliance leaders planned to encircle the town, lay siege to it, and compel the surrender of this massive Taliban force. Although only about 120 miles as the crow flies, it was a full day's drive from Mazar-e-Sharif to Kunduz across featureless terrain. There were no roads, just some dirt paths, and travel was difficult at best.

In November 2001, the majority of the Northern Alliance forces and the Special Forces elements on the ground were moving east toward Kunduz. (I had remained in Mazar-e-Sharif with a small group of U.S. soldiers in order to prepare for future operations.) As the convoys of Afghan soldiers and their U.S. advisors departed early that morning, they encountered approximately six hundred enemy soldiers in trucks just minutes east of the Mazar-e-Sharif airport. In comparison to the approximately fifteen thousand Taliban forces reportedly in Kunduz, this was a small, and at first glance inconsequential, force. On closer inspection, the enemy wasn't Taliban; they were almost all foreign fighters and they eventually said they wanted to surrender, but a Mexican standoff of sorts ensued as the terms of their surrender were hashed out.

In the course of the initial surrender negotiations, a suicide bomber blew himself up and killed General Abdul Rashid Dostum's intelligence chief. [Dostum was one of the most senior Northern Alliance commanders and a key figure in modern Afghan history, feared by his enemies but loved by his mainly Uzbek troops.] In retrospect, that should have been the first indicator that something was wrong, but, again, our main focus was on Kunduz. Although I was not physically present during this attack, we dismissed the suicide bomber as just one more fanatic. During the "negotiations," the enemy kept demanding to be taken to the Mazar-e-Sharif airport as one of the terms of surrender. The Northern Alliance leadership, however, especially General Dostum, realized that the airport wasn't a suitable place to incarcerate six hundred prisoners. The only place that made sense was the Qala-i-Janghi fortress, so that was where they were sent.

The flatbed semi-trailers on which the prisoners had arrived were packed to the gills with men, just overflowing with enemy prisoners. As they headed toward Qala-i-Janghi, they drove by our newly established headquarters, which was set up in an abandoned high school that had been donated to the Afghani people by the government of Turkey. For reasons unknown to this day, the convoy halted directly in front of our headquarters for nearly twenty minutes. From the flat-bed trailers, the prisoners could easily see over the walls surrounding the school. As a result, the enemy soldiers knew right where we were headquartered. Following the unexplained halt, the convoy made its way through the heart of Mazar-e-Sharif and continued westward to the fortress at Qala-i-Janghi. It was already getting dark and the Northern Alliance soldiers simply placed the prisoners in the southern half of the compound, allowing them to drive the trucks into the fortress.

Much has been made about the fact that the prisoners were not thoroughly searched prior to or even immediately after entering the fortress. There were a lot of factors that conspired to bring this situation about, however. First, neither the Northern Alliance nor the very small U.S. contingent were prepared to incarcerate that many prisoners. It is a resource-intensive undertaking, especially when attempting to meet the requirements of the Geneva Convention. Second, the Afghans themselves have very little history of taking prisoners. Usually, one of two things would happen in the Afghan military culture: either the enemy would surrender and be shot, or they would surrender and would switch sides. Nevertheless, we demanded that they adhere to the spirit of the Geneva Convention and treat all prisoners humanely; we threatened to cut off any aid or military assistance if they summarily executed or mistreated prisoners. Third, the Northern Alliance was not a professional military organization. They were a ragtag militia, effective in guerrilla tactics but untrained in the basics of handling prisoners of war. Further, the pace of operations left no time for training on these subjects.

Most important, the Northern Alliance, leaders and soldiers alike, had cultural habits that precluded them from dealing effectively with these prisoners. The first was the Afghan emphasis on honor. Within any tribal culture, honor is a key component. It's the cornerstone of tribal relationships and it drives many things. If you give your word, if you lay down your arms, if you say you will no longer fight, people take that at face value. In retrospect, however, we were not dealing with Afghans who honored this protocol; we were dealing with many non-Afghans, most from a younger generation very comfortable with the concept of *taqiyya*—lying to an enemy to advance the cause of Islam. They had no inhibitions about lying or pretending to surrender as a ruse. The second cultural issue was a belief prevalent among the Northern Alliance that searches and pat-downs would be an offense to the dignity of the prisoners. In this Muslim culture of honor and shared brotherhood, the Northern Alliance soldiers refused to strip-search the prisoners or even pat them down for weapons. From the perspective of the Northern Alliance leaders and soldiers, the prisoners had given their word—searching them was unnecessary and would have been offensive to their Muslim dignity.

Still, the Northern Alliance soldiers did attempt to restrain many of the prisoners by tying their elbows behind their backs with their coats—what we called chicken-winged. We did not have enough flex-cuffs, basically heavy-duty zip ties that made very good field-expedient handcuffs, for the prisoners. The fortress at Qala-i-Janghi didn't have any type of confinement facility or prison cells. So, many of the prisoners spent the night in the open courtyard, while some found shelter in the basement of an empty building in the center of the compound, which we called the pink schoolhouse. This building, which was constructed of reinforced concrete, had one story aboveground and one story belowground.

The number of Northern Alliance soldiers actually guarding the prisoners was a fraction of the total number of prisoners. The vast majority of Northern Alliance soldiers had departed for Kunduz, leaving only a small guard force, many of whom were unfit for the long trip to Kunduz. All these factors conspired to create a volatile situation. I strongly believe that this was a planned uprising by the prisoners—a Trojan horse of sorts. It was part of their strategy to re-capture Mazar-e-Sharif, which would have dealt a huge blow, tacti-cally, strategically, operationally, and morale-wise, to our efforts in northern Afghanistan. It could also have served as a catalyst for re-newed resistance.

The next morning some of the U.S. intelligence officers went over to the fortress to interview the many foreign fighters among the pris-oners. Their focus was on finding Osama bin Laden and the senior al-Qaeda leadership. Any time there was a foreign, non-Afghan pris-oner, they were a priority for interrogation, because it was assumed they had come through one of the al-Qaeda camps and may have known the whereabouts or intentions of the senior leadership.

On the morning of the twenty-fifth, the prisoners were being inter-viewed, and one of them was John Walker Lindh. There is a video of Mike Spann interviewing him, asking him questions, and, of course, Lindh is uncooperative. Not long after that interview, there was an explosion from the basement of the pink schoolhouse and then an im-mediate eruption of gunfire. It was chaos. In retrospect, we believe the prisoners smuggled in some weapons and explosives in the trucks. Like the individual prisoners, these trucks were never searched—again, because we were stretched too thin and all our focus was on Kunduz. That morning, the prisoners seized control of the southern half of the fortress, and in the opening minutes, I believe, Mike Spann was killed.

Though I didn't witness it myself, the other U.S. intelligence offi-cer present, known publicly as Dave, said that the prisoners in the courtyard rose up in unison immediately after the explosion and, even though a lot of them had their arms tied behind their backs, began running toward Mike. Dave and Mike weren't next to each other. Dave had been walking toward their car, which was parked on the north side of the compound when the explosion and gunfire erupted. He turned and saw Mike already engaged with three or four prisoners. Some prisoners freed themselves and others simply began kicking Mike; it quickly devolved into hand-to-hand combat. Dave shot a couple of them, turned, and then another prisoner was coming at him with an AK-47. The guy fired several shots but missed Dave. Dave shot him. He turned back and Mike was on the ground, underneath some prisoners, wrestling. Dave turned back again and there was another prisoner running at him with a hand grenade. He fired at that guy, turned back, and Mike wasn't moving. At some point, Mike Spann had been shot, possibly with his own gun. The situation was getting worse—very quickly. Dave took off running for his life. He ended up getting away to the northernmost part of the compound, where the headquarters building was, and he got pinned down there with some journalists and local workers.

Nearly every room of the fortress was stocked to the ceiling with arms and ammunition: rockets, rocket-propelled grenades, mortars, artillery shells, land mines, heavy machine guns and other weapons, including boxes of Russian .45-caliber submachine guns. Regardless of who controlled Mazar-e-Sharif—the Communists, the Taliban, the various warlords, including General Dostum—the fortress at Qala-i-Janghi was used as a military headquarters and its stockpiles had been maintained. In the opening moments of the uprising, the prisoners overpowered most of the guards, killed them and seized their weapons, enabling them to seize the stockpiles of other weapons. They caught the Northern Alliance unaware and killed a lot of them, quickly gaining control of the entire southern half of the fortress.

A confidant of General Dostum, Mr. Alim Razzim, left the fortress and drove the twenty-plus kilometers to our headquarters at the Turkish School to notify us of the situation at Qala-i-Janghi. Visibly shaken, he said, "You need to come to Qala-i-Janghi now, with every man you've got!" His account of events essentially confirmed what we had discovered only minutes before based on a report Dave made to the U.S. embassy in a neighboring country using a satellite phone borrowed from a journalist.

Although I was not the most senior officer, it was decided that I had the most intimate knowledge of the fortress, since I had been living there for the previous two weeks, and should lead the mission to retake the prison. I grabbed a group of soldiers, including a newly arrived eight-man patrol from the British Special Boat Service [SBS], and led them over there. As we approached the fortress there was a cacophony of gunfire, explosions, and RPGs going off. It was a very intense battle between a small group of Northern Alliance Afghans, who had consolidated near the gate of the fortress, and the former prisoners, who were now combatants again. I tried to ascertain what had happened to Dave and Mike. Even though I didn't see Dave personally, I talked to him on the radio and I knew that he was still alive and that, based on Dave's assessment, Mike was probably dead.

With the help of one of General Dostum's lieutenants, Commander Fakhir, I attempted to get to Dave's location. Leading a group of three other soldiers [two U.S. and one British], we made our way around the exterior of the fortress. Dodging mortar fire from the prisoners, we made our way to the northern side of the fortress and scaled the walls, climbing the last section with the help of a turban from a Northern Alliance soldier. In the parapet, we found a small group of Northern Alliance soldiers effectively pinned down by the fire from the prisoners. From that vantage point, we engaged the enemy with direct fire and I assessed the overall situation.

I was unable to link up with Dave personally but it was clear that the situation was dire enough that it led me to call in air strikes. I was concerned that if the whole fortress fell we could possibly lose control of Mazar-e-Sharif as the balance of power there shifted back to the Taliban and their allies. I informed Dave over the radio of my intentions and told him that if possible, he should take the opportunity to get over the wall during one of the blasts. U.S. Navy F-18s had already been alerted and were circling overhead. We dropped seven two-thousand-pound JDAM bombs into the southern portion of the courtyard to attempt to destroy the enemy. As the last of the JDAMs was dropped, another intelligence officer and I made our way to Dave's last known location, scaling the walls again but without assistance and in direct view of the enemy positions. Scrambling over the wall and then dashing to a stairwell, we went room to room searching for Dave. The building had been heavily damaged by machine-gun and RPG fire and was still being targeted by the enemy. After searching unsuccessfully, we learned from some locals trapped in the building that Dave had gone over the wall. At this point, darkness was beginning to fall. Frankly, I thought that the JDAMs had been pretty effective, but with night closing in and our very limited numbers, I thought it was still too dangerous, just not smart business, to stay in the fortress, much less assault into the southern compound.

So I pulled everyone back to the Turkish schoolhouse to regroup. We were worried that some of the foreign fighters had escaped over the walls of the fortress into the surrounding buildings. Because of the stop in front of our headquarters the previous day, they knew where we were located and there was always the possibility that they would attack the Turkish schoolhouse. We found out later that that was the case: some prisoners had actually escaped. Fortunately, many were hunted down by local villagers who were sympathetic to General Dostum and the Northern Alliance. We didn't know that at the time, however, and assumed that they were still a threat. With our limited numbers, we spent the entire evening pulling guard shifts, watching for signs of the enemy and planning and preparing to go back to

Qala-i-Janghi the following morning at first light. It was a pretty chaotic night as we also received some reinforcements—including an infantry platoon—and a few more Special Forces soldiers from a base in Uzbekistan.

When we returned the next morning, I was surprised to find that there still was a great deal of resistance. We could hear gunfire. In our absence that night, some of the Northern Alliance forces had tried to enter the southern portion of the compound through a gateway in the wall, and that became known as the fatal funnel. Al-Qaeda and the Taliban had set up machine guns to cover that entrance, and the Northern Alliance soldiers just got mowed down.

On the second day, we started to implement our plan, and as so often happens in combat, it didn't survive the opening moments. CPT Paul Syverson, my second in command, was forced from his initial position when it came under intense mortar fire. He had to move from an overwatch of the southern portion of the compound to a northern wall. During the same period, I was leading another small group around the western side of the fortress and we had taken up positions that allowed us to look directly over the wall into the southern compound. I was not aware that Paul and his group had actually moved. We had aircraft overhead and I'd given instructions to Paul as to where to target the air strike. When I talked to Paul, he simply confirmed the desired location of the first JDAM and informed me that he had already passed the coordinates to the aircraft overhead. At this point, I was approximately 125 meters from the desired point of impact. Normally, "danger close" for a bomb that size is 500 meters, to make sure you're clear of the shrapnel and bomb blast. But I needed to be close to assess the situation accurately. So we were "danger close" the whole time. Being that close to a two-thousand-pound bomb is an unforgettable experience; the shock of the blast wave, the sound, the heat. I got a call that Paul and his crew were in position and we got a thirty-second warning before impact. I had my fingers in my ears, my mouth was open, and since I didn't have any helmet or body armor, I was as low to the ground as I could possibly go.

I heard the explosion and I gave it a second or two for the dust to settle and the shrapnel to fly overhead. I peeked over the wall into the southern compound and realized the bomb didn't impact there. Almost immediately, an enormous dust cloud engulfed the eastern half of the fortress. Although the huge cloud of dust made it difficult to see, I sensed that the explosion was actually to my rear. I couldn't tell exactly where it hit, but I knew it didn't hit where it was supposed to, and I worried that it hit close to Paul and his men. I tried to contact CPT Syverson on the radio—without success—and searched through my binoculars, hoping to catch a glimpse of my men. My initial assumption was that it hit so close to Paul and his crew that their ears were buzzing and they couldn't hear anything. I also considered that it may have burst their eardrums and that was why they couldn't hear me. As the dust settled some more, I could make out the shapes of my men; some of them were moving and some of them weren't. But I thought that any minute someone would contact me on the radio.

Then I got the call from one of my NCOs with the Quick Reaction Force, located about a half mile east of the fortress. They had a clear view of the impact of the JDAM; the NCO said the bomb landed right on top of CPT Syverson's position and estimated that we had at least five KIAs and four more seriously wounded. My heart just dropped, but I quickly recovered and realized that this was one of those situations where I didn't have time to be emotional. Of the twelve soldiers that I had inside the fortress, at least nine were wounded, meaning that my small force was rendered incapable of continuing— for the moment at least.

I had to pick up and immediately call in my QRF, which consisted of several Special Forces soldiers and an infantry squad. I directed them to request medical evacuation for the injured and the dead and then immediately go to the designated rally point and assist with casualty evacuation from the fortress. As I moved to link up with them at the rally point, I also contacted the aircraft circling overhead and informed them that we had friendly casualties. As in many cases in combat, the initial report was incorrect. The number of KIAs changed from five to one, and finally to zero. Although nine of my soldiers were wounded, all of them were still alive, thank God. There were some Northern Alliance soldiers killed, but no Americans. I had lost over half of my team in an instant. That obviously disrupted my plan for the day and I had no choice but to pull back out of the fortress and ensure that my wounded soldiers received the medical care they needed.

I had an opportunity years later to read the investigation into the incident. There were two aircraft in the flight, the lead aircraft and his wingman. The lead pilot in the F-18 entered the bombing coordinates correctly, but the wingman actually entered the position of the observer. When the lead pilot had a mechanical malfunction, he passed the mission to his wingman, who released his JDAM—programmed with the coordinates of CPT Syverson and eight other soldiers. Given the fact that this enormous bomb landed less than one hundred feet from their position, it is nothing short of miraculous that anyone—let alone everyone—survived. It is all the more incredible because the portion of the fortress directly beneath them was stockpiled with rockets and artillery, yet not a single secondary explosion occurred.

At this point in the war, there were no U.S. bases in Afghanistan, only small bands of Special Forces soldiers operating with our Afghan allies. Further, the runway at the Mazar-e-Sharif airport had been severely cratered during the initial bombing campaign, rendering it unusable. This meant that the only way to get in and out of Mazar-e-Sharif, and all of northern Afghanistan for that matter, was by helicopter. And the nearest helicopters were a three-hour flight away in Uzbekistan. So, after waiting nearly four hours for the helicopters to arrive, we were able to evacuate our wounded soldiers.

By this point I was pretty frustrated; I was determined to find a way to win this thing and be done with it once and for all. I received some great news that afternoon, shortly after seeing off my wounded soldiers: the AC-130 Specter gunships had arrived and would be available for the first time. This was a significant addition to the weapons that we had available, especially because of our small numbers. The errant JDAM had spooked our Afghan allies, however, so during the planning and coordination that afternoon, we agreed that the Afghans would pull back, under the cover of darkness, just prior to the start of air strikes by the AC-130.

I led a small team of six, including myself, back into the fortress that night, the second of the battle, to direct the AC-130 strikes. The withdrawal of all but a handful of the Northern Alliance soldiers went off without a hitch, but unfortunately the arrival of the first AC-130 was unexpectedly delayed by a mechanical malfunction. The result was that we were left virtually alone in the fortress for about two hours. They were long hours during which the prisoners, if they had realized the situation, could have overrun our positions. Throughout the night there was a lot of incoming mortar fire all around us. Considering the situation, it was very accurate and getting closer and closer all the time.

When the AC-130s finally arrived and entered the fight, they were a very welcome addition. We talked them through the targets we had identified and they systematically engaged them, hitting the enemy without hitting us or our Northern Alliance colleagues. The first AC-130 expended all its ammo, and it definitely had a suppressive effect, but they were unable to stop the mortar fire—the enemy was still firing away. The second AC-130 took over and it too expended nearly all of its ammo. The crew informed us that it was down to its last six rounds of 105mm artillery.

We were still taking mortar fire and asked the crew to identify the source. Despite their sophisticated sensors, they had been unable to identify the mortar crew. As the mortars dropped closer to our position, and the gunship began to run low on ammo, my frustration rose. But just when it seemed as though they would run out of ammo before knocking out the mortars, we got a break. The crew spotted the enemy running into a building after firing a couple of mortar rounds. They had apparently been doing this all night, making them very difficult to spot. But we had them now.

I cleared the AC-130 to target the building where the enemy was hiding, a building that ran lengthwise along the center dividing wall in the fortress. It was one of the few buildings that we had not yet targeted. The AC-130 fired into the center of the building and flames immediately leapt out of the hole in the roof. Seconds later we heard a gigantic explosion and we watched a mushroom cloud skyrocket about 150 or 200 feet into the air. With one of its last remaining rounds, the AC-130 had hit the building where the mortar fire was coming from, and it also happened to be their major weapons cache. It was packed with mortars, RPGs, and rockets, and as the two-hundred-foot ball of flame was ascending, debris from the explosion was descending. We were just showered and pummeled with debris. We felt the shock waves and intense heat from the blast. Soon, the rockets began to ignite and fly out randomly, screeching into the blackness and exploding in the distance. At this point, our position was untenable: as the ammunition and rockets began to cook off, my small team was at great risk. I felt as though we had accomplished a major objective by destroying the arms cache and decided to pull back to the safety of our headquarters until the fire and explosions had burned themselves out.

That night, the blazing fires from Qala-i-Janghi were still visible from our headquarters over ten miles away. As word of the battle had reached Kunduz, where the anticipated siege turned into a massive surrender, some Northern Alliance troops started filtering back into the Mazar-e-Sharif area. On the third day, we once again returned to the fortress, this time prepared to recover the remains of Mike Spann. And once again, I was surprised to hear the sound of gunfire. Despite the air strikes, the explosions, and the fires, not only had some of the enemy survived but they were unwilling to surrender—apparently willing to fight to the death. As the Northern Alliance numbers grew, they began to take on more of the task of rooting out these hard-core enemy fighters. Despite their superior numbers and firepower, they were unsuccessful in dislodging and killing this determined enemy. The third day of the fight saw some gains for the Northern Alliance, but nothing decisive. So the fight continued into the fourth day.

On the fourth day, the enemy resistance continued but their numbers were dwindling and the cold November weather, a lack of food, and the constant fighting were beginning to take a toll on them. Still, as Northern Alliance soldiers began to clear room to room, a suicide bomber emerged and detonated two hand grenades, killing himself and wounding four Northern Alliance soldiers. The situation had settled enough that we were able to locate and recover Agent Spann's body. It appeared that he had been shot in the head at point-blank range. We returned to our headquarters with Mike's remains and waited for the helicopter to arrive. Later that evening we held a small ceremony at the airfield and escorted the remains, covered by a flag provided by one of my sergeant majors, onto the waiting helicopter. It was a gut-wrenching experience for us all. Afterward, I went back and collapsed on my bunk—physically, mentally, and emotionally exhausted after several days of intense combat. I slept for at least fourteen hours.

The die-hard enemy at Qala-i-Janghi continued to resist to the bitter end—for another forty-eight hours, in fact. The last of them were holed up in the basement of the pink schoolhouse and had resisted every attempt to be dislodged. At one point, they were assumed to be dead, and several Red Cross/Red Crescent volunteers entered the basement to begin retrieving bodies; two of them were killed. As a last-ditch effort, the Afghans flooded the basement of the pink schoolhouse. After enduring days of bombardment and bitter cold, the prospect of hypothermia induced by standing in waist-deep icy water coerced the remaining enemy combatants to give up the fight. In all, eighty-six of them emerged; among the survivors was a filthy, disheveled, and frightened Johnny Walker Lindh. Tragically, they had apparently expended the last of their ammunition on the Red Cross workers. Mr. Lindh and the other eighty-five were transported to Sheberghan, a town about a three-hour drive from Qala-i-Janghi, and incarcerated in a small prison there. He was eventually brought back to Mazar-e-Sharif and later transferred back to the United States. He avoided a trial by entering a plea bargain and is currently serving a twenty-year sentence in a federal prison.

In the end, I was exceptionally grateful to have had the opportunity to serve and participate in Operation Enduring Freedom. I think I would have been livid if I had been sitting at home on the sidelines or somewhere else in the army. It's one of those inexplicable impulses experienced by professional soldiers—you always want to be where the action is. The men who volunteer for Special Forces training and duty do so because they want to participate in those challenging, exciting, and dangerous missions. There are periods where you train for a long time and you may or may not get to be part of any specific operation—it is often just timing. I think that in the aftermath of

9/11, it was important for me personally to have the chance to serve in Afghanistan, and I am just grateful for that opportunity.

You may have heard this elsewhere, but I don't think it received a lot of attention from the press: each Special Forces team that entered Afghanistan during the initial stages of OEF was given a piece of the World Trade Center. We carried those with us with the instructions to hold a ceremony, at an appropriate time and place, during which we were to bury that piece of the World Trade Center as a symbol of our victory and that evil would not be allowed to stand. Each team did that and recorded the location using a highly accurate ten-digit grid coordinate provided by GPS. The locations were reported to our higher headquarters for posterity and eventually all locations were plotted on a map with the date, time, and location it was buried. We had those maps framed, and they took them to New York City and gave one framed copy each to the City of New York, the New York Police Department, and the Fire Department of New York as a token of our appreciation for their service and sacrifice.

We buried our piece at a girls' school in Mazar-e-Sharif, only about six-tenths of a mile from the famous Blue Mosque that's a sacred landmark right in the heart of the city. Shortly after the liberation of the city, hundreds of foreign fighters had holed up there in the girls' school. One of the Special Forces detachments engaged in a very intense firefight there and eventually called in air strikes. Initially, there was a lot of concern about collateral damage due to the proximity of the Blue Mosque. But the air strikes were precise and the enemy was defeated, while the Blue Mosque was unscratched.

We did the ceremony there because we thought it was a very appropriate place to bury the piece of the World Trade Center. We managed to find a backhoe and dug a hole that was eleven feet deep, and we buried it at 11:00 a.m. on the morning of January 11, 2002. We took a body bag that we had with us and treated it as an honor guard would carry a casket. We lowered the body bag into the hole and buried it there as a solemn remembrance of our fallen comrades and a symbol that America could not be bowed by the attacks of September 11, 2001.

Mark Mitchell continues to serve our country, now as a lieutenant colonel in the U.S. Army Special Forces.

APACHE SIX, THIS IS DOG SIX

★

Daniel Hibner, Captain, U.S. Army
Alpha Company of the 11th Engineers
Michigan City, Indiana
SILVER STAR; IRAQ; 7 APRIL 2003

Enduring sandstorms, dismantling bridge explosives, invading and securing Baghdad International Airport, and clearing minefields were all part of Dan Hibner's job description. "You couldn't find a more challenging environment to work in," recalls Hibner. For his resourcefulness, leadership, and bravery, he—like his twin brother— earned the Silver Star.

David Hibner (left) and Daniel Hibner

David and I are identical twins, and we're the same in a lot of ways, like our values and the way we think. He's a great guy, a great brother, and as a family man, he's exceptional. In the army, David is one of the best officers they have, and I'm not just being biased. I hear it from a lot of others. He's well respected among his peers, and he's got a special talent for doing what he does. As far as our leadership styles, I guess I probably "show" a little more. I get a little closer to my soldiers and the leaders in my company. I'm a little more emotional, and he's a little more even-keeled.

Even when we were kids, he and I always did the same things. We started a paper route and split the money. We'd get jobs shoveling snow, mowing lawns, raking leaves, and we always did it together. We always had the same interests, the same likes and dislikes. What was good for him was good for me, and we always looked out for each other. David is my best friend, no doubt about it.

We come from a family of eight with six kids, my dad was a steelworker, and my mom did a lot of different jobs to help make sure the family was provided for. College was important, but paying for college was a big question mark. My brother and I knew we wanted to go to college, but finding the means to do it was another story. We were both banking on baseball or football scholarships and a few offers trickled in, but we needed them to be good offers, full rides or close to it.

One offer came from Kemper Military College in Missouri. Our football coach talked to me about it, and I thought it sounded like a horrible idea. I thought that was the kind of place parents sent troublesome kids. But we were looking into everything and wouldn't take any opportunity off the table without carefully considering it. I ended up talking to Kemper's ROTC department, and they mentioned going to basic camp and the possibility of getting a U.S. Army scholarship. We decided we'd try basic camp for a summer, and it was something that David and I could do together. Our senior drill sergeant had it in for David, and that didn't go over well for either of us. He and I were "battle buddies," and we shared a bunk and everything for six weeks. One day the drill sergeant came in, picked up my boots. They were immaculate, except for a tiny piece of mud in one of the crevices, and he threw the boots across the room and then did what drill sergeants do best—some remedial training via calisthenics and plenty of yelling. He made me carry my boots all day that day, and whenever we stopped, I had to shine my boots. That was fine for remedial training. The problem was whenever I started shining my boots, another drill sergeant would come by and tear me up for shining my boots. They were messing with me pretty hard, and it happened all day long until David couldn't take it. He went to the senior drill sergeant and yelled at him and said what they were doing was wrong, unfair, and unprofessional. I didn't know he'd done that until he came back to the barracks and said with a little chuckle, "Well, I don't think I'll be getting a scholarship."

When the scholarship offers came in, I got one and David didn't. We both decided to opt out, because if that was the way the army worked, we weren't interested. We talked with the assistant professor of military science at Kemper, Major Lepore, and explained our decision and he said, "If you ask me, you just showed me you're exactly the kind of guys the army needs as officers." I'll never forget him. He was a good guy and a squared-away officer. We went back home to Michigan City and were supposed to report to Kemper that fall, but we were thinking we probably wouldn't do it. The night before we were supposed to attend Kemper, we went out and partied. When we got back, our mom was pretty much done packing our bags. She knew Kemper was really the best opportunity we had, and she wasn't going to just let us throw it away. If we really didn't want to go, she wouldn't have made us, but Dave and I both knew she was right. Our mother really influenced us all of our lives, but this time it was at a critical point, because it put us on a good track and a track that would lead to our chosen careers in the U.S. Army.

We spent two years at Kemper Military College, and it was a great experience. Jumping ahead ten years to the invasion of Iraq, I have to admit I was exhilarated. My brother was deployed to Kuwait in September, and when he came to my house to say good-bye, Dave said, "Well, I guess this is it. I'll see you in Kuwait." We both figured the whole division would be there shortly, which was good because I didn't want to miss it. I was convinced it was going to happen, so I wasn't the least bit surprised when I received a phone call from my battalion commander, LTC Thomas Smith, saying we needed to return from leave a couple days early.

As a company commander, I couldn't have dreamed of anything better than this, taking my unit into combat. It was the Super Bowl, and I wanted to be there. I had a young organization but we were well trained. After numerous training exercises at Fort Stewart and a solid National Training Center rotation at Fort Irwin, California, we could make a plan, prepare for combat, and execute the plan almost instantly if we had to. When you throw in the confidence that comes with that training, it's easy to get excited about doing your job. Of course, there's apprehension too. There's that question: "I know I can do this in training, but what about in combat, when the bullets are flying?" I'd say it was 95 percent confidence and 5 percent apprehension. We knew that this was what our country was calling us to do. It's our job and we're ready.

The focus of the operation was speed. We would move as fast as we could, fight our way through areas of expected resistance but always keep our mind on the prize: Baghdad, the center of gravity for Saddam Hussein's regime. Our goal was to quickly get to the Karbala Gap and "shoot the gap" so we could make a beeline to Baghdad. To do that we had to go through An Najaf, and that was a beehive. The terrain was tough but we kept right on moving. There were times when enemies wanted to surrender and we'd just drive by them. We were very careful not to shoot innocents. If we couldn't see a weapon and they didn't seem to have hostile intent, we always erred on the side of caution. Unless it was obvious that this was an enemy troop acting in a hostile manner, we didn't engage them. Those are easy decisions to live with.

We'd been moving for a few days nonstop, conducted some missions, and were in contact with the enemy a few times, and we had a "planned tactical pause" to let the support trains catch up with us. That gave us time to get our equipment cleaned up, do vehicle maintenance, and get everything reloaded. We slept and refueled, which took three or four hours. At this point, we were south of Karbala when a huge storm blew in. It was unbelievable. I'd seen desert sandstorms before, but let me tell you, this was the sandstorm to end all sandstorms. It was absolutely insane. One morning, as the sandstorm was just kicking up, I was sleeping in my Armored Personnel Carrier and I started to catch wind of an operation going on in the town of al Kifl. An air defense artillery unit had been sent there to look at a bridge and test the waters for enemy presence. A couple of Bradleys crossed the bridge when the bridge was destroyed and they were cut off and under a pretty heavy enemy attack.

This was a fast-evolving mission. They were going to send in an infantry company and an engineering company to help. We came up with a plan. We were going to link up, and that was when the sandstorm hit. By the time C Company, Thirty-seventh Infantry, got to my location, we couldn't see them and they couldn't see us. We were getting ready to go into a fight with almost zero visibility. Al Kifl was just a beehive of mortar and small-arms fire. Our mission was to figure out a way to cross the destroyed bridge to reinforce the other side. There was a huge "V" in the bridge where the supporting columns were blown up and spans dropped down. I went under the bridge and checked it out and the dropped spans looked structurally sound. We drove across the bridge ourselves and continued our reconnaissance. We dismantled the enemy's remaining demolitions so they couldn't blow up any more of the bridge. We learned an important lesson about the way they rigged the bridge and how they wanted to delay the ultimate detonation of the bridge until we had armor going across it. The big mission was coming up. We had to cross the Euphrates River to reach Baghdad and the entire Third Infantry Division needed to cross it.

We were now on the enemy side of the bridge when the first mortar hit. Our task force commander, "Rock" Marcone, was wounded and had to be evacuated to the friendly side of the river, only it wasn't that friendly. The storm was really kicking up, and I received orders to facilitate a relief in place with another unit and take my company back to the perimeter we came from that morning. Late afternoon, about 1530, all of a sudden everything went dark. The sand pelted us, literally sandblasting us. We put chemical lights on our antennas but still couldn't see one another. We put on our night-vision goggles and that worked for a few minutes, but then the storm got worse. It became pitch-black, we were in enemy territory without any way for another unit to support us, and we couldn't see each other. We had to stop moving before we had a break in contact or one of the vehicles in my company drove into a wadi. We could only hope the storm would lift. No army technology can see through an Iraqi sandstorm except infrared, and we had only three infrared sights in my entire company—but the infrared sights were used to look for any enemy activity. We were just blinded. I was concerned about our situation, but the thought occurred to me that if we were blinded, then so was the enemy. All of a sudden, what seemed to be a strange faint yellowish light appeared in the sky, and we could just sense that everyone's eyes were drawn to this light. It got more and more pronounced, more orange and then a fiery orange, and I thought, *Wow, this is amazing.* One of my lieutenants from my Company HQ rode in my track and asked, "Sir, what is that light?" I looked at my watch and said, "Lucas, that's the sun."

Then it started raining and it rained mud. It was the best thing that could have happened because it clumped up all that fine sand so we could actually see again. We looked like mud people. We got back to our Tactical Assembly Area and breathed a sigh of relief that it was done.

Shooting the Karbala Gap was a night assault, and that was one tough piece of terrain. At night it was brutal trying to get through with all the crevices, steep cliffs, cracks, and undulating terrain. "Objective Peach" was the bridge objective on the other side of Karbala Gap and it was a critical bridge that we had planned for and the time was near. It would be no walk in the park. The weight of the world was on our shoulders because the entire Third Infantry Division was depending on us. In fact, the whole Corps really depended on us. If the Third Infantry got out of sync, the timing of the whole mission would be thrown off. Worst of all, it would slow everyone down, and speed was something we were doing everything we could to maintain.

As our Task Force, 3-69 Armor, arrived in the area, we were getting a lot of enemy reports. We could see air force A-10 jets strafing the far side of the bridge, and they didn't seem short of targets. We secured the near side of the bridge, and my company was called forward. We would do an "assault riverboat crossing" with fifteen-man rubber Zodiac boats. We set our vehicles two hundred meters behind the bridge in a concealed position, and then the bridge began ascending about another two hundred meters before the shoreline of the river. I moved out with a reconnaissance force to check things out. We heard a lot of firing and fighting going on but not directed at us, so I knew we had got there without the enemy seeing us. It wouldn't last, and if they saw us, they would tear our little element apart. It took a long time for the boats to arrive, and I was getting anxious. We carefully scanned the bridge from a concealed location and one of my squad leaders, SSG Coleman, pointed out something hanging from the girders of the bridge, probably explosives. I knew we had to dismantle the explosives before they destroyed the bridge. Once two boats arrived I made the decision that we couldn't wait any longer—we had to move. I gave some quick directions and changes to the plan that included getting some of my engineers and some of the attached infantry into the first boat and under way. I have to give the enemy credit for showing tactical patience because they waited for us to get the first boat in the water and then they opened up on us.

We fired all we had back at them; the volume of fire was just incredible. We needed Bradleys in there to protect our guys, but the terrain was so marshy and thick they had a lot of trouble getting in there. We had our A10s strafing the area and that bought us some time. We'd been taking mortar fire up until now, and for the first time, we took heavy artillery fire, which just shook the earth. All their artillery landed in one spot because, for some reason, they weren't adjusting fire or they didn't know how to adjust fire. Everything was landing about two hundred and fifty to three hundred meters south of us.

The guys in the boat were firing their weapons, which meant they couldn't row. I worried that we were going to lose a boatload of engineers and infantry soldiers. Finally, somehow, the Bradleys made it through and they helped fire on the enemy positions on the far side of the river just in the nick of time. You couldn't believe the relief I felt. With the Bradleys in place, I could move this mission along. We got two more boats in the water, and as we arrived at the far side, I saw that the enemy had destroyed a span on one side of the bridge, although it didn't drop down. It was a four-lane bridge, and half of it was out and the other side was ready for detonation. The enemy was just waiting for the armor to come across. We quickly cut the electric and explosive detonation systems they had rigged, and rendered the rest of the explosives useless. We secured the far side and there was a high volume of enemy fire, but they didn't hold the terrain they needed to effectively engage us.

We pushed our toehold out a bit farther, and I called Lieutenant Colonel Marcone and told him the north side of the bridge was clear but not to use the south side. I repeated not to use the south side because a seventy-ton tank on such a damaged span would almost certainly be catastrophic. I also called my Second Platoon forward to mark a lane so no vehicle would attempt to cross on the south side of the bridge. We couldn't see it but we could hear the armor rumbling as it arrived. Then we saw just the tops of the vehicles. It was so damn noisy, but it was a beautiful thing to hear. As the Bradleys crested the bridge, they immediately engaged enemy targets. The enemy was dug in. They had at least a battalion-size element of several hundred guys on the other side, which was why we were taking so much fire. They had armored vehicles dug in, heavy artillery, and mortar support. They had one hell of a position there.

We managed to sneak in and move fast enough that they couldn't destroy the bridge. Once we could safely bring the armor across, it was over. Our armor was just raking them. Once our armored vehicles peaked across the bridge, they were engaging targets as they were moving; they didn't stop. For hours we fought that battle. The enemy had every advantage to beat us in that fight, but we won.

We spent the majority of the next day removing the explosives from the bridge. That was no easy task because the enemy still hadn't given up on the idea of destroying the bridge. We secured the area to prevent that from happening, and we exhausted every option to try to get the explosives from the undergirders of the bridge. The problem was the height of the girders. Finally, Sergeant First Class Brian Raines volunteered to try something new. I just kind of looked at him thoughtfully and said, "You got the job." We rigged up a rappel rope on the underside of the bridge, and he hung upside down, seventy-five feet above the water, and took out those explosives from the bridge columns. He definitely earned his pay that day. It was dangerous to hang from the bridge like that, but to top it off, those explosives could have been booby-trapped.

That day we received the orders that we were going to attack Saddam Hussein International Airport (Baghdad International Airport). It took us the better part of the day to get there, and from there on out, we were in continuous contact with enemy forces. At times we couldn't see the enemy but it didn't matter. We had a more important mission, one that might topple the regime, and we just kept moving.

We got to the airport, and my company's job was to dismount and clear out one section of the airport called the VIP Village—a kind of resort complex within the airport. The task force was going to secure the airfield itself. Things were dangerous. The airport was built like a fort with fences and concrete walls everywhere. We expected a lot of resistance. When the sun came out, so did the enemy. We broke down a wall and I looked to the left, and there were fedayeen soldiers running across the rooftops of the next area we were going to clear. We thought the fight would be over when morning came, but it was just beginning.

We cleared out these buildings. Some had been looted but most were untouched. There were guard towers throughout this area, and we were launching grenades into them because they represented our biggest threat. If a fedayeen popped up in the guard tower with a machine gun, he could control the entire area. We saw foxholes with fires still burning. There were signs of the enemy everywhere. We dismounted and one of our grenades fell short and hit at the base of a guard tower. I got hit by one of the shrapnel pieces in the left knee. It knocked me down and the pain was excruciating. It sent my left knee backward and I collapsed. I just tried to shake it off and keep moving. We cleared for a couple of hours, rooting out some of the enemy. We came in contact with one of Saddam Hussein's elite elements but the Iraqi regulars were just running. They were leaving weapons, letters, photos, and everything behind.

My knee ballooned up. We were clearing the airfield and using earthmovers so we could start using the airport for our strategic operations: bringing in supplies, landing heavy aircraft. I didn't have much time for my injury, and I wasn't going to let it take me out of the fight. I could barely walk. It was getting worse and worse to the point that I couldn't move my left leg into my HMMWV [Humvee]. I had to pick it up with my arms and move it. I definitely wasn't feeling top-notch.

I found out that my brother's company was part of the task force with the mission to feel out the enemy in Baghdad by doing what was referred to as a "Thunder Run." His company took Highway 8 from the south to the airport. I caught wind of it because I was monitoring the radio. I took a shower; it was just a birdbath really but I got myself cleaned up. Then my brother got on the radio and said, "Apache Six, this is Dog Six." It was just so refreshing to hear my brother's voice. We hadn't seen each other since Kuwait six weeks earlier. Dave told me where he was. I went to him. We looked different to each other. We'd both experienced so much in a short period of time and

Dave's company had just finished a tough fight. Most of his company was out of ammunition and they were getting resupplied. Dave hadn't been wounded at that point but I was limping around. He didn't make a big deal out of it. We knew the fighting wasn't done.

Things seemed to be coming to a head, and we wondered where this was all going to end. We owned the airport. The way it ended was my brigade attacked the heart of Baghdad from the west, and my brother's brigade attacked from the south. My company would end up in the lead for the First Brigade and his company was in the lead for the Second. We would both breach minefields to get our task forces into the heart of Baghdad, this time to stay.

We moved out early in the evening, still daylight, and we didn't expect many minefields. An unmanned Ariel vehicle flew our route just hours before we left and detected no mines. I left my breaching assets at the assembly area. Charlie Company 369 called back and reported that there were minefields the enemy had laid twelve hundred meters deep on both sides of Highway 8. We tried to bypass it but we couldn't get past it. I was reconning it. It was unbelievable how fast the enemy had laid those mines. How they did it so fast, I'll never know. But I did recognize the mines because they were the same ones we saw at Objective Peach that were used as additional explosives on the bridge. They were Italian-made mines with anti-handling capability, which means they could be booby-trapped. They're dual-primed, so you can't defeat just one priming system; there are two. They're blast-resistant, so even if you put an explosive right next to it, it won't necessarily detonate. When I saw them, I just about puked.

I called my task force commander and told him I would be bringing my breaching assets forward but that it would take some time. He sent Bradleys forward to try to shoot the mines. I wasn't thrilled with the idea because it might make the minefield even more dangerous since the mines are now partially destroyed and even more sensitive and hidden in the debris where you can't see them. The Bradleys were having little success. I called my Armored Combat Earthmovers (small armored dozers) forward. They worked better but it was also taking a lot of time. I really wanted to employ my MICLICs, hoping the overpressure would kick the mines off the road since the overpressure would probably not cause a blast-resistant mine to detonate. I also called forward two D9 Armored Bulldozers that were attached to my company from a national guard unit. One of my best staff sergeants, Brian Clark, came up with his squad, and he employed the MICLIC like clockwork. Eighteen hundred pounds of C4 high explosive tethered to a rocket like sausage links flew threw the air, perfect centerline down the road. I gave the command to fire and the line charge shook the earth; mines and trees caught on fire. The problem was the mines were still there. With the arrival of the D9s, I wasted no time putting them to use.

It was getting dark when we put the national guard guys to work trying to clear the minefield in D9s. It was very slow going and I was getting impatient. We were four to five hours into the job and it was 2300 hours (eleven p.m). I was losing radio communication with the soldiers in the D9 and you can't do that in combat. I climbed up into one of the dozers myself in the middle of the minefield, and the enemy started firing at us. I was completely exposed and I was a long way from my vehicle. I jumped off the vehicle and did the hundred-yard dash through this minefield with my bum leg. Their crew-served weapon kept firing in my direction while I was running, and I wasn't too concerned about it. I knew they were probably firing at me but I didn't care anymore. I jumped up into my vehicle from the ground to the turret in a bad mood. I had a lot of adrenaline rushing through me.

I got in. We had a Mark 19 and it's a beautiful weapon. I told my driver, one of the best armored vehicle operators in the army, Specialist Jared Hart, to get into the minefield and he drove as far as he could. We stopped, and I unloaded an entire canister of grenades into the whole area. I had my night-vision on, and it was the most amazing scene, like fireworks going off all over the place, and that was the last we heard of those guys. Either they got into the game late or they had been waiting until we were in a position that favored them, but I was the lucky guy who got their attention, I guess. We cleared the rest of the minefield at daybreak. Second Brigade was in the center of Baghdad, and with the minefield breached, First Brigade owned the west and was meeting Second Brigade in the center. The marines were in east Baghdad. We had accomplished our primary objective.

Are things better in Iraq now than before? It depends on who you are. When you talk to Iraqis, everybody has a horror story about Saddam Hussein. You don't have to go looking for them; they are just offered to you. In the big picture, the instability in Iraq is horrible. There's a fear of the unknown. There's a fear of what the future will bring. I do believe Iraq has the chance to be a true sovereign nation under elected, competent rule. The potential for Iraq to be better is huge. This is a period of transition, and you can't compare Iraq before to Iraq now. In history, when you take over a country via invasion, there's unsettling and instability, and it's almost unavoidable. It takes time. The way Americans are, we love e-mail and digital photos; we are addicted to instant gratification. But when you're talking about transforming a nation into something bigger and better, there is no such thing as instant gratification.

The question is, do we have the patience to see this mission through and do it right? We must stick with it and that's coming from someone who's been there a year now. I just finished up my second deployment to Iraq, and I'm not looking forward to my third.

But I signed up for this, and whatever the nation calls for me to do, I'll do.

★

Dan Hibner is now a major. He has some nerve damage to his left knee so that it feels like it's asleep, which he finds "annoying." He says he'll be with the U.S. Army "until the army feels it doesn't need me anymore."

THEY COULD NO LONGER TELL THE WORLD WE WEREN'T THERE

★

David Hibner, Captain, U.S. Army

Company D, Tenth Engineer Battalion

Michigan City, Indiana

SILVER STAR; IRAQ; 7 APRIL 2003

Identical twins David and Dan Hibner went to war together in March of 2003. Assigned to Task Force 1-64 Armor, Dave's engineering company captured prisoners, cleared minefields, braved firefights, and helped capture Baghdad International Airport. Waiting for him in Baghdad was his twin brother, Dan. Both brothers were awarded identical medals, the Silver Star for bravery and the Purple Heart for their leg wounds.

DAVID HIBNER

Dan and I both wanted to go on active duty and attend Army Ranger School. We got everything we wanted. Everything. We trained hard for Ranger School and we reported to Fort Benning, Georgia, in November 1996. Ranger School was tough; it lived up to all the legends, but it was the best training in the world. Only about half of those going through Ranger School graduate. It was the best training in the world, and I find myself going back to my experience to figure out the best way to teach and train my guys. What I discovered about myself is that my body can go much farther than my mind thinks it can, and I didn't really know that until Ranger School. Years later, when we were getting close to Baghdad and the tempo was so intense, we went three days without much sleep to speak of and there was no shortage of challenges, and I was able to focus more on the mission because I'd experienced all that in Ranger School. I absolutely believe that it saved my life.

When the war in Iraq was inevitable, we went to Kuwait in September 2002 and we had the chance to do what every leader in the army dreams about doing. Our training was absolutely world-class. I don't know if anyone in history trained the way we trained. We were confident and we were ready to apply the training to what needed to be done in Iraq.

Morale was high. On March nineteenth or twentieth, we saw our cruise missiles screaming overhead. It was five in the morning and every single guy in our unit was on top of the vehicles yelling and cheering because the cruise missiles were like the gun being fired at the start of a race. We weren't happy for war necessarily but we were ready to go and apply what we'd trained to do for so long. There was a feeling of confidence that never went away.

We didn't see many people at first, and then about thirty hours into the movement we came into a town and had a truck that needed maintenance work. Six Iraqi soldiers in uniform came running out with their arms to surrender. These six were the first and last prisoners to surrender to us the whole time we were there.

We kept going and we drifted through a couple of small towns. People would come out of their houses to watch us file through; that was kind of eerie. No one reacted. They weren't cheering or waving but they weren't shooting at us either. They may have been happy to see us but there also may have been some people in town watching them.

A recon unit up ahead had come under attack and so our mission was changed from a clearing mission to an attack mission. We continued to move forward and found a deliberate defense setup. There were about 110 loyalists dug into fighting positions, and their vehicles with mounted rifles and machine guns were hiding behind the berms. The fight was on. By then it was dark and our tanks were just thumping down on these bunkers. There were cannons and Bradleys firing into the enemy positions and mortars were raining down on these guys, and some of the loyalists were leaking out. It's hard to beat a unit that's dug in; plus, these loyalists were fighting like crazy. They were fanatical. Even with all the firepower hitting them, they were trying to sneak forward to get a closer shot at us. They next morning, we found some of their wounded on the battlefield, and our intelligence officer asked them why they were fighting so hard. They said that farther back behind them were special Iraqi Republican Guard officers, and if they tried to retreat they'd be killed, and after that their families would be killed.

After that battle, in the middle of the night, my battalion commander, Lieutenant Colonel Eric Schwartz, gave my company permission to occupy a certain sector and an order to take charge of a road intersection. There were two major roads coming in and I was given the one on the southeast. I put my company in a crescent, facing An Najaf, because that's where we figured the danger would come from. By two thirty in the morning our company had been without sleep for two days, so I decided to put half the company down for a rest. I put myself at the most decisive point. At three a.m. we noticed a light coming out of An Najaf, a single vehicle that was about eight kilometers away. They were coming right at us. In about half of these instances it's a legitimate target, and the other half of the time it's a civilian. The fact of the matter is that we put ourselves in danger so that we would not make a mistake and have a wrongful death.

I was thinking that because the vehicle had its lights on, it was a civilian who just happened to blunder onto the battlefield. We could have destroyed it from a very long distance, but that's not how we were operating. We didn't want to kill anyone that didn't need to be killed, who wasn't a lawful combatant. So we waited. We tried to see with our thermals and naked eyes what we were dealing with, but we couldn't. They got to around three hundred meters. By then, the whole company was feeling kind of desperate, but I was adamant. Everybody held their fire. The vehicle crept forward and crept forward, and at that point we knew it was a pickup truck, which raised my suspicions, but I was not ready to start firing. I had my machine gun tucked under my shoulder, desperately trying to figure out what the vehicle was. I had the feeling that something wasn't right.

Tate turned and yelled to me, "They got a machine gun!" As soon as he yelled, for the first time I could see them and they could see me and we were about ten feet away from each other. We looked each other in the eye and recognized that the other was the enemy. We realized that the next few seconds would decide who lived and who died. Thank God we came out with the upper hand. I don't remember putting the selector switch on fire or cocking my machine gun;

I don't remember anything. Tracers were flying everywhere and the bullets were slapping the sides of our vehicles.

We trained on the machine gun to have a break once in a while or else it would ruin the cyclic timing and jam the weapon. But, man, I didn't let go of that trigger the whole time. I unloaded a drum of my ammo into that truck. It literally rolled through our company perimeter and out the back side and then it just kind of drifted to a stop, probably about three hundred or four hundred meters behind us. And that was it. I grabbed our radio and called in the report that we'd had contact and that a tactical vehicle was destroyed and at least three loyalists were killed. LTC Schwartz—God, is he a good leader—he just came back on the net, just as calm as he could be, and he said, "Roger, Dog, you've got this fight so continue to fight and report." All of a sudden, my adrenaline level just dropped and that's what I needed. Obviously it was a life-defining experience.

We heard reports that the enemy was crawling toward our area. We had a report that the loyalists were in this mud hut. Our thermals told us there were "hot spots" in the hut so we knew there were people. We could have just destroyed the hut, but we couldn't confirm whether they were enemy or friendly. Nothing happened. Finally we decided to move back and stick with our company objective of protecting this intersection. The next morning I came out and the first thing I did was look at that hut. I saw two little kids and a woman walk out of there. Maybe there were loyalist soldiers in there that night, but if there were kids in there too, boy, am I glad I didn't fire at that hut. Our entire task force continued to put ourselves at risk rather than mistakenly kill civilians. Did it put us at extra risk? It sure did. Was it the right thing to do? I think it was.

We got reassigned; we were in the lead and happy about that. We moved into a mining area with a huge conveyor system. About this time it started raining, and because there was so much dust in the air, it was raining mud. Visibility was zero. The next morning it looked like Mars, mud and muck everywhere. It turned out we were right next to an Iraqi outpost, but we couldn't see each other. We went to clear this outpost and it was empty, but there was a fish frying in a pan and there were ledgers and documents all over the place. There were bunkers used to store massive amounts of explosives and ammunition and we blew them up. Whoever had left, had left in a hurry.

The battalion commander came and said to get ready to go to An Najaf. We had thirty minutes to get loaded up. Shortly after entering An Najaf, we were ambushed. The shooting started and the kill zone was probably seven kilometers long. The shooting never stopped. They were shooting at us from both sides of the road. We had RPGs coming at us from the right side and left side. We couldn't get a fix on the enemy because the enemy was everywhere. The only way we could pick up on where they were was catching their muzzle flash, and even that was hard to see in the dust. All the tires on our trailers were getting shot out and we were starting to bog down and get stuck. It seemed like the enemy fire was intensifying, and then all of a sudden there was this *zing* sound, and I felt something hit me on the side of the face. It was a flash, sparks right off the side of my face and a bullet divot nearby. There was only one place it could have come from, the tops of the buildings. I told everybody to shift their fire to the tops of the buildings. Doing that suppressed some of their fire, but we needed to get out of there.

We crossed a bridge and occupied it and the intersection for several days, doing checkpoint operations. We were quite a sight. We had flat tires, leaking fuel, and a transfer case that was grinding because the top had been shot off. The batteries had been shot through. Every trailer had four tires on it and every tire on every trailer was flat. All the equipment and rucksacks were riddled with bullets.

Sergeant Lucas, God bless him, thought he'd been hit by something, but he never imagined it was a bullet. He'd been shot through the triceps. PFC Northcutt had been shot square in the middle of the back but his body armor had swallowed it up, and his squad leader used a Leatherman to pull out the bullet, which of course he saved. He got the breath knocked out of him, but other than a nasty bruise on his back, he was fine. Without the body armor, he'd have been instantly killed. I had a driver who had been hit in the head and the bullet just planted itself inside his helmet. Except for an excruciating headache, he was fine. Given the circumstances, we came out smelling like a rose. But for weeks afterward we were discovering more problems with our vehicles from bullets having penetrated them. One of my platoon leaders told me that his soldier was eating an MRE and the pound cake had a hole in it, and there was a bullet buried right in the middle like a little chocolate surprise.

By this point we'd been immersed in enemy territory for eight straight days and we were under sporadic mortar fire with occasional RPGs whizzing by us. A bus of women and younger men came through our checkpoint. The men were very protective of the women and we tried to respect that. We had what nobody else had: a female medic. She inspected the women on the bus, and when they lifted their black dresses, there were machine guns, buckets of ammo—I mean, you name it, they had it—strapped underneath their dresses. That piece of intelligence spread like wildfire.

I'd send my platoons out on missions and we'd find fighting positions, weapons and ammo everywhere. We started using Iraqi explosives to blow up their weapons and ammunition. We didn't have any problems with our weapons. We kept them clean and they performed for us, which is a testament to the discipline of our soldiers, because they had been in an ambush situation where it was pure dust. The air was filled with it; if we breathed it into our lungs, we'd choke on it. We had to breathe through rags.

We got a break, and then around April first we were on the move to Karbala. It came to be known as the movement from hell. It was so slow, so hot, and the fighting was intense. There were narrow canal roads and it was like being in a traffic jam. On the far side of Karbala we started taking mortar fire. We started out at eight in the morning and we didn't get done until four the next morning. I got an hour and a half of sleep and then woke up for our operations meeting.

They told us we were going to move across the river and occupy "Objective Saints" just south of Baghdad. When we reached our destination, we found the headquarters where the Iraqi army did the battle planning. We saw maps, sketches, and sand table models. We found diaries and ID cards. That night we got our orders that we were going to do our first "Thunder Run": a running tank battle against the enemy's Medina Division. We destroyed all kinds of equipment, vehicles, you name it. It was a running gun battle the whole way and we met little resistance. It was like a turkey shoot. The biggest danger was the secondary explosions from their artillery rounds going off. LTC Schwartz was hit in the arm with a piece of shrapnel. We came back to Objective Saints feeling at the top of our game. From our initial planning, I'd heard about the necessity of destroying the Medina Division a million times. We destroyed the Medina Division and we felt pretty good about it.

I remember getting a call that night at nine to come to a task force meeting for an order. I walked into the planning tent eating my trail mix, chewing away, and looked at a map that was laid out on the table. The majors were pointing to the center of it and I said, "Why are you pointing to the center of Baghdad?" LTC Schwartz walked up and said, "Okay, by now I'm sure you realize what's going on. We're going into Baghdad." Then he said, "You know, you gotta have faith that there's someone out there who knows more than we do about what's going on and that they wouldn't send us on a mission that we can't succeed at." Then he told us it wasn't a brigade attack, just a raid, our battalion going in alone. My heart sank. I felt we'd done a lot of heavy fighting and it was time to share the wealth a little bit. Going into Baghdad wasn't going to be an easy fight. We had more wounded than most units and more destroyed equipment. I don't think they cared how much fighting we had done, or maybe they liked the fact that we had fought so much before we went to Baghdad. The bottom line was, we were going to go.

My troops reacted the same way I did: "You've got to be kidding me." We were an engineering outfit and we hadn't breached one minefield yet. Just as LTC Schwartz had done with me, I told my men that this was our mission, we were going to Baghdad and we needed to focus on the mission. We got the mission because it was a hard mission and we were going to do it and we were going to succeed.

We didn't know the enemy's strength or what weapons systems they were going to use. We were being sent on this mission to figure all that out so the units that came in next would know the answers to all those questions. Call it a raid, call it combat reconnaissance, call it whatever you want to. We were out to show the Baghdad regime that they could no longer tell the world that we weren't there. We were going to prove our presence by driving right through the middle of their city.

This was an order and we had to come up with the best plan to execute it. So we did. We were moving into a city with a population of 5.5 million and we knew the hardest fight of the war was going to be in Baghdad. We would be surrounded the whole time. We couldn't evacuate wounded or broken vehicles. We didn't have air support. We didn't have artillery support. We were alone. We finished planning at three in the morning and we lined up to leave at four thirty a.m.

We lined up and I could smell the fumes from these huge engines and hear the M1 tank diesels and turbine engines whining in the foreground and background. I was in my 'trac with all my weapons as clean as they could be, ammunition stacked as high as it could go, and explosives that were rigged and ready. That was the only time, standing there that morning, that I thought to myself that I might not make it home. I knew that if I was thinking that, then my soldiers were thinking it, too.

Waiting was the hardest part. If you've never seen an armored task force moving in battle, then it's hard to describe the firepower, the lethality, the capability, the proficiency, and the professionalism all coming together to form this unbelievable unit. Everything that we'd done since December had come to this. We knew it. LTC Schwartz said that if we wanted to test our weapons, we could do it. Everybody peeled off a few rounds and we had that little extra confidence.

Two minutes later the fighting started. We'd never seen this level of intensity of fire and determination before. Those guys didn't want us to make it through and they knew this was their last chance to stop us. This was their chance to prove everybody wrong, that they could beat the American forces in conventional warfare. They lined the streets with machine guns, RPGs, and machine-gun nests that they'd burrowed into the overpasses. They were shooting at us with everything they had, so we were moving along as fast as we could. Charley Tank Company had a vehicle hit in the engine, which started a fire in the back of the tank. They tried to put out the fire but that caused a problem: we weren't moving targets anymore. It was loaded to the gills with ammunition and the fire wasn't going out and the commander had trouble figuring out what to do. I don't think Colonel Schwartz wanted to leave the tank, because even one piece of destroyed equipment would be a small victory for the enemy. But the situation was deteriorating and the enemy fire was getting heavier and the fire was getting worse. It was time to let go. We left the vehicle. Twenty minutes had gone by, but it felt like an eternity.

We started taking casualties. One soldier was shot in the face. One got shot in the chest or neck. We were feeling the pressure of combat when things go wrong. We still had a long way to go. The sting of battle was starting to get to everybody. We put a tank round through the disabled tank and the air force dropped a couple of two-thousand-pound bombs on there, but when the smoke cleared, sure enough, there were Iraqis with their RPGs dancing on top of the tank they'd destroyed.

Halfway through the battle, I'd gone through ten thirty-round magazines. Everybody was laying down suppressive fire. There were lots of enemy everywhere. I remember seeing a truck carrying Iraqi troops speeding to our flank, trying to get ahead of our column. I called it in, and five seconds later one of our tanks put a round through it and just disintegrated it. That was just one small example of what was happening all over Baghdad.

We were getting hit with a lot of RPGs up and down the column. One soldier got his leg wounded pretty badly and they couldn't handle his wound inside the vehicle. He needed a doctor. We stopped the column again and an ambulance pushed forward, and everybody was providing suppressive fire for the doctor to go forward and treat this guy. That worked well, but the problem was we were stopped again and that gave the enemy time to reinforce. We were probably an hour into the battle at that point. We'd expended a lot of ammunition, suffered several casualties, and we'd stopped a couple of times. The air force did some strafing and that helped take some of the pressure off us. But everybody wanted to come in and get their licks on us. For every casualty we took, they probably took a hundred.

They were relentless about sending in reinforcements. They kept coming. The fire kept intensifying. We were quite a mess by that time. As we approached the airport we found the icing on the cake: the enemy had erected these big concrete barriers, and as an engineer it was my job to figure out how to get our sappers forward to get rid of them. We could blow them up or try to ram them with the plows on our M1 tanks. Colonel Schwartz said, "Roger. Ram it!" Our M1 tank got up a whole head of steam and was traveling at thirty-five miles per hour when it hit the concrete barriers with the plow. The tank went airborne. If the intensity of fire didn't scare the enemy, then seeing an M1 tank fly through the air must have. The tank landed on the other side. The crash destroyed their plow but they had managed to move the concrete bunkers enough that we could weave our way through. First Brigade was already there and they were a welcome sight. We arrived with vehicles on fire, everything bullet-riddled, a trail of spent shells behind us everywhere we went.

Our men performed flawlessly. They were absolutely amazing. We were fighting a bunch of loyalists, a bunch of dismounted troops, people in windows, from every fighting position imaginable. We eliminated a lot of targets and contributed a lot of precision to the battle. The way an engineer vehicle is configured, we could shoot in all directions at the same time. Here is another twist of irony: up until that time my company was the only one taking casualties. Then we headed into the heaviest fighting of all and suddenly my company was the only one that didn't have any casualties. There we were in the middle of it and we didn't take one casualty. Not one.

If I spent a day trying to explain it to you, I still couldn't give you an idea of how bad it was. We did what we did because that is what had to be done. We had some serious vehicle issues that needed to be taken care of. Everybody was low on ammo. We had a lot of weapons maintenance that needed to be done before we could move again. Everything had been shot up. But we came in, lined ourselves up like we always did. We aligned in perfect formation on the tarmac and started rebooting right away, the way we'd been trained. We began cleaning out our vehicles, and literally thousands and thousands of spent shell casings were being swept off the vehicles onto the tarmac.

I went around and checked on my soldiers. Some of them were writing in their diaries, others were making jokes. Some were real quiet and subdued and wanted to be left alone. I think I felt every emotion they were feeling. I was proud of my soldiers. Everyone started to focus on getting their vehicles squared away, checking fluids, getting our weapons cleaned, getting rearmed, filling our magazines, doing all the things we have to do to move again.

I knew my brother, Dan, was in the First Brigade. I thought maybe he was in radio range. I switched to his frequency and I said, "Apache Six, this is Dog Six." He came up on the net. I'm certain he was happy to hear me and I was happy to hear him. Within fifteen minutes Dan and I met right there at Baghdad International Airport. That was the first time we'd seen each other in a long time. It was just another example of the way it has been all our lives: when we need each other the most, we're always there for each other.

Later LTC Schwartz came on and said, "You guys can't really understand now the significance of what you just did. What you have to believe is that we sacrificed a lot but we made history today. You gotta understand that." And I think we did. That was the first blow and we put the regime on their heels and now we were coming for the knockout punch.

It was a quiet night, not a lot of action. We got some decent rest but 50 percent of the company was still on security detail and we had a lot of work that needed to be done on our vehicles.

It turns out that just a few hundred yards from us, this Iraqi infantry company was camped in a date grove. We had to pull all of the vehicles out of there and destroy them without destroying the farmer's date grove. We spent that entire day pulling fourteen vehicles out of there, pulling out their ammunition, blowing up the vehicles. Then we set up separate caches to blow up the explosives and ammunition because that has to be done in smaller blasts. We did that all day long. It was getting dark, we were finishing up, and we were exhausted. The date farmer came out and brought us huge tin bowls of dates. These were gigantic bowls, enough dates so that everyone could eat until their stomachs hurt. We did that. I'd never had a date before, but once I had my first one I couldn't stop eating them. I think that's exactly what that guy wanted. They were so good. We didn't speak the same language but we had an appreciation for each other.

As the day was winding down, I got another call. I went to the task force and they looked at me and said, "We've got another mission for you tomorrow." I thought they had to be kidding. I told LTC Schwartz that I thought our company got really lucky yesterday and I didn't know if we were going to fare as well tomorrow. Like any good leader, Colonel Schwartz took his soldiers' questions seriously. This decision was kind of hanging in the air and then it turned out the mission was made for us. The intelligence reports said that the enemy had laid out a minefield where we had attacked the day before. At that point, it wasn't even up for debate. That's our game.

The intelligence report came in at eleven p.m. and we had to leave at five a.m. There were different kinds of breaching techniques to consider that night, but this minefield posed a special challenge because it was in the middle of the city on a highway. Everybody was debating the best way to do it. Every possible option was discussed that night. Finally Colonel Schwartz turned to me and said, "Look, we don't have that much time to debate about this. We simply need to make a decision and just go with it. Bottom line is, you're the one who has to breach this minefield so I'm going to leave it to you to decide how to do it. No more debate."

That's one of the things that made him such an incredible leader. He was decisive and he trusted subordinates. I stepped up and said, "Sir, you might think this is going to sound a little crazy, but I think we should do a covert breach." My plan was to do it right under the enemy's nose. We left at three in the morning and we went three or four miles into enemy territory. We just crept forward about as fast as a person can walk. We kept our engines as low as we could. We moved to the minefield completely undetected, and as we got close I stopped the company. We went forward with the least amount of power possible so we didn't blow our cover. We stopped and I pushed the sapper platoon forward and we started doing the lasso technique to pull the mines out. The minefield was 550 meters deep and there were something like eight hundred mines. Time was of the essence, and I could see we weren't going to make our deadline. We needed to speed things up. This was the mission and everybody was counting on us. This was it, the attack on Baghdad. We were going in first and we had to clear the way for the rest of the troops. If we couldn't get the minefield breached, it wasn't going to happen, so we made the decision to pick up the mines with our hands as fast as we could.

We got done at 4:50 a.m. and I breathed a sigh of relief. We made it with ten minutes to spare. The Iraqi guards who were supposed to guard the minefield could have spotted us. I guess they never dreamed we were going to walk up there and remove them by hand.

The next day we were on the move again, heading toward downtown Baghdad. There was some pretty decent fighting going on and an RPG hit one of my vehicles. It was just to the left of me. They got us. I could feel the blast and feel the heat. The vehicle that was hit drifted off course and I thought the worst, that everyone inside was dead. But they were just knocked out; they came to and went right back into formation. The RPG didn't penetrate the vehicle because we put as much crap on the outside of our vehicles as we could. Rucksacks, MRE boxes, tents, if it could be strapped to the outside, we did it, because it gets the RPGs to detonate early and it ruins the blast effect. The whole front of the vehicle had peeled off, as if God had come down and just slapped everything off the front of it. It was gone, splattered everywhere, pitted and burned. As we were driving along, we could see underwear and trousers spilling out of the rucksacks that had holes in them. But that's a small price to pay for the hit we took.

We kept moving to the center of the city; our mission was to occupy a sector outside the Tomb of the Unknown Soldier. We all had the feeling that it was too easy and there was something wrong. We expected to have to fight our way into that position. I think the enemy realized they couldn't hurt us when we were on the move so they waited until we stopped. Then we started getting hit from everywhere. I was standing outside when the first mortar round landed. I had a media team with me. The mortar landed nearby and I'm surprised none of us got hurt. Everybody scrambled into the vehicles, and the mortars fell continually from that moment on. They never stopped. We were drawing small-arms fire and we were trying to find out where it was coming from. Just when things started to quiet down, we'd hear a round whiz through the air. I thought, *Here we go again.*

I got a report that a private had been hit and I wanted to see how he was. I went over to his 'trac and saw that he was pale and bleeding bad. The medic was trying to take care of him. By the way, my female medic was the first female to go into Baghdad. I told the private he was going to be fine, but I really didn't know if he was going to be fine or how we were going to get him out of there. It was getting ugly.

We knew that the mortar fire was being carefully aimed and that someone was directing the fire on us. We got so used to it that, based on the sound of the round as it came in, we would try to estimate how close it would be. It wasn't a fun game to play but it helped pass the time. When there was finally a break in the mortar fire we went into a nearby building just to stretch our legs. We cleared that building and downed a little chow before we were going to get back in our vehicles. The media team I was with was standing by the door. I was always uncomfortable when they would do stuff like that. The cameraman was filming mortars coming in and our mortar platoon trying to put counterfire on them, and he thought it was pretty good footage. I looked over the cameraman's shoulder, and sure enough, I heard it. Before I even had time to think, *Boy, this one is close*, it exploded right in front of us and we just got blown away. We got blasted to the far side of the room, about fifteen feet away. There was dust and broken glass everywhere. They got us. I had a chunk of mortar round go into my left thigh and it felt like someone was driving a nail that was on fire into my leg with a baseball bat. The cameraman was wounded in the buttocks and we were stuck inside the building. I quickly came up with a plan to get us out of there. I sent us out by twos, back to the vehicle, and then once we were there, we threw our flak protection back so that if a mortar round landed while we were climbing into the vehicle, we would at least have flak protection. So we got back in the vehicle and our medic came out. She had been treating my leg and the cameraman's butt.

Once it got dark inside the city, we got a resupply patrol out to us and got fuel and ammo. The next morning, life was different for everybody. There were other problems to deal with but it was different. I stayed with the company another two days before I went to the hospital to have my leg looked at. They shot an X-ray and the hunk of shrapnel had planted itself right next to my femur. The doctor looked at the X-ray and he said, "There it is and there it will stay." He said it would do more damage than good trying to take it out. I have a little souvenir that I brought home with me, that's all. It just happens to be inside me.

Two and a half years later, I think about the things we did and sometimes maybe what we could have done differently. For the most part, I look back and I'm proud of it and I'm proud of my guys and I really miss what we had at that time. I wonder if some of the other guys in the company feel that way too. We really had it going. We were quite a team. We were more than a team, we were a family. I miss it. I don't know if I will ever have that again. I sure hope so.

★

David Hibner is attending graduate-level international business classes and learning Arabic at the University of South Carolina as a member of the U.S. Army. He'll finish his schoolwork and then get back into a brigade. He says he will stay in the army as long as they'll keep him. He hopes the next ten years are as good as the first ten years.

BO PEEP

★

Thomas Parks III, Warrant Officer Two, U.S. Marine Corps

First Battalion, Fourth Marines

Dover, New Hampshire

SILVER STAR; IRAQ; 3 APRIL 2003

Parks served as the battalion infantry weapons officer for the First Battalion, Fourth Marines during the march to Baghdad. For a twenty-day period from March 20 to April 10, 2003, he was in continuous contact with the Iraqi Regular Army, the Republican Guard, and Saddam's fedayeen forces. Parks and his company came under intense small-arms and rocket fire while escorting the battalion command element in Al Kut. Reacting instantly to the enemy ambush, Parks is credited with single-handedly destroying an enemy T-55 tank, a sniper ready to fire upon a fellow marine, two other enemy fighters, and the captor of a little girl.

THOMAS PARKS III

I recently retired from the First Marine Division out of Camp Pendleton. I'd been with the Marine Corps for twenty years. My wife, Christine, is still in the Marine Corps and she received orders to go to Kansas City, so I came along like a good and faithful husband. The school system is great for our kids and Christine is doing important things for the Marine Corps here at the mobilization command for all the reservists going to Iraq. She's the toughest and prettiest marine in our corps, I might add.

I grew up with my father and stepmother in Dover, New Hampshire. When my dad was seventeen and a senior at Dover High School he got in a fight at Monarch Diner in Dover, which is now a Dunkin' Donuts. That was on a Friday night after a bunch of beers and he broke another kid's nose with Officer Thompson standing ten feet away. They didn't arrest you then, but the next day he had to go see the chief of police with my grandfather, and five days later he was at Parris Island, South Carolina, to finish his senior year of high school, 1962, at Marine Corps boot camp.

When he got out four years and four months later—extended for Vietnam—my mother, father, and I moved back to Dover. He got a job at Brady Ford in Portsmouth, New Hampshire, as finance manager, where he stayed for two years, until the opportunity to buy into Tri-City Dodge came up thirty-three years and two months ago. He has since retired; he is my hero and the smartest man I have ever known. He started a tradition when he broke that kid's nose.

I enjoyed Marine Corps boot camp. I was a very athletic kid so it fit me quite well. My father was always at the forefront of my mind and I wanted to make him proud. At the very beginning, I was living it for him, but I discovered that I had found my niche. My dad says that if they didn't have a Marine Corps, they'd have to invent one for me. The marines were exactly what I needed: the honor, the courage, the commitment to something bigger and brighter than myself.

In 1990, I was with an outfit called Third Battalion, Ninth Marines. We were on our way up to Vancouver to enjoy some time off and show the public some military might by giving tours of the ship and showing the latest and greatest of military might. It was while we were on our way that Saddam invaded Kuwait. I could feel that big ship do a U-turn in the Pacific Ocean. It just did an about-face, and we steamed back to Camp Pendleton.

I think we had one day back at our home station, Camp Pendleton. We were issued our desert camouflage, our gear, our ammo and weapons, and we were gone. We went to Twentynine Palms for about four or five days of training and then we were on the plane over to Saudi Arabia. We landed there on August 12, 1990. They weren't ready for us yet so we dropped off all the heavy equipment. They kept us in these steel buildings, which made the temperature feel like 150 degrees. We were in a holding pattern for about a week. Then my unit ended up moving north into defensive positions. We were part of a larger unit called Task Force Ripper and then we ended up becoming Task Force Papa Bear. We kept moving forward and forward.

For about eight months we lived out of the deepest holes that we could dig. Once eight months was up, we got on our amtracs and started moving toward Baghdad and taking lots of Iraqi prisoners of war. We cleared trenches, made our way through them, and we'd find the enemy burrowed in and hiding. The vast majority of them we took as POWs. I looked at the enemy as capable but they'd been left out there in the middle of the desert with no supplies. The ones that fought, we killed, but the ones that didn't, we took prisoner.

When that war was over, we pulled back. Kuwait International Airport is where we consolidated and then we knew we were done. It was over. I remember just sitting there in my fighting hole and feeling displaced and unable to grasp any sign of victory. A hundred hours is what the books say, that's how long Operation Desert Storm lasted. For us it was one hundred hours of being awake. That was my first taste of combat.

When we returned home, I became an instructor at the School of Infantry. I took all the leadership skills I'd learned in combat and I started teaching it to entry-level and senior-level marines. I moved on to Third Battalion, Fifth Marines as an infantry squad leader. I must have shown some promise, because the battalion commander asked me to be the squad leader for the annual rifle squad competition. I took thirteen men and a navy corpsman—the Marine Corps called it Super Squad—and we won the competition. They sent my squad to Washington, D.C., to meet the commandant of the Marine Corps. The commandant asked me what I wanted to do. For some reason I said, "I want to be a drill instructor, sir." The next day, I had orders to the drill field. That was January of 1996 and I was back on Parris Island, South Carolina.

While serving as a Marine Corps drill instructor I was promoted meritoriously to staff sergeant. I continued to train raw recruits into tough marines, and in 1998 I became the drill instructor of the year. They promoted me again meritoriously to gunnery sergeant, E-7. I continued to mold young men into marines until I was ordered back to Camp Pendleton. I was taking college courses while a part of the Third Battalion, First Marines when I decided that I wanted to become a marine officer. At that point I'd been in the Marine Corps for thirteen years. I wanted to become a battalion weapons officer, and I finally achieved that in 2001. I was assigned to First Battalion, Fourth Marines, and we were getting ready to go over to the Western Pacific.

Instead of WESTPAC, as part of the war on terror, One-Four was ordered to Iraq. My battalion commander was Lieutenant Colonel "Cowboy" John Mayer. He is the most inspirational leader I've ever come across. We would have followed this guy anyplace. His call sign was Pale Rider. Our motto was, "Behold the Pale Rider and Hell follows." He was a very knowledgeable commander, a good man, and a great leader. Wonderfully inspirational. Humble would be the best word to describe him. The climate he created was, you train hard, you work hard, you love your country, the corps and God. My worldview wasn't so myopic anymore. I saw the big picture. And I saw it through the eyes of the Pale Rider. He is a full-bird colonel now, commanding the Thirty-first Marine Expeditionary Unit. I am very proud to have served under Cowboy John Mayer. He was the best man at my wedding.

We were in Kuwait for our preparatory training, getting ready to cross the line of departure to go into Iraq. We were doing our shooting, all our training. I set up ranges and had them bulldoze mounds of sand into berms so we could practice shooting into them. Rehearsing, rehearsing, rehearsing, every day for about a month. My job was to prepare us for combat. We did this until March 19, when it was time to pack up our stuff and go. I had one machine gunner, a hardback Humvee with a machine-gun mount, and a driver. The driver was a young guy from Atlanta, Lance Corporal Cobb. The machine gunner was from Chicago, another city kid by the name of Carlos Rochel. I nicknamed him "Taco." We forged this special relationship, the three of us.

Cobb was just as cool as the other side of the pillow. I was thirty-eight and he was twenty. I taught him how to navigate in the desert using the stars and he taught me how to be twenty again. Once we got into the Iraqi cities, I didn't have to teach Cobb anything. He's got natural instincts from the streets of Atlanta. Cobb could get us to a gunfight at the drop of a hat in the city because that was his background. Taco was loyal and dedicated to the machine gun and its employment.

We made this hundred-mile march through the barren desert and we kept each other awake. I sat shotgun and Cobb was in the cockpit driving. It was cold this time of year and we were driving a hundred miles from Kuwait, all the way into Iraq. It kept getting colder as we drove north. Taco was up in the turret 24/7 freezing his ass off. Cobb and I were down in the vehicle singing silly songs to stay awake; whatever it took to get to the fight. We were navigating with our night-vision goggles. Colonel Mayer started calling me Bo Peep because we were driving a fifty-vehicle-long log train, and some drivers toward the back of the column would doze off and go off course and the chain of vehicles would be broken. He'd call me and say, "Gunner, this is Pale Rider. Bo Peep, go get 'em." I'd have to retrieve the sheep. It could be miles and miles of open desert. I had the navigational skills to go get them and then try to catch up with the rest of the log train.

There were plenty of fights to be had. Once we crossed Kuwait it was barren desert. After a while we started to see a few mud huts. We were taking a lot of prisoners and killing many insurgents. There were a few roadside bombs. We also saw some orange-and-white taxi-cabs or old Toyotas. The insurgents and fighters would hail a taxicab to go to the front lines of the battle. They'd do anything they could to disguise themselves. We'd see their green fatigues shed off and strewn about the desert. We'd see a boy in a dress with a turban on his head wearing combat boots. We knew where he was coming from. We could see the disdain in their faces but they were there to fight another day.

This was early in 2003 so there were just pockets of resistance here and there. They had tunnel systems that they would fight from, then hide. Our first firefight as a battalion was with eight snipers who were about five hundred meters away. Every unit has to be christened by fire, but our whole battalion opened up on these eight snipers five hundred meters in the distance. I ran about the battlefield telling everybody to stop. I was the only one with combat experience there. They yelled at me, "Gunner, get down." They thought I was going to get shot by a sniper who was five hundred meters away with a worn-out weapon system. We learned together. They were concerned about their people and I was concerned about using up our ammo. They weren't the cagey veterans they would become within mere days.

In the southern portion were the Shiites. They welcomed us, waving and saying, "Give us money." The little kids would ask for candy. We'd give them pieces of our MREs. Once we got to the Sunnis farther north, we could tell they were ready to fight. We happened upon a lot of Baath Party headquarters.

First we moved through Al Kut and then we got closer to Baghdad. Our outpost was a cigarette factory. We were happy to be there and we smoked like chimneys. At the cigarette factory, we had the high ground and we put snipers on the top. We worked out of Saddam City, now called Sadr City. That was my stompin' grounds. Saddam City was a place where ambushes happened every day. Saddam City was this wretched slum. Garbage and open sewers everywhere. No electricity. No running water. No infrastructure whatsoever.

During the day we'd see teenage kids all together waving at us and wanting money. Then in the nighttime, they'd be shooting at us. It was very challenging because my emotions went in every different direction.

My mission the whole time was to influence the fight, to be more or less the eyes and ears for the commander. Wherever the fight was, I was. Our mission was to control the area, to take charge of what went in and out of the eastern part of Baghdad. I would go out with no more than six vehicles and cruise around looking for the enemy.

We'd go where the action was. I wore a weapons officer's insignia of a bursting bomb on my left collar—the coveted sign of the marine gunner—and I'd wear my warrant officer pin on my right collar. Cobb was pretty good at artwork so he painted white bursting bombs on either side of our Humvee doors. The enemy would soon look for these bursting bombs as a target for a very pissed-off marine gunner who was out to get them.

Lieutenant Colonel Cowboy John Mayer utilized me every day as the most experienced infantryman in his unit. I would teach the captains on the go. We were in the early stages of the fight and it was a pleasure to work with these young folks and be able to pass on some of what I knew. Inside me, I'm still a kid. But they see me as the old gunner.

Of the enemy, we saw their best and their worst, from guys with hoes or rakes in their hands all the way to the guys with RPK machine guns and snipers. I respected them because they knew the area; they were adept at their surrounds. They knew how to move around. They had a great tunnel system and plenty of escape routes.

In Al Kut, we were ambushed. An insurgent took a young girl as a hostage and used her as a defensive shield. It's hard to have much respect for a person like that. I put a bullet through the captor's head. That's all there was to it, an instant reaction. It's just an instinct. This little girl could have been my daughter. She was about four years old. When her captor fell, she ran over to her parents and obviously was rattled by the whole incident. The surrounding insurgents hunkered down in a hole and the fighting continued. Even in the heat of all that had just happened, I could not stop thinking of my two beautiful daughters, Tina and Suzy, and how they were once four years old. I fought on holding that thought.

The next thing I did was grab an AT-4 rocket launcher, and I killed a tank that was right next to us. It was just seventy-five meters away and the shock from the blast threw my equilibrium off. I disabled the tank, threw down the expended AT-4. Colonel Mayer called a squad of tanks up from the First Tank Battalion and they were now out on the streets. We were on one side of the street and the enemy was on the other, shooting at us from houses and a hedgerow about a hundred meters away. I used one of those cool tank phones on the back of the tank and told the first tank, "Turn to your left and blow a hole in that house." I told the second tank the same thing with the cool phone on that tank. The third tank didn't have a phone so I was at a loss. I utilized the tanks as cover. I ran to the second tank and told them to tell the third tank what I wanted them to do. I never had as much respect for tankers as I did then.

They started putting 120mm shells into the buildings, making holes, which unfortunately the enemy used to shoot at me. Obviously, I had my machine gunner just going crazy. We located, closed on, and destroyed the enemy. Like I said, we were being shot at from the north, south, east, west, northeast and northwest. It was a flip of the coin where we were going to take cover. We had a company of marines about five hundred meters to our north. I was with the regimental commander and the company commander and I was trying to protect them. John Mayer will tell you all day long that I saved his life. It was an adrenaline flow. I just wanted to kill the enemy. I enjoyed it. I continued to kill the enemy and the last thing I did before we got out of Al Kut was to run over to the destroyed Iraqi tank and grab a big old machine gun off that thing. I figured that would be a good idea because the enemy wouldn't be able to use it again. Through the grace of God, I have no idea how, I am alive. I live each day with the mental wounds of hard-fought combat; however, it is worth it for this country, for our freedom and our honor.

We fight for our buddies. We fight for our fellow marines, soldiers or sailors. Right now, I'm looking at a picture of a marine who's saluting with no hand. He's got gauze on his arm and he's standing there in his dress uniform. Obviously he's been through the treatment center at Walter Reed or Bethesda. He's crisply saluting, and where his hand would be, where his fingers would be extended and joined, his thumb along his forefinger, and his forefinger touching so gently the brim of his Marine Corps dress cover, there is air. But he is saluting. His upper arm is in line with the ground. He is so intently saluting the flag of his country, the country that he honors and has given his right hand for.

I have another photo that I'm looking at of a young staff sergeant who has a hook for an arm—you know, the kind they give you before you get a decent prosthetic. There's an older gentleman with a VFW hat on and he's obviously a World War II veteran. The old veteran is crying. He's holding on to this staff sergeant with all he's got, just telling him how much he appreciates what he's done for his country. The staff sergeant is just as proud as he can be, holding on to this older gentleman. These are my heroes, and all of the men and women who have not made it back alive. I do not consider myself a hero. I consider myself to be one of the lucky ones who have the ability to tell a story.

★

Thomas Parks retired from the marines after twenty years of service. He is the Director of Business Development with a technology and support company. His wife, Christine Glynn, is still with the marines as a chief warrant officer. They have four children: Christina (seventeen), Suzanne (sixteen), Kyle (fourteen), and Morgan (thirteen). They live in Raymore, Missouri.

THE ONLY WAY OUT IS THROUGH

★

Brian Chontosh, First Lieutenant, U.S. Marine Corps

Rochester, New York

NAVY CROSS; IRAQ; 25 MARCH 2003

After a three a.m. breakfast of beef enchiladas from a plastic pouch, twenty-nine-year-old platoon commander First Lieutenant Brian Chontosh and his unit headed north toward Ad Diwaniyah. It was March 25, 2003, the sixth day of the war. Two hours after they had hit the road, they were caught in the kill zone of an ambush. They came under fire from a hundred-plus-soldier unit of the elite Iraqi Republican Guard armed with AK-47s, machine guns, rocket-propelled grenades, and mortars. Brian Chontosh earned the Navy Cross. Armand McCormick and Robbie Kerman were awarded the Silver Star. Thomas Franklin and Ken Korte were awarded Navy and Marine Corps Commendation Medals.

BRIAN CHONTOSH

I was just an average happy-go-lucky high school guy in Rochester, New York. I played baseball, I wrestled for a year, and I skied with the ski club. I lacked direction coming out of school. I originally went to an air force recruiter, who said, "Nah, you're not what we're really looking for; we're not interested." I left discouraged, and a Marine Corps recruiter who happened to be right there said, "What's wrong?" I started talking to him and he set me right up.

When I was a young eighteen-year-old kid, I didn't have much maturity. I needed someone to kick me in the pants and tell me what to do. That's what helped me get to where I am today. Basic training at Parris Island was like a vacation. I wasn't getting incentive PT like everybody else, and I wasn't getting yelled at like a lot of the people, so I figured I was doing pretty decently. The toughest part was getting used to the regimented routine, getting up at the same time every morning. I wasn't fazed much by the yelling. I went into boot camp thinking, *The marines, those guys are tough and I don't know if I'm worth it. I don't know if I can make it, man. I don't see myself as that caliber.* But I was realizing my own potential, gaining that confidence. I've grown so much over the last thirteen years.

Starting with boot camp and continuing through my years in the Marine Corps, I learned a dedication to something that was greater than I am. Up until that point in my life, I'd probably been a pretty selfish kid. The marines gave me leadership skills, a sense of self-worth, and an understanding that there are things out there worth more than myself. The Marine Corps definitely gives you something to believe in.

Marine Corps training gives you the ability to recognize patterns in warfare based on things that you've experienced in the past. You understand immediately how to make decisions, consciously or sub-consciously. You do the training so you can build a team that has trust, confidence, and faith in one another; you form a cohesive unit. Together the unit develops a thought process that will allow it to con-front problems, solve them, adjust, and then make right decisions, even when you're up against the unpredictable.

My job as the leader was to bring out the best in my team. I did that by making them feel like human beings, by making them feel like they were worth something, and by having them take pride in themselves and in others. I let them know that I cared about them and valued their thoughts, beliefs, ideas, dreams, and wishes. I prefer to lead with my personality, not my rank or authority. Having ma-rines do things because they believe in themselves or in me and be-cause they have faith in their unit is so much purer than just telling them what to do.

On March 25, 2003, we were heading north and I looked ahead and saw something I didn't like. I turned to my driver and said, "Man, I'm nervous about that berm right there." No sooner had the words left my mouth than we were in the thick of an ambush. We were getting slammed by RPGs flying everywhere. Mortars started landing off to the left, and machine-gun and small-arms fire came in: the works. Iraqi soldiers were positioned behind a berm, a fifteen-foot wall of sand. Tanks and AAVs took direct RPG hits, and one of our Humvees was hit. Corpsman Michael Johnson was killed and Corpo-ral Quintero was seriously wounded in the abdomen. We were in the kill zone for what seemed like forever but was actually only minutes. The only way out was to drive straight at the enemy's machine gun and attack the emplacement. I wasn't looking for a medal; I just wanted to save my marines. I was just doing my job, the same thing every other marine would have done.

★

*Under ambush from a well-trained and deeply entrenched company of Iraqi Republican Guards armed with mortars, rocket-propelled grenades, and automatic weapons, Chontosh ordered his driver, Lance Corporal Armand McCormick, to head directly into the firestorm. With his machine gunner, Corporal Thomas Franklin, returning fire, they took out the enemy machine-gun nest. Chontosh saw a small groove or access alley in the trench line, and without thinking twice he ordered his driver into the enemy trench, where their Humvee careened and caromed off one wall of the ditch and then the other. The vehicle slammed into the side of the wall and stopped. Chontosh, Corporal Robert Kerman, and Armand McCormick jumped out of their Humvee. Thomas Franklin stayed on the machine gun for suppressive fire and Lance Corporal Ken Kolte got on the radio to alert the rest of the battalion that "friendlies were on attack in the trench." They were running, shooting, scattering, and killing the enemy as they worked down the trench line. Having used all the bullets from his M16A2 service rifle and 9mm pistol, Chontosh picked up a discarded enemy rifle and continued his attack using an AK-47. When its ammunition supply was depleted, he picked up another and did the same. Finally, McCormick handed "Tosh" an enemy shoulder-fired rocket-propelled grenade launcher, and after a short discussion about who should fire it, Chontosh fired away. It did not detonate. But it sent a red fireball through the two-hundred-yard trench and routed the enemy. Chontosh, McCormick, Kerman, Franklin, and Kolte had overrun a company of Iraqi soldiers, killing more than twenty and wounding several others. Five marines had single-handedly disrupted an elaborate Iraqi Republican Guard ambush. The firefight lasted fifteen minutes. Up

---

* At this point in the interview, Captain Chontosh said, "I don't want to tell war stories." He instead wanted to talk about his marines. The following account was compiled from various newspapers and official sources.

until that point, the war had gone on for five days and Chontosh's platoon hadn't faced any significant contact.

Kerman and McCormick saved my life. They had as much to do with winning the firefight as anything I did. I want to tell you where I came from and what I believe in. And I represent only myself but I feel thousands of marines feel the same way. I'm proud of my marines.

I see a lot of myself in Armand McCormick. He's special. I knew when he first checked into our unit he was motivated, aggressive, very personable, and physical. He's just an all-around good guy, too. I worked with Armand for about two or three years before this happened. He was a brand-new private who came into my platoon when I was the platoon commander. Here was this new guy checking in all by himself, so I made him my radio operator and our relationship just grew from there. We just had a tighter bond. He was someone I could always depend on. He was always looking out for me, always watching my backside when I was looking at something else. There were a lot of times I wouldn't even talk on the radio; he'd just talk as if he were me and he'd make decisions. He was gifted for a private. He drives like a maniac but that's a compliment.

Robbie Kerman was very young. He'd been with our battalion only a short time. He was fresh out of boot camp so his nickname was "Boots." Whether it was PT or something else, he was the little kid and he got picked on the most. But he never let it get him down. He lived the Marine Corps life. He didn't want to let his father down. His dad had also been in the Third Battalion, Fifth Marines a long time ago. Robbie tried as hard as he could in everything he did because he didn't want to disappoint anybody. He couldn't hit a thing with rockets. He was a terrible tow gunner. We made him a rifleman, and he was a damned good rifleman.

Thomas Franklin was in the vehicle that day and he's truly selfless. He doesn't care about himself whatsoever. He was actually on terminal leave in Miami, Florida, taking college classes when I called him up on the cell phone. I said, "Dude, I need you to get back here and go to war with us." He said, "All right, I'll see you in a couple of days." He got back in; we canceled his terminal leave. His wife wasn't too happy, but we needed him and he needed us. He's a big boy, 260 or 270 pounds. Muscular as can be. He definitely saved our lives that day.

Another marine in the vehicle with us was Ken Korte. He was the radio operator in the back of the vehicle. While we were attacking the enemy, Korte got out of the vehicle and walked around providing security and giving ammo to Franklin. That was when he found three enemy soldiers alive. They'd been hiding in a little cubbyhole. He could have killed them but he didn't. He took them prisoner. I couldn't figure out how we could have prisoners after all we'd been through. I thought everybody would be dead. It turned out that one of the prisoners was a brigadier general in the Iraqi Republican Army and he was responsible for the defense of the entire area. As soon as Intel started questioning him, he sang like a songbird. All of the information he gave us about insurgent strongholds and the whole nine yards probably saved hundreds of our guys. Korte took the moral high ground. It was the right thing to do and he did it under some pretty extraordinary circumstances.

I don't see my time in Iraq as a stream of continuous memories. More like snapshots. Some days I see the pictures and some days I don't. Some days I see different pictures that I haven't seen in a few days or haven't seen at all. Smiles on little girls' faces. Taking soccer balls to kids in the cities. A lot of good along with the horror of war. I just don't know if I've realized the full impact it'll have on me for the rest of my life.

I admire and love the people of Iraq. For the past thirty years they've had to endure the harshness of life under Saddam Hussein. During that time they had zero opportunities. They had so much taken away from them on a whim. They are good, wholesome, salt-of-the-earth people. There is so much going on over there that the general public doesn't see. The only way to experience it is to go over there and live it, feel it; then you'll understand it. There are great things in store for Iraq. I can't even imagine what will be going on in its future.

★

Captain Brian Chontosh remains on active duty with the U.S. Marines as an instructor in its junior officer corps. He received two Bronze Stars for actions in Fallujah in November 2004. He is a husband and father of two children.

MARINES ARE A DIFFERENT BREED

★

Justin Lehew, Platoon Sergeant, U.S. Marine Corps

Second Marine Regiment, Task Force Tarawa

Columbus Grove, Ohio

Navy Cross; Iraq; 23–24 March 2003

On March 23, 2003, a group of marines were riding through An Nasiriyah when they received a distress call and came upon the aftermath of the ambush in which Jessica Lynch was captured. After rescuing the wounded, they returned to the task of taking the southern bridge, when hundreds of insurgents swarmed their position. When the amtrac from another company was destroyed by enemy fire, Lehew sprinted seventy meters to save a wounded marine. With plenty of wounded but no weapons at the casualty collection point, Lehew helped the wounded, rallied the troops, withstood withering fire to collect weapons, and fought back until the rescue helicopter arrived.

My childhood was almost picture-perfect, like you see on *Leave It to Beaver* or *My Two Dads*. I had a great life. I was lucky enough to have both my mom and dad in the household until my dad passed away when I was thirteen. Then my mom raised me. My father had been in the military. He went into the army in 1941 and he was part of the Twenty-ninth Infantry that hit Omaha Beach on June 6, 1944.

Originally, I wanted to join the air force. After serving in the army, my dad joined the air force because he wanted to go to Japan. I grew up going to the different military bases and commissaries. When I signed up for the air force in Columbus, Ohio, I took the classifications test and passed and was sworn in. Then this major ran downstairs and pulled me off into a room and said, "I'm sorry, we can't offer you the job we just offered you because you're color-blind. We made a mistake." Instead of being qualified for about four hundred jobs in the air force, I was only qualified for two of them, and those weren't anything I wanted.

I was sitting around in Columbus with my head between my legs wondering what I was going to do with my future when this big burly gunnery sergeant came walking down the hall. "Sit up straight," he yelled at me. "Get your chin up. You look like somebody just kicked your dog in the ribs. What the hell's the matter with you? Get up on your feet when you talk to me." I explained to him what had happened and he said he was sorry things hadn't worked out for me in the air force. Then he said, "If you don't mind, I'll give you this recruiter's number and he'll pay you a visit at your house."

That was the best thing that could have happened to me. I was pretty disciplined up until then. My parents made me who I was, but the marines really instilled discipline. Basic training was on Parris Island, South Carolina, and I did fine. I wasn't like a top-notch recruit, and I wasn't at the bottom end. I was in the middle. My recruiter's advice was to keep my head down and blend in so I wouldn't take as much fire. I tried to do that but I slowly figured out that every recruit has his day. They made sure they got to every single one of us.

Your parents are responsible for you up to the age of eighteen and then you're pretty much sent out to make a life for yourself. Boot camp was the start of my own life. Now I'm responsible for my own actions. I have to answer to me alone. Right out of basic training, I was thinking of trying to do twenty years in the Marine Corps.

The final day before graduation the senior drill instructor handed out the jobs, and I was given "amtrac." I thought that meant I was going to work for Amtrak loading railroad cars. I went home to Ohio for ten days and I found out my training would take place at Camp Pendleton in southern California. I quickly found out what my future was going to be like. This was the fall of 1988.

My first tour of duty was in Iraq fighting in the Gulf War in 1991. We all knew that when that war was over it wasn't complete. Without taking Saddam Hussein out of power, we were eventually going to be in Iraq again. We also knew that the next time wasn't going to be like 1991 and that we weren't going to cross the border and have everyone just throw up their hands to surrender.

My guys were an awesome bunch of marines and they took their training seriously. We had around forty marines who could be trusted with the mission. I wouldn't micromanage. I would supervise and be there for whatever they needed and I trusted them to take the job and run with it. If they didn't have an answer, they knew I was there to get it for them.

I told my guys straight up, "This is what we've trained for. There's no better coach to take you to the big game than me." I never felt like

I had to tell somebody to do something because of my rank. I got out there with my men and they could see that I knew what I was doing and that I'd done it before.

I wasn't able to talk to my wife from early February until mid-April 2003, because every kid in that platoon got a phone call before the officers got one. We take care of our people first. When I made my call on March 17, my family wasn't at home. A friend of my wife's called her on March 23 and told her to turn on the TV because there were burning amtracs in Iraq and she thought they were ours. My wife sat there for two weeks not knowing whether I was alive or dead.

I can remember March 23 vividly. I had a twelve-vehicle platoon of forty marines heading to An Nasiriyah in southern Iraq. We left at three a.m. and our job was to secure two bridgeheads to open up a zone for the entire First Marine Division to come through the following morning. That was the game plan. About five or six in the morning we were on the outskirts rolling toward the city when we heard radio traffic coming from the city. Our tanks had come across a few burning army vehicles. Everybody thought that was really weird because we were the forwardmost unit of the entire spearhead and there wasn't supposed to be anyone in front of us. Captain Mike Brooks told my platoon commander to grab a couple of vehicles and take them up north to find out what was going on.

He gave us the grid where the lead tanks were and we stopped and asked them, "Hey, have you guys seen any army soldiers around here?" They looked at me like I was nuts.

We kept driving forward for about two and a half kilometers and we saw two tanks off to the side of the road engaging the enemy with their .50-caliber machine guns. I jumped off the side of my vehicle, ran to the unit commander, and said, "Sir, have you seen any army soldiers around here?" He said he thought he saw them back where the burning trucks were.

My first sergeant spotted some soldiers off in the field about two hundred meters away waving their hands in the air. We headed toward them and started taking small-arms fire. There was a group of six soldiers and two of them were wounded. One of them had four gunshot wounds and the other one was shot in the leg. This was the first time my corpsman had ever seen anything like this. The young man who had gunshot wounds was just smiling, like he was thinking, *Boy, am I glad to see you guys here.* The other kid was barely nicked and he was screaming like a stuck pig.

They were a maintenance company that had been ambushed, gotten scared, made a wrong turn and gotten lost. They weren't trained for any of this but they did what they could for an hour until we arrived. Half of their people, including Jessica Lynch, had been captured and taken hostage and the rest had fled into the field and put up the best defense they could. Corporal Miller defended that entire group by himself until help arrived. He was awarded the Silver Star.

The enemy started pushing across the field toward us as we were trying to medevac the wounded out of there. There was one good way to get rid of these guys, so I jumped up into the weapon station and started engaging all over the field with the .50-caliber machine gun. They turned around and hightailed it out of there. We medevaced eight soldiers back to the rolling aid station.

We got the call over the radio that the rest of our company was going to start stacking and move into the city. It was surreal because we were going into a major city of 220,000 with just the infantry, no air or artillery support. We didn't have satellite imagery or anything, just a road map. An Nasiriyah is as big as a major U.S. city. The streets are tight and the buildings are close together, which decreased our maneuverability. There was a lot of apprehension about firing artillery rounds into a huge city. I heard over the radio, "Forget the artillery, forget the air, we need to get infantry into the city now!"

The game was on. We passed tanks that were on fire and their ammunition was starting to cook off. We rolled to the top of the first bridge, which was a railroad bridge, and we didn't receive much fire at all. It was really quiet. We started to roll into the major portion of the city. When we got to the main bridge, it was still quiet. As soon as we got all the vehicles over the southern bridge to the northern side of the city, a hand grenade went off. It was like somebody started a track meet. All at once it seemed like Armageddon opened up from all angles of the street.

We started seeing masses of people in the alleyways coming at us. We saw people jump on the balconies with AK-47s. RPGs were flying through the air. We couldn't adjust our fire to engage any specific enemy because they were everywhere. We spilled the infantry out the back of the vehicles and our guys took cover and tried to figure out where the fire was coming from. The main thing we needed to do was hold the bridge. We were ten thousand miles from home in the middle of nowhere and we had to support ourselves and hold the bridge until the next unit came up to relieve us. It was 140 degrees, we were wearing our chemical suits, and we were starting to run low on water. After two hours into the battle it seemed like ten minutes. We got calls from the amtracers that they were running low on ammunition and fuel. Two units were trying to push through to reach our position. They had a straight push up what we called Ambush Alley. There were buildings up on both sides of the road and it was a straight shot of a kilometer and a half. The enemy was running across the street in between vehicles. The enemy numbered in the hundreds.

About the two-hour mark, the tanks rolled in. I can still remember hearing the marines, like something out of a movie, putting out the loudest cheer because they knew that nobody was going to mess with those tanks. We also knew that tanks are the biggest things to shoot at, they're a prime target, because if the enemy can take out one of them, they feel like they're starting to win.

I jumped up on the turret of the tank and peeled off the marine's earpiece and told him that we were taking a lot of fire from this building across the street that had red windows. I jumped off the turret, and the instant my feet hit the ground he leveled that building. The enemy got the picture that there were bigger things to mess with here.

I was looking down the alleyway and one of the lance corporals ran up and said, "Gunny, there's a lady out here that comes out of the building with a baby, and every time she goes back into the building, an RPG comes out. Their aim keeps getting closer and closer." Sure enough, she walked out with a baby in her hands, walked back into the building, and an RPG came back out. We had a sniper, and the next time she came out we got her. The marines ran down and picked up her baby. We never received another RPG round from that place.

We were running low on supplies. Captain Brooks was running all over the place with the radio, trying to get some air support in there. Miraculously, up until this point, we didn't have any casualties.

Sergeant Collins yelled out over the radio that there was an ambulance driving on the road straight toward us. He said he fired a warning shot but the ambulance wouldn't stop. I figured it was a vehicle with an IED. He and I fired into the cab with the .50-cal machine gun. It went off to the side of the road and I'll be damned if as soon as it got off the road there weren't six guys clad in black with AK-47s. They were attacking us with ambulances and that's hard to train for. There were other insurgents in black jumping out of cars and heading toward a weapons cache under the bridge.

As soon as that happened, I turned to my driver, a good ol' boy from Georgia, and he was laughing at one of our amtracs that was going the wrong way with its ramp open, dragging on the ground, shooting up sparks. I can remember thinking, *Please don't let that be one of mine.* Everything was in slow motion. I saw a rocket trail come straight down the street behind it and I saw another one come off the rooftop into the top of the amtrac. I saw a marine fall out the back. The vehicle came to a rolling stop in the middle of the intersection.

It was an instantaneous decision. It wasn't anything I planned. I told the chief mechanic to get in the turret. I didn't know whether he'd ever fired that weapon or not but I assumed he had. I grabbed my corpsman, got on the street, and started running the seventy meters toward the vehicle. There was just a horrendous amount of fire going through the intersection. We heard this big *thump* and looked down, and a piece of pavement was missing. It was a dud RPG. When we got to the vehicle, the young doc from Puerto Rico was with me and he said, "I'm here as long as you are, Gunny."

We came to the vehicle and the first thing I saw lying on the back of the vehicle was the leg of a marine. Everything was hazy. There was black smoke billowing out from the inside. Doc and I went inside the smoking vehicle and it looked to me like everyone was just dead. Everything was a twisted mangled mess and we started sifting through it all, triaging any marine we could, grabbing wrists and trying to feel for a pulse. All of the grenades and ammo were stacked up all over the place; it was a time bomb. I said, "Hey, I think everybody is done in here." I was going to see if their weapons still functioned, pull them out, grab the radios, and get out of there. We were going to have to blow this vehicle up. As I was sweeping through the center of the vehicle, I heard somebody gasp for air. I yelled up, "I think we've got a live one."

We dug through the pile of bodies. The live marine was under another dead marine and his body was in an L shape. I felt for a pulse and he had a faint one. His head was split open from the base of his neck all the way up to the top of his head. I mean, you could see into his head. I told the doc to grab him. We started yanking him out of there. This guy was a big boy. It took five of us to pull him out and run him over to where my vehicle was. Doc started to treat him.

I heard the company XO had set up a house to receive the wounded and I ran over there. There were two other wounded marines inside the house. We gathered up all the weapons we had. This one kid hobbled up to me and he was gray from head to toe. Half the back of his ankle and foot was shot out and I can distinctly remember him saying, "I can still fight, Gunny. I want to stay here." I had a rifle in my hand and I racked a round and I put him on the door. I said, "I'm going to get some help and grab some more weapons. If anybody comes from this direction, don't shoot them. If anybody comes from that direction, shoot 'em."

We could hear the enemy talking from the other side of the wall in the back of the house. There were two wounded marines in the corner of the house completely shell-shocked and bleeding from the ears. I ran out into the street and gathered up a couple of weapons and a few more marines and stuck them in the house. The intense fire never let up. When I got back the doc told me, "Gunny, we've got to get the hell out of here. This kid is gonna die if we don't go now."

The battalion XO told me he had air support coming in and asked if we had any pyrotechnic rockets to mark a landing zone for an evacuation helicopter. Unfortunately, the helicopter landed smack in the middle of the intersection, and that was the hottest zone in the battlefield. There were power poles and power lines all around. That pilot needs to get a Distinguished Flying Cross. We ran the casualties a couple of football fields to the helicopter. This kid must have weighed three hundred pounds with all his gear on, and we dropped him on the floor. We were all exhausted and knew the helicopter would make a very inviting target, so we had to get out of there fast. The helicopter pilot didn't understand the gravity of the situation and they told me to put this guy on the top rack. I just looked up at him and said, "Do you know what an RPG is?" He said, "Are they shooting them?" I yelled that I didn't think they had any left, they had shot so many of them. I made my point and the helicopter took off. The minute we lifted off, the enemy started shooting everything they had at us. I don't know how they didn't hit us.

I told my boys to cherish every day and not to waste any of their time. I said that there are so many good things that they can learn from their time in the military and this action, so many different friends, so many different networks that they have out there. I try to impress upon them an understanding that you have to take a personal interest in others. Just because something isn't important to you, you're not the only one living on this earth and that means whatever is really important to another person deserves your time and interest.

I always told my boys that no matter where they go in life, they'll always be my boys. So if something happens twenty years from now and you're down on your luck, I'd better be getting a phone call letting me know what's going on with you.

The boys used to make fun of me when we were in training evaluations and the amtracs were acting up. Before we would get going, I would go down and rub every one of our vehicles on the side and give them a pat on the back of the rear ramp. It was like a little send-off. Whenever any of them were having maintenance problems I would be in there with a wrench, talking to the vehicles, yelling, "Why are you doing this to me, honey?" I grew up around farm machinery, and you take care of your equipment and you take pride in owning it. If you treat them right, they're going to treat you right. I taught that to all the guys.

Having the Navy Cross is a big responsibility. There's a prestige that comes with the Navy Cross. It represents what the military is and what a lot of people did who came before me and wore the medal. Most of them are in graves. I don't think of myself as a hero. I'm just a marine. When I hear the word "hero," I think of a little girl who is fighting cancer. My mom is a hero. When she was diagnosed with cancer, she said she didn't want any more chemotherapy because it was too painful, too much of a burden on her family. I think the word "hero" gets tossed around too loosely. My wife is in the U.S. Navy and she looks at me and says, "I could be married to you for a hundred years and I will still never know what makes you tick." Marines are just a different mind-set. We're a different breed. We are fighting with men we totally respect and we call them our brothers.

★

First Sergeant Justin Lehew is currently serving with the U.S. Marine Corps' First Reconnaissance Battalion at Twentynine Palms, California. Having received the Navy Cross and the Bronze Star for valor, Lehew remains one of the most highly decorated marines in the global war on terrorism.

SHOCK MEDICINE

★

Luis Fonseca Jr., Hospitalman Third Class, U.S. Navy

Second Marine Expeditionary Brigade

Fayetteville, North Carolina

NAVY CROSS; AN NASIRIYAH, IRAQ; 23 MARCH 2003

Luis Fonseca Jr. is the first navy corpsman to receive the Navy Cross in thirty-two years. He was assigned to Marine Company A, First Platoon. Their mission was to capture and hold the northernmost bridge in An Nasiriyah. The marines started taking RPG fire, mortar rounds, and machine-gun and small-arms fire. A direct mortar hit disabled one vehicle and left five marines wounded. Fonseca evacuated them from their burning vehicle, applied tourniquets, administered morphine, and loaded them onto his amtrac. When it in turn was hit, he evacuated his patients again. One seriously wounded marine he carried across open ground under intense enemy fire.

U.S. NAVY

When I was in high school, I was into a little bit of everything. I played soccer from the ninth grade to my senior year. I was in band. I was part of a Hispanic Club that put on shows in traditional Latin-style dances. I think I always had a girlfriend.

But I was just kind of stuck. I was eighteen years old and I felt I needed a change in my life. I didn't want to be at my ten-year high school class reunion and have my friends ask me what I was doing and have to answer, "I'm not really doing anything." I wanted to do something with my life. I wanted to feel some sense of accomplishment.

I've always been intrigued with medicine. I have always liked helping people, even as a little kid. In fact, I was CPR- and first-aid-certified at the age of thirteen. When I went to talk with the Marine Corps, I found out that they didn't have a medical section. They use the navy's. I didn't want to join the army because my dad had already done it, and I wanted to create my own path.

When I decided to join the navy, I thought to myself, *What is the hardest thing someone can do in life that everyone always talks about?* Of course I thought of the medical services. Since I had dropped out of high school, I wanted to prove to people I could still do what I really wanted to do in life. Just like any enlisted guy, I went to basic training. Then I went into what's called the Navy A School, where I learned my primary job. I am a general-duty corpsman, so I learned the basics of what a corpsman does every day: dealing with medical records, dealing with drugs, everything from Tylenol to morphine. I learned the basics of IV punctures, how to start an IV line, draw blood, and give immunizations.

After that training, I got what's called a "dream sheet," where I listed my top three priorities that I wanted to do. I always knew I wanted to be a field medical corpsman. I always knew I wanted to be with a Marine Corps unit. I wanted to do trauma medicine and shock medicine.

I had been trained well, but the question remained: How well can you train to go to war and prepare to die? It's just something you have to accept. I tell junior corpsmen when they're getting ready to go over to Iraq or Afghanistan for the first time, "You know, you could die in your sleep tonight or you could die a hundred years from now. You don't know. Because you know that you might die doesn't mean you should stop living life."

Everything you do in combat has to be second nature. You do not have time to stop and think about what's next in the process. You can't pull out a book and look up the answer or ask a buddy what to do next. The one second that you stop to think about what's going on could cost someone their life. In the heat of battle, that one split-second decision could cost a life or save a life.

By March 23, 2003, in An Nasiriyah, I'd been in Iraq for just two or three days. It started off pretty much like any day. We woke up in the morning, cleaned ourselves up a bit, and prepared to push forward. We knew what our mission was and we knew that we would be securing a bridge later on that day. It was the Saddam Canal Bridge over the Euphrates River near An Nasiriyah, about two hundred miles southeast of Baghdad. I don't think anyone in their wildest dreams really thought it was going to get as bad as it did.

We pulled up and stopped on the southern part of the town. I remember seeing all these Iraqi tanks on fire, so we knew that our air support had been there and pretty much demolished all of their mobilized units. We stopped and crept forward a little bit. That was the same time and place where Jessica Lynch and her convoy got ambushed, so one of our tanks and one of our amtracs got diverted to go help them.

Word came over the radio that we were still supposed to push forward to help secure the northern bridge. A lot of question marks went up in the air. We didn't have tanks. We didn't all have armor plating. My platoon sergeant got on the horn to verify the command. He verified that we were still supposed to push forward. He gave the order.

When we got to the southern bridge, all the locals were smiling and waving at us, saying "Hi" and giving us the thumbs-up. Real friendly. All of a sudden, it was like you see in the movies, where you have daylight and then it turns black. We crossed a point where everything was gloomy. No one was on the streets anymore.

Our convoy was twelve vehicles deep and we were number twelve. Our lead vehicle was taking small-arms fire. I was standing lookout and my platoon sergeant said, "Hey, Doc, get back in the vehicle." As soon as I sat down, I heard the first small-arms rounds ding off our amtrac. Then we heard, "Rocket in the center lane." Seconds later our vehicle diverted to the right and then came back up to the left. We were moving out of the path of the RPG that an insurgent had shot down the road toward us.

I wondered what our enemy could have been thinking. They weren't going to do anything to us with this small-arms fire. I knew we were going over to secure this bridge in five or ten minutes and nothing could stop us. Then the rest of the First Marine Division could push forward to Baghdad. Unfortunately it didn't play out like that.

As soon as the first RPG hit, we heard mortar rounds coming in at us and heavy machine guns. Artillery was striking down on us. We were getting hit from the left, the right, from behind, from the front and from above. About five minutes after the fight started, my platoon sergeant called over the intercom system: One of our 'tracs got hit, number 211, the one right in front of me. There were hurt marines and instinctively I knew it was my job to go out there and help them. In the three years before this moment, I had never done what I considered to be my real job. This was my time to show my guys that I knew what I was doing.

My platoon sergeant told me he was going to open up the back hatch for just a second. I thought about my family and something along the lines of *Lord, help me.* In the time it takes you to turn a doorknob and step out of your house, that's how long I thought about all that. Then my mind went blank and all I thought about was that I had to get to my guys.

I ran about thirty-five to forty meters north toward the amtrac. When I got there, I saw that it was engulfed in flames. There were five wounded and I helped get them out of the amtrac. Two of them had partial lower limb amputations; three had shrapnel or flash burns. One guy had a broken leg. Once we got them out, we set them on the deck and I did the basic first aid, stopped the bleeding, and put splints on. We had to move the men, though, because their amtrac was on fire and it was going to blow up due to a secondary explosion, from their own ammunition going off inside.

Right before we moved them, I heard a crackling from above. I looked up and saw scatter bombs. Once the scatter bombs went off, I gave the order to move the five casualties into my amtrac. When we got there, I reassessed and redressed the wounds. I flushed out people's eyes who had flash burns. I decided to give them sedation, and the two that had partial lower leg amputations, I went ahead and gave them morphine for the pain. Using a black permanent marker, I put a big "M" for morphine on their foreheads along with "12:31" for the time I administered it. This way everybody down the line knows what is going on with this patient.

These were definitely life-threatening wounds. With amputations, especially ones that happen so quickly and aggressively, all the veins and arteries retract into the muscle. The muscles contract to stop the bleeding. That's the perfect time to apply the tourniquet. But if you don't, the muscles will naturally begin to relax and the veins and arteries open up and all the blood rushes out just like water from a hose. That will send your body into shock.

I had been taking care of these patients for about ten or fifteen minutes when they called me over the intercom and said that number 206 had been hit. I ran north about two hundred to two hundred and fifty yards with my medical bag. I couldn't find number 206, but I stopped and helped out some other grunt corpsmen who were attached to the infantry unit. We set up a collection point to help them medevac their casualties.

I kept running another two hundred yards, trying to find 206, but I still couldn't find it. I ran into the commanding officer for Charlie Company and I said, "Hey, sir, I got word that 206 had been hit but I can't find it. Do you have any word on that?" He told me, "Doc, I believe that is a message in error so go back to your amtrac. You're doing a great job and keep up the good work." "Roger that, sir," I said and went back to my amtrac.

I stood outside of my amtrac, taking a pee. The crazy thing a person does. I don't want to say I was shell-shocked but I didn't really grasp the enormity of what was going on. I heard everyone shouting, "Doc, get back inside," and I said, "Hold on, I've got to finish peeing." As soon as I got back inside and closed the hatch, a mortar round landed on our amtrac. We took two more hits: another one on the right side and one on the top. Then an RPG struck the front, blowing out our transmission and disabling our vehicle.

At the time, I decided to take the casualties out of my now-disabled vehicle and get them somewhere safer. We opened up the hatch and moved four patients to another amtrac. The fifth marine

I personally fireman-carried over open ground under intense machine-gun and rocket fire. I made it to a ditch, and he and I hung out there for a while.

This was the sixth hour of the firefight. We were in the ditch for about ten minutes. Sometimes it feels like we were there two hours. The badly wounded marine was one of the guys who had a lower leg amputation. I kept monitoring him and he was doing well. I kept talking to him, keeping him alert and awake. Then we saw an amtrac come by. I flagged him down, ran up the road, and told him to follow me. I ran back to the ditch and we loaded up our casualty. We went south through the city, offloaded our casualties to the Second Battalion, Eighth Marines, cleaned up our amtrac, and proceeded back north to regroup with our platoon, which was engaged in the fight. We took fire on the way. By the time we got there, things had calmed down. There were little sporadic firefights here and there. Air support was coming in. The tanks finally caught back up with us.

We lost eighteen marines that day. Fifteen others were wounded and had to leave the battlefield. Ten others were wounded slightly and didn't have to leave the battlefield. That had to have been one of the worst days of the war.

The one thing that surprised me, and it surprises just about everyone, was that I weighed 150 pounds at the time. I'm five feet five and I carried a two-hundred-pound marine on my back, plus all of my equipment and my medical gear. I was also surprised by how much knowledge and training I retained. I was able to make split-second decisions.

Honestly, I thought I was going to die. I knew there was a bullet with my name on it. I thought, *I'm going to do my job until I get hit.* I needed to save my boys. I needed to take them back home. I was running up and down looking for number 206 for an hour or an hour and a half, just coming up on wounded and, unfortunately, deceased marines. I didn't think I was going to make it out of this alive. But it wasn't an overwhelming feeling. I would honestly say it was more of a calming feeling, like *I can't believe this is where I'm going to die.* But then I'd hear marines crying in pain and think, *I may die but these guys need me right now.* I was doing my job, which is not to think about my safety but to think about the safety of my marines. I wish I could have done more.

Because I was in the navy and was assigned to a marine unit, I felt like an outsider at first. They had earned the title United States Marine and I hadn't. I had to prove myself, that I could hang with them, do PT with them, hump with them. One of the greatest honors, believe it or not, is hearing my marines tell me, "Doc, regardless of what branch of the service you're in, you are a marine in our eyes." Marines are some of the best people I've ever met. Guys trust me now.

★

Luis Fonseca still serves in the navy. He is preparing to go to navy deep-sea dive school and is training as a medical technician.

TRUE TO HIS MISSION

★

Paul Smith, Sergeant First Class, U.S. Army

Second Platoon, Bravo Company, Eleventh Engineer

Battalion, Third Infantry

Tampa, Florida

POSTHUMOUSLY AWARDED THE MEDAL OF HONOR FOR ACTION NEAR

IRAQ INTERNATIONAL AIRPORT; 3 APRIL 2003

Charged with transforming an airport courtyard into a holding area for Iraqi prisoners, SFC Paul Smith assessed the best location to be behind the masonry wall along the highway. Two guard towers along the wall were ideally situated to provide overwatch to the holding area. An M9 Armored Combat Earthmover (ACE) knocked a hole in the wall to create an opening to a large courtyard with a

U.S. ARMY

louvered metal gate on the north side. With the help of a squad leader and team leader, SFC Smith checked the far side of the courtyard for enemy, found none, and posted two guards. From the guard post at the gate, small groupings of buildings were one hundred to two hundred meters to the northeast. To the northwest, a large white building with a white dome was visible. The location seemed perfect, as the courtyard was along the northern flank of the blocking position and enemy actions to this point were mostly from the east.

While an engineer squad began to clear debris in the courtyard, one of the guards saw ten to fifteen enemy soldiers with small arms, 60mm mortars, and rocket-propelled grenades. These were the lead elements of an organized company-sized force making a deliberate attack on the flank of Task Force 2-7. SFC Smith came to the position and identified twenty-five to fifty more soldiers moving into prepared fighting positions. Smith instructed a squad leader to get a nearby Bradley Fighting Vehicle for support. While waiting for the Bradley, SFC Smith had members of Second Platoon retrieve AT-4 antitank weapons and form a skirmish line outside the gate. By this time, the number of enemy identified rose to hundred soldiers, now a confirmed company-sized attack. Three of B Company's M113A3 Armored Personnel Carriers (APC) oriented .50-cal machine guns toward the opening in the wall and the surrounding guard towers, which were now occupied by enemy soldiers.

SFC Smith's actions to organize a defense against the deliberate attack were not only effective but inspired the B Company, Eleventh Engineer Battalion soldiers. He then began to lead by example. As the Bradley arrived on-site and moved through the hole in the wall toward the gate, SFC Smith ran to the gate wall and threw a fragmentation grenade at the enemy. He then took two soldiers forward to join the guards and directed their engagement of the enemy with small arms. The enemy continued to fire rifles, RPGs, and 60mm mortars at the soldiers on the street and within the courtyard. Enemy soldiers began moving along the buildings on the north side of the clearing to get into position to climb into the towers. SFC Smith called for an APC to move forward to provide additional fire support. SFC Smith then fired an AT-4 at the enemy while directing his fire team assembled near the front line of the engagement area.

Running low on ammunition and having taken RPG hits, the Bradley withdrew to reload. The lead APC in the area received a direct hit from a mortar, wounding the three occupants. The enemy attack was at its strongest point and every action counted. Not only were the wounded soldiers threatened, but also more than one hundred soldiers from B Company, the Task Force Aid Station, and the mortar platoon were at risk.

SFC Smith ordered one of his soldiers to back the damaged APC into the courtyard after the wounded men had been evacuated. Knowing the APC's .50-cal machine gun was the largest weapon between the enemy and the friendly position, SFC Smith immediately assumed the track commander's position behind the weapon and told a soldier who accompanied him to "feed me ammunition whenever you hear the gun get quiet." SFC Smith fired on the advancing enemy from the unprotected position atop the APC and expended at least three boxes of ammunition before being mortally wounded by enemy fire. The enemy attack was defeated. SFC Smith's actions saved the lives of at least one hundred soldiers, caused the failure of a deliberate enemy attack hours after First Brigade seized the Baghdad airport, and resulted in an estimated twenty to fifty enemy soldiers killed. His actions inspired his platoon, his company, the Eleventh Engineer Battalion, and Task Force 2-7 Infantry.

Father of Paul Smith, Bill Smith:

Five of my six brothers served in the military. Myself, I'm a twenty-year man. The longest we ever remained in the United States at one time was eighteen months. Paul, he was pretty much bouncing around the world: Germany, Korea, Greece. I've got a videotape of Paul and his sister in the backyard in a three-foot hole in the ground. If you look closely, there's a military canteen sitting to the side of the hole. That was their foxhole. Paul's about six at the time and his sister was four. Paul and his friend Roger were always scrounging for wood and using big cardboard boxes to make forts in the backyard. That's just something they did.

More than our other children, Paul was sort of like a chameleon. Some people described him as shy but I think he was reserved and thoughtful. He was a tall, skinny kid and he always fit in. He was a pack rat, collecting seashells, rocks, and bottle caps. He went his own way. He was exposed to a larger world. He could tell you what was going on in other countries.

Probably one of the contributions I'm proudest of was protecting the president of the United States. I was with the missile site that gave coverage over the top of President Nixon's summer home. We would be "locked down" or restricted for weeks at a time. The other kids would say to Paul, "Where's your dad?" or "What's your dad doing?" Paul would say, "Well, he's protecting the president." The other kids would laugh and say, "Yeah, right," but Paul would just let it go because he knew their backgrounds were different and they just didn't understand.

When Paul was growing up, he liked to fish and hunt, take things apart, fix cars, do carpentry. Off the Florida coast, we'd fish from shore because we didn't have the financial resources to take out a big commercial boat or anything fancy. We'd catch a few fish and fry them up in a pan. Or we'd tie a chicken neck on a string and throw it on and retrieve it slowly and get some crabs. We'd boil them in a pot and watch a movie at night. Paul would see lots of things: poisonous snakes, manatees. Once we saw a black panther.

When he was seventeen, he spent the summer with me at Fort Bragg and we'd have PT formation every morning at 6:00. This was the Eighteenth Airborne and they are a little tougher than the regular army. The standards are tighter. We'd run as a battalion, five hundred or so men altogether, sweating and yelling in the dark. That's not the obvious place you'd expect a seventeen-year-old kid, but Paul wanted to be there. He'd get up with me, go to PT. He stayed with me on those runs. By golly, he'd finish those runs. He'd give it his all. Just a wonderful boy. And the men just loved him. At the time, none of us would have chosen to be there, but what a way to start your day!

As far as his decision to be a soldier, he made that decision himself. We had many a conversation because I was concerned and I didn't want him to become a soldier just because I was one. I urged him to become a carpenter. Although there's a very good side to the military, it takes a toll and sometimes soldiers don't realize it at the time. Soldiers are paying a price of separation and loneliness. I wanted him to have a realistic picture of what he was getting into, and then he made his own decision. His eyes were wide open. He matured to the point of deciding to make it a career.

In the First Gulf War, he lost an acquaintance of his. The man was guarding a bank. One shot, one soldier dead. That hardened Paul a lot, plus learning firsthand what went on in Kosovo and Albania. Just seeing other people oppressed. Not having the freedom to make their own decisions. His men described Paul as a "hard guy" or a "hard-ass." When that is said about a career noncommissioned officer, it's a compliment. It means he's a by-the-book, hard-core leader of men. That's what Paul became.

He was a stickler to the point where he'd have his men do things over and over until they got it right. Before the battle even started, Paul knew that his unit would be right up front, the tip of the spear. That's why he trained his men as hard as he did. He loved those boys. He wrote that it was a privilege to be leading these men. They were all good men, one and all.

Captain Mike Bliss:

PAUL WAS THE ULTIMATE SOLDIER. He was an extremely right-or-wrong, black-or-white guy, no shades of gray. No situational ethics. He was true to his mission, true to his soldiers. He was all business. With Paul as your platoon sergeant, you were put to a higher standard than the rest of the company. If they understood that standard and what was expected of them, they enjoyed it and excelled because it was consistent. Whenever he held his platoon back or stayed late, he'd be there with them. If they were doing a run, he'd be out front pushing them. His philosophy was "If my men are here, then I'm here." Because of that, I think they were better prepared for what happened that day.

We had pushed through the Karbala Gap by the afternoon of April 2. The rest of the brigade seized the bridge crossing the Euphrates River and the 2-7 was sent a little south to attack a part of the Medina Brigade. Our tanks got stuck in the mud and we had limited sleep. That evening, we crossed the Euphrates and headed to the Baghdad International Airport. As the sun started to go down, we got sidetracked on these raised roads in the farmland, between the bridgehead and the airport. The farmland had been saturated so we couldn't really go off into the fields. We spent the better part of six hours just trying to get the whole task force turned around on a single raised dike. It was a real mess. It was pitch-black. The moon was off-cycle so there was no illumination. I saw Paul's Humvee and I looked in the passenger side and there was someone asleep there. I went to investigate and lo and behold, Paul was in the driver's seat. He let his driver get some sleep, and Paul was up on the dike guiding amtracs around and guiding the platoon right to the airport. That's how I know Paul didn't get any sleep that night. As daylight broke, we ended up at the intersection to the east side of the airport. It was pretty quiet.

All the palaces were around the airport and there were eight-foot masonry walls lining the roads with guard towers to protect the palaces. The sun came up and that's when the Iraqi Republican Guard realized, "Oh, no, the Americans are here." All of a sudden, we started hearing resistance and gunfire and gradually we heard it closer and closer, sporadic fire from every direction. It must have been about 0800 or 0900. We got a call to construct a holding area for prisoners. Paul immediately came back and said he had the perfect spot. "Let me do it, sir." When he said that, I knew I wouldn't have to worry about it again. That was the last thought I had to put into it. I knew he had the mission.

Casualty reports started coming across the net. I couldn't see into the courtyard but I could hear the fighting. We'd taken mortar rounds that had injured three of the soldiers. We needed to evacuate them. At that point, I had no way of knowing that things in the holding area had escalated to an all-out fight. As far as what Paul did, it's kind of incredible to hear. He came up and told someone to go get a Bradley to help fight. He threw a grenade. He fired an AT-4. He fired the .50-cal. Reloaded it. His proficiency in weapons alone to do all that, without even thinking about it, is amazing. While he did all that, he was ordering his platoon evacuation and coordinating fire from the Bradley. If you think about it, it's unbelievable. But knowing Paul, it's believable.

He took the fight to the enemy at the farthest point and he really squashed the attack there. It could have been a lot worse; let me put it that way. They could have mounted long-range fire into the first-aid station. They could have created more chaos and done more damage than they did. These were trained soldiers we were fighting, Saddam's elite unit. I would argue that Paul repelled the enemy and he certainly saved us a lot more casualties, including me. While I don't dwell on it, it certainly comes back to me. I think about Paul's sacrifice and I'm grateful that I'm here and that he did what he did. I don't steer away from talking about him. I think it's an important story. His soldiers would tell me pieces of what he did that day and I was able to put it all together. They just laid out the facts. They didn't need to exaggerate it. He really had performed an incredible act of valor.

Bill Smith:

I TALK WITH SERGEANT TIMOTHY CAMPBELL quite a bit and he told me that when they removed Paul from the Armored Personnel Carrier, he had thirteen holes in his armor vest where the rounds had hit him. He was aware that he was being hit but he chose to stay on that gun. He could have dropped inside the APC and been protected.

Sergeant Campbell is the soldier that led Paul's men to the tower and finally took it out. That's basically where the battle ended. I believe Tim Campbell is the man that killed the soldier that killed my son. I communicate with him regularly and he's a darned good man.

I have a $200 deer rifle, nothing fancy. That's the gun that Paul liked to shoot. I think Paul would have wanted it to be in the hands of Sergeant Campbell, so that's where that gun is going to end up. Some fine day I'm going to visit him and I'm going to put that gun in his hand. I think Paul would like that.

I had a pastor tell me something that really comforted me. He told me, "I believe that Paul lived his life as he chose and he died as he chose. A lot of people don't have that option." I believe that accurately describes Paul. I think he did live his life as he chose and I think he died as he chose.

I wrote a little something, perhaps I could read it:

Paul Ray Smith was a 100 percent red, white, and blue American soldier, doing from the bottom of his heart what he believed in, not a naïve young man that was overwhelmed by the events around him. His men, whom he called "my boys," described him as a hard-ass NCO. He loved those men, and as their leader would do nothing less than what he did. His actions, the day of his death, would surprise no one that knew him. When his all-volunteer force of men was attacked by an outnumbering force, Paul had seen his men bleeding, in pain, wounded, hurting, and suffering and he just could not let this stand. These were his men and he owned them body and soul. He would do nothing less than give his all. I knew he felt he did what he had to do that day. Paul was personally reserved, quiet, thoughtful, kind, and gentle. He would have preferred to live in a world of peace, love, security, and happiness. But that is not the world he was exposed to. The son of a German farm boy from Swanville, Minnesota, with a mother from El Paso, Texas, who was the daughter of a Lebanese fruit peddler, is awarded the Medal of Honor by the United States of America. Only in America could this happen.

Paul was a hero because of the way he lived his entire life, not just those thirty minutes of heavy fighting on a machine gun. And then I ask the question, Was it worth it? The answer will not be written by Paul or by Americans. That answer will be written by 27 million Iraqis, who for the first time can experience the freedom of democracy. Our country made many mistakes as it grew and I expect the free people of the Middle East will also. They will probably express their freedom in a way very different from the Western world, and that is okay. I ask them not to forget my son. He felt freedom was worth dying for. I ask them to live in peace and tolerance. We all share the same world and it can be made a better place for the next generation. And then I ask the question, What greater reward is there to pass on to one, once we are gone?

★

Paul Smith leaves behind a wife, Birgit, a daughter, Jessica, and a son, David. At a White House ceremony, David accepted the Medal of Honor from President George W. Bush for his father's valor on the two-year anniversary of Paul Smith's death.

TAKING CARE

★

Dennis Caylor, First Sergeant, U.S. Army

Eighty-second Airborne

Tonawanda, New York

SILVER STAR; AS SAMAWAH, IRAQ; 30 MARCH 2003

Soft-spoken and self-effacing, Dennis Caylor has spent his adult life in the U.S. Army. Fluent in Arabic and a father of a young son, Caylor brought a professional's precision and a deep sense of humanity to his service. He earned the Silver Star for his actions in As Samawah.

DENNIS CAYLOR

My father was originally from Pennsylvania and his family farmed and mined coal. He transplanted to New York. I was born and raised near Buffalo, and went to school in Tonawanda. My parents had six kids and I've got a twin brother. When my twin brother and I were five, our parents began taking in foster children who were blind or mentally retarded. My mother was definitely a saint. All thirteen of us used to go camping. At home, you could see a long line of bicycles along the driveway. It was quite a sight.

I had an older brother who was in the army, got out, and then went into the Marine Corps. My twin brother, a buddy of ours, and I all joined the army together. To this day, I don't know what spurred us to do it.

We went through jump school at Fort Benning, Georgia. The second time I was ever in a plane, I was jumping out of it. Once you start jumping out of planes, you either like it or you don't. I liked it. I earned those parachute wings. Fort Bragg, North Carolina, is the major base, and I stayed there from 1984 until 1994. Then I became a range instructor in the mountains of Dahlonega, Georgia. That was a beautiful assignment for two and a half years. Then I got called to be a training supervisor to the Joint Chiefs of Staff at the Pentagon. It was an eye-opener. Big-picture stuff. I did three years there and that's where I met my wife. We married in 1999 and we've got a three-year-old now. He was six weeks old when I went to Iraq.

After I got back from Iraq, I went to the Sergeants Major Academy. Now I'm on this assignment, which is essentially running a small basic-training mobilization station for National Guard Reserves. The majority of our instructors have been to Iraq or Afghanistan, so we've got some lessons we can impart. We run them through basic first aid, marksmanship, convoy operations, and the whole gamut. It's a four-to-six-month process before they go overseas. They will listen to you a little bit more than someone who hasn't experienced combat firsthand. I've been on this assignment for a year and a half and I've only been home for about three months. In the unit that we're training now there are brothers in the same unit, sometimes fathers and sons together.

There's a structure in the military, a battle rhythm, if you will, a way we do business that brings together that family feeling. If you talk to any soldier, they don't want war. No one wants to do harm to anybody. It's like the analogy of the sheep, the wolf and the sheepdog. The bad guy is the wolf and soldiers are the ones who have to protect the innocents, the sheep. It's a good thing to provide freedom to another country.

At our training, we try to instill in our soldiers the importance of learning the language and the customs. We tell them that they represent what America and Western culture is all about. We're all the same, whether a person lives in South America, Europe, or the Middle East. Everybody loves their family. Everybody loves their kids. Humans are humans. Our cultures may differ a bit but we're all the same.

We spend a lot of time focusing on the ability to employ the weapons systems or to use the vehicle so that it's second nature, almost a muscle reflex. We're looking for a calm, cool, collected fighting force. We also want them to understand that as soldiers they are the diplomats for the United States. Our unit, the 325th, was proud of the way we trained. We knew our equipment, hands down. When we were attached to another unit, we knew they were getting the best of the best. We were ethical and valued leaders. We understood humanity and the diplomacy that was going on. We were bighearted Americans; that was who we were. My soldiers would give you the shirts off their backs and then turn around and protect those people who were in need with a vengeance that you wouldn't want to be on the other end of.

The people in Iraq would invite us into their homes, and in turn we had to show respect for them and understand their culture. We were there to provide them with whatever they needed to get back on their feet. We needed them to know that we were not invaders, that we were there to help them have a voice and have a choice in whatever they wanted to happen.

We were in As Samawah, south of Baghdad. It was a predominantly Shiite town and the first battle area of the war. We went around and visited with the local citizens. There were lots of farmers. In the Arab tradition they invited us in and we joined them for a meal. Initially, they were wary of us, reluctant to open up. But we were there for three weeks of stability operations, fixing their schools and things like that. When we left, they actually lined the streets and waved good-bye. They were sad to see us go. I think each unit has its own personality, and the people in As Samawah identified us by the patches on our shoulders. They told us that some patches they enjoyed working with more than others. That made us feel good. We were in As Samawah from March 30 until April 21. Then we went to Fallujah on the twenty-third of April.

We set up in an abandoned house in the center of Fallujah and we made that our compound. A man brought his son up to the gate, they looked at me, and he said to his son, "That's what an American looks like," like I was a zoo animal. They had never been outside their hometown so they treated Westerners as a different species. I speak Arabic to a degree. I learned it through the Defense Language Institute. I went through all their language tapes, about fifteen hours of them. I picked it up pretty quickly and had a good base knowledge. I ended up learning more Arabic through the Bedouins in the Sinai. They lived near a trash landfill and I'd go out and bring them some food and we'd sit and have tea. They'd run out to the trash and bring me a Sears catalog or something and they'd point to a picture and they'd tell me how to say it in Arabic and I'd tell them how to say it in English. I received a lot of my Arabic training through the Bedouins. Anyway, I was able to talk with that man and his son and make a connection with them.

We got reports that four thousand enemy troops were back at As Samawah. We flew aircraft into the Tallil Air Force Base south of the city and did a ground assault convoy for the seventy-three kilometers to As Samawah. It took us thirteen hours. It was dark and we didn't have night-vision goggles. It was a huge convoy and there was a big Slinky effect, a lot of stopping and going, stopping and going.

We got into As Samawah at five a.m. local time on March 30. We offloaded in a landfill outside of town. They'd been receiving mortar fire that morning. The logistics train with fuel, water, food, and other supplies was being ambushed in the towns en route to As Samawah. Our job was to establish a wagon wheel around the town and set up a blocking position. No one was allowed in without passing through a checkpoint.

About seven or eight enemy soldiers with weapons were moving toward us. We engaged them and they started shooting back. Then they opened up with preplanned mortars, multiple RPGs, machine guns, and snipers. We all had our chemical suits on. Charlie Company was off to our right flank. We were in the center, in the middle of everything. Alpha Company was off to our left flank and battalion headquarters was to our rear. Alpha Company was shut down. Mortars were just raining in on them.

We maneuvered up and were going to flank what we thought were a squad of enemy fighters. We got up to that point and mortar rounds started coming in. The whole battalion was under fire. PFC Light was hit; he was the first casualty. PFC Yeoman was our machine gunner and he was firing from a berm of sand, but the enemy machine gunners were shooting back and their bullets were kicking the sand up in his face like a rooster tail. The bullets were just missing him, and he said to Sergeant Miller, who was sharing the berm with him, "Could you scootch over a little bit," just that calm.

Mortars were bursting all around us and a mortar round came into our position and threw mud all over me and Sergeants Panera and Hatcher. Sergeant Panera was grabbing his face and yelling, and I said, "Did you get hit? Did you get hit?" And he said, "Yeah, with mud." It was that close. Sergeant Raymer and Sergeant Tomes were working on PFC Light and I asked them to give me the thumbs-up or thumbs-down as to whether he was going to make it. They gave me the thumbs-down. I said, "Well, he's still breathing so I'm getting him out of here." All the while bullets were whizzing by us, making bee sounds. RPGs were blowing up all over the place. They must have had a good pile of them waiting for us. I went over to the gator, which is a little four-wheel-drive golf cart, and my guys used handheld smoke grenades to conceal my position since I was running out in the open. They laid down suppressive fire, too. We loaded Light up in the back of the gator and I grabbed the platoon's medic, Doc Wilson, and he and I drove back a mile and a half to the battalion headquarters. My only concern was to deliver Light breathing. He had been shot in the cheek. We kept pressure on the wound and tried to clear an airway for him to breathe.

Everyone at the battalion headquarters asked us if we needed anything. I threw handheld smokes, ammo, and a .50-caliber sniper rifle into my little gator and drove back in to where my platoon was. Mortars were still coming in. I said, "Okay, stop. Let's pull back and reassess." We pulled everybody out of RPG range. The mortars couldn't reach us. We replenished our ammo and set up in a defensive position.

We thought we spotted the sniper in the tower of an old cement factory and we fired a tow missile at this big smokestack. We all sat back, watched it fly through the air, and waited for the missile to go off. It hit the smokestack dead-on. The missile didn't do anything to it, just knocked some dust off it. We thought if there was a sniper up there, at least it shook him up. That thing was really built. Later I think we dropped a bomb on it and it was still standing. The walls were three or four feet thick.

There was a van with insurgents coming at us. We hit them with a rocket and blew up the van. Throughout the next three days, there were little fights and skirmishes. In As Samawah no Americans died. There were many injuries. I credit our training and our muscle memory. And the hand of God. And luck. We had twelve mortar rounds fall on our position at one time. It was like there was a shield around us.

We had enemy prisoners and enemy wounded who had given themselves up. We had 502 detainees altogether. This was just our battalion trying to manage that many people. We weren't prepared, but we built tent cities and got them stabilized. We fed them hot chow and talked to them about why we were there. I think we won some hearts and minds by the way we treated people and showed that we understood their culture and their needs.

Then we basically cleaned the town out of the rest of the bad guys. A lot of the prisoners who came out were working people, like truck drivers, and they told us they'd been forced to fight. They told us there were fifty Syrian Baath Party members who said they should fight the American infidels and threatened their lives or their families if they didn't. They were members of the Kudus Party, real hardliners. They kicked everybody out of the schools and hospitals and used the buildings as operating bases. We found a lot of ammunition piles and weapons caches in the schools. We cleared every house and building as we went through. We stayed there for three weeks.

We established operating centers and the Iraqis would come and ask for our help. We had eighteen Delta Special Forces medics attached to the unit and they made sure all the clinics were up to speed with supplies and the hospitals had power and what they needed. We got the water and sewer back online. We had a reverse osmosis water purification unit that we used to help get water out to the locals.

A man came up to our gate with his uncle and his mother. They were pleading for our help. His wife had some metal shrapnel in her neck and she was paralyzed from the neck down. The Iraqi doctors at the hospital said they couldn't do anything more for her. Our command said that the hospital had everything they needed from us and she wasn't our responsibility. I said, "Screw that." The executive officer, Lieutenant Dave Smythe, wanted to do something. We told them to go and get an ambulance with a crescent moon on it and meet us at the water tower at the center of town right before curfew. We escorted them to the brigade surgeon. He found out that her neck was all infected. She hadn't been given antibiotics. He cleaned her up and gave her antibiotics and said that there was a neurosurgeon at Tallil Air Force Base and we'd take her down there tomorrow. We took care of it.

It's a tribal system over there and if you take care of one family member like that, they don't forget it. I took the husband back home. He brought his three-month-old daughter out to show us and it just made you feel good inside. The word about what we'd done spread all through town the next day. There were other acts like that the soldiers did. After that, we could do no wrong. We were part of their family now. We used our ability and power to help them.

There were land mines in the town. They knew I spoke Arabic so they came up and told me where the mines were in the farmer's field. There was a five-hundred-pound unexploded bomb on a porch. We cleared the farmer's field and we loaded the five-hundred-pound bomb up on the back of my Humvee. I named the bomb Bob. We got it out of their neighborhood. They didn't look at us as evil. They knew that when the fight came, there was going to be some collateral damage. I remember pulling out a picture of my six-week-old son, Conner, and they understood.

I remember being down in the center of Baghdad. We were working on the third-holiest mosque there. Vendors started setting up around the holy ground selling everything from ladies' panties to CD-ROMs. The imam came up to us and he said that he couldn't control it. There were no police around. We set up guards all around the mosque to keep the booths and bazaars away and keep the traffic flowing, because cars were parking wherever they wanted. People would come out of the mosque and lean over and quietly thank us and keep walking.

There was an elderly lady coming out of the mosque, probably in her eighties, and she walked with a cane. She couldn't step down from the curb. She had to sit down, scoot off the curb, and stand back up. One of the soldiers directing traffic saw this and he stopped six lanes of traffic, went over, put his arm around her arm and helped her off the curb and across the street. Everybody stopped and looked and watched. I remember it; it's so vivid in my mind. Because he respected her and knew she needed help, the people appreciated that. That's the way we were brought up. A lot of us were brought up by the last great generation, the one that Tom Brokaw wrote about, and their ethics and morals filtered down to us.

I'm a career soldier. Seeing the wounded always causes me to reflect and think about how ugly war is and wonder why this ever had to happen. But then you look at that three-month-old little girl the

Iraqi father brought out to us. There are a lot of sad hearts about people getting wounded and killed. Because I've had close to twenty years in the service, it didn't affect me as much.

I remember Staff Sergeant Raymer. He had Light's blood on his hands. I took my canteen out and we were washing the blood off his hands and I asked him if he was all right. He said he was. But you have to revisit those guys. When we got to Baghdad, we had a psychiatrist visit the guys in our unit. The chaplain played a big role. And just the camaraderie. You have to talk about it. I don't reflect on it, wondering if I did this right or did that wrong. We just executed what we had to do. Some soldiers will question the decisions they had to make, and that's where their buddies come in and say, "Hey, we did what we trained to do as best we could."

The biggest heroes I know are the families back home. The support from wives, mothers, daughters, sons, dads, uncles, sisters, and brothers. They're the ones who sent the letters we got in the mail and they're the ones we talk to on the phone. They keep us going. They let us know people care. It has a big effect on us. God bless them.

As for winning the Silver Star, it wasn't "I" who did it. It was "us." I did nothing more than what others did. We did our jobs. Somebody witnesses you doing something and they write it up. I told them to put the write-up in the trash several times. I never read what the two witnesses wrote about me. I don't know who wrote what or what they said. I never even saw the award. I've got a Xerox of it. When I came back to the Sergeants Major Academy, they said, "You won the Silver Star." I never had an awards ceremony because, frankly, I didn't want one. I'm not a big ceremony person.

★

Recently promoted to sergeant major, Dennis Caylor is now stationed in Hattiesburg, Mississippi, where he's doing what he does best: training other soldiers. He runs a basic-training mobilization station for the National Guard and U.S. Reserve forces. He will serve two more years in the United States Army. In retirement, he says he'll devote a lot of time to his family and says he would like to do something for the government and the soldiers, "to give something back to them."

THE BATTLE OF DEBECKA PASS

★

Jeff Adamec, Master Sergeant, U.S. Army

Howell, New Jersey

SILVER STAR; IRAQ; 6 APRIL 2003

April 6, 2003. At a strategic crossroads in northern Iraq that they dubbed "the Alamo," two dozen Green Berets fought off T-55 tanks, Armored Personnel Carriers, and hundreds of Iraq's elite infantrymen. Outnumbered ten to one, and with artillery and tank shells hitting nearby, Staff Sergeant Jeff Adamec and Staff Sergeant Jason Brown used Javelin missiles to take out the enemy and secure a key intersection linking Mosul and Kirkuk in northern Iraq. Both men earned the Silver Star. Said Major Curtis W. Hubbard, commander of Company C, Third Battalion of the Third Special Forces Group, "Two guys shut down the attack. Two guys turned an organized Iraqi

JEFF ADAMEC

attack into chaos. They halted an entire motorized rifle company." For American forces moving south from Kurdish-controlled zones into the government-controlled territory of northern Iraq, this was the first major offensive of the war: the Battle of Debecka Pass.

I was a recruiter's dream. Ever since I was little I wanted to be in the military in some way. Initially it was the Marine Corps, so I went and talked with the marine recruiter and told him that I wanted to be a medic and be airborne. He said, "Well, our medics come from the navy." I didn't want to join the navy or get on a boat. I went next to the U.S. Army office. The recruiter said, "So you want to talk about the army?" "No," I said. "I'll sign up today. Just make me a medic with the airborne." His eyes lit up. I said, "Yeah, no problem, man. I'm joining." I actually left for basic training the same day I graduated from high school in Howell, New Jersey. I walked off the graduation field, got into the recruiter's car, and he drove me to the airport. I left for Fort Leonard Wood, Missouri, that night.

I thought basic training was going to be a lot harder than it actually was for me. It was challenging but I expected to be yelled at more. I had such high expectations for how tough it was going to be. I was a seventeen-year-old kid and I'd never been away from home before. There was no one who knew me. I had to rebuild my entire life from the first day I set foot in the army. I never had problems making friends.

You're isolated from the world and you are put into situations where the trainers aren't coddling you. They aren't there to be your mommy and daddy. You've got to step up and be a man or be a woman and take responsibility for something. Because you're with other people and you have to lean on them and vice versa, it creates a team bond. I think that's the best lesson the army teaches anybody who serves: the ability to work with others to accomplish something. You can never get anything done individually. It's impossible in the army. There are individual things that you do but overall there's some kind of team effort going on. That's what most people take away from the army.

Sergeant Earle was our drill instructor. The guy kind of looked like Hitler with that little mustache and real short haircut. He wasn't a big guy; he was skinny and wiry. When that guy walked into a room, he commanded everyone's attention just by the way he carried himself. He was my first impression of leadership in the military and I couldn't have asked for a better one. He made us feel like we'd accomplished something. We were no longer worms. We were soldiers.

From there I went down to Fort Sam Houston in San Antonio, Texas, and learned to be a medic. Then I went to Airborne School at Fort Benning. I learned that if you want something bad enough, no matter what kind of physical or mental condition you're in, the desire to accomplish it will drive you far past the abilities of your body or your mind. I've seen guys get through on pure desire. By the end of Airborne School and [Ranger Indoctrination Program], I was getting by on adrenaline and pure desire to get to the end. I've seen guys who were in better shape than I was just up and quit. I didn't want to quit. I wanted to be there. Those who quit didn't want it as bad as I did.

When I knew I was going to be deployed, there was a certain level of fear. You aren't human if you don't feel it. And people react to it in different ways. I sat glued to my TV set after the 9/11 terrorist attacks, waiting for my chance to go. My wife said, "Why do you guys in the army have this inner desire to go over there and do that stuff?" I replied, "Well, it's kinda like being a baseball player. You go to practice every single day of your entire life, but until you play a game you don't know if you're going to win or lose. But you want to play."

Yes, there is fear. On the plane over to Iraq, guys to the right and left of me who had been in Afghanistan before were sleeping. I looked at them like they were crazy. There's no way I was going to sleep. I was awake for three straight days.

The first days, up in the north, were really quiet. We were just cruising across the desert, taking it one grain of sand at a time. We hit the ground, and I'm going to be honest with you, I expected it to be like a World War II movie. It wasn't that way at all. The plane landed and the Kurds were there to meet us. We spent a lot of time with them those first couple of days and we were wondering, *Where's the war at?* When I got off the plane I was wired tight, and this lull calmed me down.

I've never seen people so happy to see an American in my entire life. These Kurds, every single one of them, wanted to shake our hands and meet us. They wanted to know our names and where we were from. You meet a lot of people in America who talk just about themselves. All these guys wanted to hear about was us. We got to know them, which made fighting for them easier. The Kurds didn't want to let the Americans win the war for them. They were more than willing to do it themselves.

Dawn broke and we started moving. This was about eighteen days into the war. We had Operation Detachment Alpha 391, with the motto "91 Don't Run," and Operation Detachment Alpha 392. We had half a team from the Tenth Group plus all these Kurds. We weren't in charge of them, just attached to them. At first it was like a big convoy, guys walking shoulder to shoulder across the ground. No one was there. We got through the beginning of the Debecka Pass and came across a huge minefield. That was the closest to danger I'd been up until that point. There were mines all over the place. The Kurds were so used to seeing this kind of thing they got out of their trucks and just picked up the mines and moved them to the side of the road. When you go to a country that has been in some kind of war for so many years, they know a little more about war-making than you do.

We went through the pass, where a bunch of Iraqi Republican

Guards surrendered to us. The Kurds and the Republican Guard are enemies, but you wouldn't have known it by the way they treated these guys. They gave them bottles of water. There was no hatred. Those Republican Guard guys were probably thinking they were going to get executed because they had done awful, awful things to the Kurds for years. Then they gave up and the Kurds turned around and treated them well.

When we got to the intersection we started taking inaccurate mortar fire. We set up a roadblock and looked to see where the mortar fire was coming from. They had a mortar set up in the back of a pickup truck. To try to gain better accuracy, instead of adjusting the mortar fire they'd just move the truck. Interesting theory. Didn't work out for them. We advanced on their mortar position, bounding toward them, and we stopped at one point. I was on the top of my vehicle. This is something I will absolutely never forget in my entire life: my team sergeant got out of his vehicle, looked off to the right and said, "Hey, Jeff, does that look like a tank?" It did look like a tank—a small silhouetted vehicle was coming toward us. Then he said, "Does that look like another tank?" There were ten or fifteen of these things heading our way, and I said, "Hey, this ain't good."

Everyone packed up and pulled back to the intersection. We all made a mental promise. Nobody had to yell out commands. Everybody just knew: we were not going to move back from that point. We were not going to give up that ground. We called that spot "the Alamo."

I had the Javelin missile system, which takes two minutes for the seeker to cool down on the guidance device. I was just sitting there, looking at this thing, waiting for it to cool down. Everyone else was running back to the vehicles. Finally one of the guys on our team said, "Hey, dumbass, you want to come with us? We're going." I picked my stuff up and got on our vehicle. I fell off the back of it onto the ground. Everyone started laughing, in the middle of everything that's going on. Then I tripped over the ratchet strap and fell again. By then even I was laughing. Here were these tanks bearing down on us at forty miles per hour and they were meaning to misbehave. They weren't coming to shake our hands.

We pulled back five hundred meters to the next little berm. One of my other guys and I dismounted with the Javelin missiles and we went to work. I don't know who the commander of the enemy unit was, but he'd send out four tanks or four Armored Personnel Carriers, and then when he didn't hear from them, he'd send more. They kept sending guys for the next eight or nine hours. It was odd, like shooting fish in a bucket. This was the worst tactic I'd ever seen. They had no idea we had the Javelins and that we had air support. They were just walking into a bad situation. We could see all the way across the open valley the enemy had to cross. The Javelin missiles can really reach out and touch something. The enemy was not trying to skirt around the Debecka Valley. They came straight across, right at us, head-on, every time.

This was the first time I'd ever shot a Javelin in combat. Weeks before, we were getting ready to deploy and Jason Brown, the weapons sergeant from 9-1, came in one day and said, "Hey, why don't we go down to the Javelin trainer and just train up on them real quick. You know we're going to be deploying here in a couple of weeks." I thought that sounded like a good idea. We got everyone together and took them down to the Javelin trainer. The training ended up being something that saved our lives.

Those Javelins fired off, and I'll tell you what: it was the sweetest sound you ever heard. Once the Javelin leaves the missile housing, it's totally on its own. It's heavy and cumbersome, but once you train on it and get used to it, it's very easy to use. Two days before we actually went out on this mission, I was bored out of my mind, so I grabbed the Javelin handbook and started flipping through it. And thank God I did that, because if I hadn't, I probably wouldn't have even remembered how to turn that thing on. I was lucky enough to do one thing at the right time.

We looked through the targeting device and fired it. But we had to remember to move, too, because those tanks knew where the Javelin came from. We could see their turrets turning, but by that point we'd already fired, unhooked it, picked up our stuff, and run one hundred meters in the other direction. The enemy was shooting where we used to be. Little did they know that in about two seconds they were going to get hit with the missile we just fired at them. Altogether we had eighteen hits. Tanks or Armored Personnel Carriers. Every time. What made it worse for them was that every time the aircraft would fly over, the enemy would dismount their vehicles and just run off. But we had the .50-cal machine gunners on the top of our vehicles just waiting for that to happen. For them it was just bad luck. Whoever was in charge made a series of bad tactical decisions. The day was ours.

During the attack, an errant bomb of ours was dropped on a bunch of Kurds. Because I used to be a medic, I went to help with the sixty or seventy casualties. I grabbed my bag and we beat feet up there. You couldn't make a movie more graphic than the scene we were about to run into. I can't even explain it. Guys were blown to pieces. Ammo was exploding all around us. Everything was on fire. I worked on a BBC guy who was embedded with the Kurds. I was getting yelled at because I was working on this guy without my gloves. I didn't have time to dig through my bag and look for gloves. I did everything I could for him, but he had a lot of injuries and ended up dying.

We finished with all of that and were cleaning up to come back down to where our vehicles were. One of the guys on our team had got binoculars up. He said there were Iraqi Republican Guards down there who wanted to surrender. We tried to signal them to come on up. Just as they stood up to surrender, these white pickup trucks pulled up. The fedayeen in robes were in these trucks. They lined up the Republican Guard troops and began executing them. They were being slaughtered on their hands and knees, begging for their lives. The fedayeen scumbags were shooting these dudes in the head, one by one. There was nothing we could do to save them, but there was something we could do for them. We dropped a 750-pound bomb on the whole thing. We just erased that intersection. The guys who were trying to surrender were soldiers like us. They followed orders. They fought. These fadayeen, I tell you what, I don't detest anyone like I detest those guys.

My pants were soaked with blood. I was sitting there mentally drained. My medic, a good friend of mine, walked over to me. He opened up a soda and he set it down. He opened up the cookies. We sat there and ate cookies in front of our vehicle while the sun was going down.

The media inaccurately reported that six Special Forces guys, Green Berets, got killed. The story hit the morning news cycle back in the States, and of course everyone's wives and girlfriends were freaking out. When we got done with the battle, the sergeant major said, "You need to call home. Just let them hear your voices, tell them you're okay." And that was what we did.

It was a great battle. Twenty-four Special Forces guys went up against two hundred and fifty Iraqi Republican Guards and not one of us got scratched. For the first year afterward, it was all I heard about. A good friend of mine who I really respect in the army said, "Don't let this define who you are. Don't sit back on your laurels, because we're about to go back to Afghanistan and we've got to be ready to go." He said we needed to think about the next combat zone and he was absolutely right.

There's a guy in Baghdad right now who is a baker. His entire life he's been making bread for the Iraqis. He's seen his people suffer. He knows that when the Americans came and he watched Saddam's statue fall, it was the happiest moment of his life. He remembers looking over and seeing American tanks and Americans handing out water. Then he turned around and saw American soldiers dying, in his country, by the hands of insurgents who are not from his country. That baker has two daughters and he'd rather not send them out of the country, but he would if he had to. Yet he trusts the Americans and he knows they are there to help and he doesn't leave. He stays there every single day, while there are car bombs going off in front of his shop. He trusts that the Americans are going to help him get his country back on its feet. We aren't fighting Iraqis over there. We're fighting terrorists who are coming from other places. We're fighting for his freedom, and that's our gift to him. We're fighting them in Baghdad and not New York City, and that's his gift to us.

★

Jeff Adamec remains on active duty serving with the United States Special Forces.

NO BETTER FRIEND, NO WORSE ENEMY

★

Timothy Tardif, Lance Corporal, U.S. Marine Corps
Second Battalion, Fifth Regiment, First Division
Huntington Beach, California
SILVER STAR; AL TARMIYAH, IRAQ; 12 APRIL 2003

Even by marine standards, the Second Battalion of the Fifth Regiment is a legendary outfit. Tim Tardif trained to be a sniper because he was determined to be the best of the best. On April 12, 2003, Tim was functioning as the squad leader when their three amtracs came to a bridge and were ambushed. Without any cover, Tim and his fellow marines "kissed the ground" and advanced toward the line of four houses where a mixture of fedayeen and Republican Guard were firing. Even though he was badly injured in the leg by a grenade, Tim and his men pressed on and won the fight. Medevaced to southern Iraq and then Germany, Tim finagled a way to get back to his men, back to the combat zone.

TIMOTHY TARDIF

A good marine adapts and overcomes. You give everything you do 100 percent, no matter what. You don't give up. You work hard to learn everything. You just shut your mouth up and do your job. You don't talk back to senior people. I don't care if you're a PFC and the other guy is a lance corporal, you don't talk back. We're all together all the time and we know everything about each other. You get really close to them. They're your brothers.

When I enlisted, I walked into the recruiter's office and I said that I wanted to be a grunt. It's hard mentally and physically, definitely not a nine-to-five job. We're in the field all week and we're hooking and jabbing, sweating. That's what it means to be a grunt. I wouldn't trade it for anything in the world. I noticed that once I got into the civilian world, there were no skills that I could apply, except a whole lot of self-discipline and a love of challenges.

When we deployed, we flew a big 747 charter jet with our weapons and everything. We got to Kuwait on January 28, and we stayed there for two months. That was the worst time. In that country there is nothing. No vegetation. Flat. Fine, gravelly sand. We set up camp and slept under the stars for two or three weeks. Then we got tents. We ate MREs and went to these refresher classes on land navigation, weapons, and every little thing. Later on we were allowed to have dice and cards. There was nothing else to do so we played some serious blackjack and poker. I didn't get into it very much. There was one chess board that everybody was always fighting over. There were a couple of guys who were really good at chess and we would try to beat them and they'd just whup us. Getting mail was huge. We didn't get any mail for the first month and we didn't get any packages until the fifth month. There was a lot of time to think. We smoked a lot of cigarettes. There were lots of rumors about when we were going to invade Iraq or whether we were just a show of force to try to get Saddam to cave.

We were close enough to the border that our command was convinced the Iraqis were constantly watching us. It was cold at the time but they didn't want us to put our hands in our pockets. They didn't want us showing any weakness. They'd take us out four miles from the camp and set up a tactical defense. We'd dig fighting holes and set out sandbags. They were afraid we'd lose our combat edge, so we'd be on watch for two hours, sleep for three hours, get up for watch for another two hours, and on like that.

Once we got closer to the line of departure, we went up to a pre-staging area and waited for orders to punch through into Iraq. We crept right up to the border, dug holes, and waited there in our chemical suits. This is when Saddam was firing SCUDs and they were landing in Kuwait, in the desert, all over the place. Then we saw our artillery opening up on the border area. It looked like something out of *Star Wars*. We crossed the border into Iraq and we first went to the oil fields. There were supposed to be twelve men in our amtrac but they shoved eighteen or nineteen of us in there for hours at a time, every day, just rolling along. Sometimes we'd get contact, get out and shoot a little bit, make sure everybody was taken care of, then back in the amtrac and we'd keep rolling. Basically, we were tired and uncomfortable. We just wanted an excuse to get out. That's when the sandstorm happened.

It was the seventh level of hell inside the 'trac because it was hot and loud and miserable. There was no air circulating inside. The smell of diesel fumes was everywhere, and when we went outside we had to keep our hands on the amtrac or we'd get lost. That's how bad it was. It was all red during the day and then the day turned into night. We tried to push on, but we heard about a couple of amtracs that collided and one that went off a slope that it didn't see. We decided it was too dangerous to go on.

After about three days, the sandstorm quit and we pushed on to Baghdad. We stopped at Baghdad University for a couple of nights. We were glad to be out of our amtracs. It was a green campus, not at all what we expected. We were patrolling along the street and someone would pop up, fire an RPG, maybe get off a couple of rounds of AK, and then they'd run like hell. We would try to chase them as best we could. A couple of times we gunned them down.

We did security patrols and had a lot of positive contact with Iraqi civilians, especially in As Samawah, south of Baghdad. One of the codes we live by is "No Better Friend, No Worse Enemy." I carried a copy of that in my flak jacket the whole way. We didn't wear sunglasses so we could make eye contact with people. We didn't fly the American flag because we were liberators, not conquerors. We wanted to help the Iraqi people get their sewage, water, power, and government back up and running. We became really tight with the people there. They would invite us over for dinner and tea. We treated their kids like they were our own. One of my buddies that I still e-mail is an Iraqi police officer. We taught the police officers martial arts and other regular police techniques, like how to restrain someone. We communicated through interpreters. We'd help the Iraqis push their carts, bale hay, whatever they needed. We tried to do whatever we could for them. If we were on patrol and saw somebody who needed help, we just did it. We gave them water and dug ditches for drainage. The Shiites were very appreciative. They loved having their freedom.

Baghdad looks pretty modern, with streetlights and freeways. But you could definitely tell there was a sanitation problem there. The Shiite section of the country had rebelled during the 1991 war and so Saddam basically beat the crap out of them. The roads weren't fixed. There were open sewers. People would go just a hundred yards from their house to dump their trash. There was no spaying or neutering of pets so there were ratty, mean dogs everywhere.

We worked out of an old train station. The insurgency was easy to smoosh because the people there loved us. They would come up and tell us where the weapons caches were. Sometimes there would be quarrels between neighbors and one would try to get the other one back by coming to us and saying, "He's got weapons."

One day we were the lead element of our battalion and our job was to make sure that a bridge in this small town was good enough for all the vehicles to make it across. We got up there and my 'trac stopped on the near side of the bridge. Two trucks crossed to the other side and stopped. We had the bridge covered from both ends. We didn't know it at the time, but a combination of fedayeen and Iraqi Republican Guards, a bunch of the enemy who had been beaten back, had decided to combine forces and gather together right in front of that town. We were trying to stretch our legs. Some people were eating chow. Well, all of a sudden, it started getting nasty. They initiated the ambush with two RPGs and just lit up this one truck. They killed the gunner, who was up on the .50-cal, and wounded the driver pretty good. Our guys returned fire and thought we had to get over there and help those guys out. As we crossed the bridge we could hear the fire coming off the amtrac. We had to button up; the hatch came down and we closed and secured it. We were trying to find targets but it was hard to tell where the firing was coming from. Then I noticed that we were getting contact from the right side because the bullets were hitting that side of our amtrac.

An enemy RPG clipped a power line, and that came swinging down and landed by our right flank. The enemy would pop up with AKs. We could see them over on the right side, shooting at us, and once in a while we'd see a muzzle flash from an RPG going off. It was chaotic and no one was giving orders. I tried to get the lieutenant on the radio but he was calling in fire. I decided we were going to go ahead and try to clear through that area. Basically, I had a machine-gun team with me and we were receiving fire from these two houses pretty regularly. We laid down an initial burst of suppressive fire and then we spread out. The houses were probably about two hundred yards away. I tried to find a good place to set up our SAW [Squad Automatic Weapon].

About five enemy fighters were hiding in the tall grass. As I advanced, I saw them right away and I got three of them. I always kept my gun on semi or three-round burst. One of the other guys popped up and I got him. I didn't see the other guy that was hunkered down in the grass, but my buddy Corporal Marco Martinez, who was coming up behind me, was able to see him, but it was too late. He'd already lobbed a grenade when Martinez shot him and the grenade went off. That's when I was wounded. We kept doing our assault up the road toward the houses. We started receiving more fire. There were probably sixteen or seventeen guys in each house and they were organized. They could see us moving forward and we could see them running out the back. I sent one fire team to go around the back of the house. We had two teams coming around the front and we were trying to move on each side of the house. When they started running out of the back of the house, our guys would shoot them. That was working well.

Then we finally got to this one house. We shot a rocket at the house to create an initial shock. We didn't want to enter these homes through a door or a window because they'd be expecting us. Our rocket made an awful nice hole and we rushed through it to clear the house. We radioed back, "We cleaned this house and we're going on to the next one. Get ready." We were receiving fire from down the street, but I posted a couple of guys out there and they returned fire just to keep them off our backs. Meanwhile, the enemy had taken up positions in this bunker behind the house. One of our guys decided to reload. He was supposed to get down, switch magazines, and stand up when his gun was back in action. For some reason, he froze and decided to do it right there, and he got shot. His situation was critical. We needed to get up to him and get him out of there because he was bleeding to death.

The enemy must have dropped their RPG launcher when they retreated to the bunker, and my buddy Corporal Marco Martinez got it. He'd never fired one before. He didn't know how to load it or fire it but he figured it out, and he was finally able to blow up that bunker. He earned the Navy Cross.

We got to our wounded marine and evacuated him out of there. I didn't think he was going to make it. It took us about fifteen minutes from the time he was shot until Martinez destroyed the bunker. He was just lucky. We were laying down enough fire that the enemy didn't have time to spray him one more time.

We needed to get out of there because they were calling in a "Jack-hammer" mission, which meant the fixed-wing aircraft were going to bomb the whole area. We started to bound back at that point. I was just too dizzy. I blacked out. When I came to, my wounds hurt a lot. It felt like my right leg got hit with a hot torch. They sent me to a field hospital in southern Iraq and they patched me up the best they could. Then I went to a military hospital in Landstuhl, Germany, and I was there for about two weeks.

I was able to cut a deal with the doctor there: if I was able to walk around the hospital for a day without crutches, then he would sign a waiver saying I could go back to my men. I borrowed a set of camies at the hospital because my own gear was all torn up. After that, I went down to the airfield and talked to the air boss to find out when there would be a flight going down to Kuwait. I waited two or three days for a flight. From there, we had a convoy of new marines going to Iraq and I was lucky enough to go with them.

If I'd stayed in Germany, I would have been sent home. As for my wife, I didn't tell her too much because I didn't want her to worry.

★

Timothy Tardif remains on active duty and has returned to the combat zone for another tour of duty.

THE QUESTION IN THE BACK OF EVERYONE'S MIND

★

Joseph Perez, Lance Corporal, U.S. Marine Corps

First Marine Division

Houston, Texas

Navy Cross; Baghdad, Iraq; 12 April 2003

In the blistering heat in an area just south of Baghdad during the opening days of Operation Iraqi Freedom, Lance Corporal Perez led from the front, taking charge of a battle in the Iraqi desert. Drawing most of the enemy fire, he pounded the entrenched enemy positions with rifle fire and grenades, and he destroyed a machine-gun emplacement. Seriously wounded with gunshots to the back and shoulder, Perez fought on, directing his unit to take cover and fire into enemy strongholds.

CHUCK LARSON

I joined the Marine Corps a little late. I was at the University of Houston for two years but I wasn't really sure what I wanted to do. In 2002, I joined the marines—for two reasons. First, when I went down to the local mall where all the recruiters were, they were the only ones open. Second, my mom was pushing me to join the marines because they have a reputation for being the best.

I'd pushed myself before. I had been an honor student in high school and I was doing all right in college. But basic training was pretty hard. Physically I was ready for it, though the mental stress was tough. I'd grown up a little bit after high school, but in boot camp I was treated like a five-year-old. Everything from my outside world was taken away. I wasn't outstanding. I didn't make a name for myself by any means. I did enough to stay under the radar and keep from getting yelled at. In high school and in college, I'd never really put my mind to anything. I did something and I moved on. But now I felt I was on the path to doing something that I liked and was good at.

I graduated from boot camp on October 18 and then I went to the School of Infantry. A month later, I was in Kuwait waiting for Operation Iraqi Freedom to take off. I felt ready. Maybe it was because I was a young enough marine or naïve enough that I didn't know what I was getting into. I thought I had all these skills and desert training. It was a rapid progression of getting to know everything that we needed to know, but I definitely felt I was ready.

I had a lot of confidence in my guys. I had been through boot camp and infantry school with a lot of the marines in my platoon. We had the sense that our superiors had been around awhile and that they'd had the opportunities to train a lot longer than we had. They showed us that they were good leaders. But our leaders hadn't seen action yet, the same as the rest of us. A lot of them were what we call "stop loss": they had been on their way out of the military as the war was about to take off and got held back. They didn't have a choice.

We all wondered how we'd be under fire. This was the question that was in the back of everyone's mind. Our superiors were worried because we were brand-new marines and they wondered how we were going to act. I didn't want any of my actions, if I faltered, to affect anybody else.

When the war started, we were packed into our amtrac. At any given time we had between twenty and twenty-five people, depending on the situation. We were told we would encounter enemy fire from the very beginning so we were pretty pumped up about it. But nothing happened. Everyone was edgy. On a day-to-day basis, we were hearing things over the radio. Something was always happening over there, somewhere else. We were expecting to be the next ones called, but for the first ten days, nothing. I think March 25 [2003] was the first time we made contact with the enemy. I wasn't a part of that and I thought, *Oh, man, I missed it.*

The southern part of Iraq is desolate. Other than the oil fields, there's not a whole lot there. We saw Bedouin families who were scared, throwing up their white flags as soon as they saw us. It wasn't until we got to the middle of Iraq that we started seeing more and more people. About a week later we had a sniper shooting at us when we were going through a smaller city.

As for the day of the battle, the day I got wounded, it started out like any other morning. We loaded up and we just happened to be the lead company. We did a herringbone, in which we patrolled up one side of the street and then down the other. We were kind of sitting there when we heard over the radio that something was going on. We got the call to dismount. We moved parallel to Highway 6, and from there we could hear the battle going on in front of us. Everyone was pumped now. We were still lying low. The unit in front radioed that they needed support from us. I thought that we were definitely getting into some action today. We continued forward and fell in just behind the other unit.

I was the lead man in our company because I was the point man for our platoon. I was mostly at the front of everything. That was the best position for me because I like to lead people. If I can't do it from a position of rank, then I'll do it by being the first in the fight or being the first one to have an opportunity to make a decision. I felt like I was safer that way.

We linked up with another company and decided to do an envelopment around the enemy position. We thought we were dealing with an Iraqi training camp where they train foreign fighters, and we just happened to fall upon it: about one hundred Iraqi fighters and upwards of two hundred to three hundred foreign fighters. We crossed a footbridge that led across a canal. It was an ideal way across the canal because it happened to be in front of the only opening in the berm leading to the field where the fighters were firing from. I could hear bullets whizzing by me as I crossed the bridge.

We made it across real quick and hung a right. We linked up with some other marines and they told us where they wanted us positioned. Just as we were doing this, ten Iraqis came from under this bridge, all very young and all with their hands up. It made me nervous because they came out of nowhere. I told them to get down on the ground and somebody behind me would take care of them. I continued on around the berm and then another berm running perpendicular to the canal on the left side. As I was running up, I saw where somebody had left sleeping bags and jugs of water. The bedrolls were so big I remember worrying that the enemy could hide in them and then shoot us from behind. We were moving pretty fast at that point, almost at a run.

Two Iraqis poked their guns out of this little grassy area and started shooting at us, just letting their AKs run free. I was probably ten feet away from them when it happened. How they missed us, I have no clue. Our immediate reaction was to drop to the ground and start shooting. I was so tense at that moment that after the second shot, I realized I was firing into the dirt. I told myself, *Calm down, calm down.* I waited for the one guy to pop up and I shot him. I waited for the other guy to pop up and I shot him. At this point I was telling myself, *I'm good now. I can do this. I just have to remain calm.*

The next enemy was probably five to seven feet behind me; my team was spread out at an angle. We eliminated him, moved on to the berm, and started clearing the field to our south. We threw a grenade, it went off, and we stormed the trench or irrigation ditch. The water was not very deep, maybe up to our knees, but the mud was deep so we were just sinking. Every step we were pulling our feet out of the thick, heavy mud, making it hard to walk. The temperature was ninety to one hundred degrees and we were in full chemical suits. About that time I almost passed out. I got real dizzy and put my hand on the side of a berm to steady myself. I looked up and saw two enemy with weapons in their hands. I didn't think they had seen us because they were looking out to the west, in the other direction. I held up our squad and called my team leader forward. I told him there were these two enemy personnel standing right there. "What should I do?" I asked. He told me to shoot them. I just wanted to get confirmation. I reared up and shot one of them and he fell down. The other guy got real scared and just stood there. I shot him as well.

We held up for a little bit. There was another platoon moving with us, kind of like a squeegee. As soon as we moved we got shot at by a machine gun and two other positions simultaneously. We brought in a helicopter, and that cleared out a little space for us by firing at the guys who were firing on us. They gave us enough cover to maneuver around to where we needed to go. At that point I grabbed my AT-4 and fired it, blowing three or four guys straight out of the bunker. There were only three of us that had scopes on our rifles, but that made a big difference. I could see everything, zero in. We halted in this area and redistributed ammo.

By this point, we'd been fighting for about an hour to an hour and a half. It seemed like five minutes. I got some water in me, turned to my team leader, and said, "Man, this is crazy. Who would have known that we were going to get into it this bad today?" But we were having a good day; we were rocking and rolling.

We needed to coordinate with the adjacent platoon. They had moved off and created a gap in the direction that we were heading. They sent me and my team leader over to link up with them at the same spot where I shot the two guys earlier. I started running along a knee-high berm. I saw this guy under a bush and I dropped down to line him up. Nobody else was shooting at him. My team leader came up and said, "What are you shooting at?" I said, "I'm shooting at that guy that's maybe five meters in front of you." He said, "Where? Where?" "Right there," I said. "I could throw a rock at him now." Finally he saw him, and between the two of us we unloaded a magazine into him.

We picked up and went about ten steps before we saw a tree with a machine gun behind it. I saw the guy and we made eye contact just before he started shooting at us. As soon as I pulled my rifle up to shoot at him, he unloaded with that machine gun and he caught me. Apparently I got shot about five times in the chest. The thing is, I had my armor on and none of it penetrated, but the last two rounds got me in the shoulder. The shots instantly knocked me down to the ground. I wasn't sure at that point if I was shot or not because I'd never been shot before. I was thinking, *Am I shot or did I just get hit in the armor and have the wind knocked out of me?*

I couldn't tell. I had a million thoughts go through my head all at once. When I tried to pick up my weapon, I couldn't. My arm was immobile. My next best move was to get off the berm so he couldn't shoot me anymore. By that time, my platoon had seen me go down and thought I was dead. This guy was still firing at me but firing over my head. I'd run out of grenades so I was out of the fight.

My squad kept asking me, "Are you okay, are you okay?" I told them, "I'm fine, I'm fine," because I figured if I could breathe I was okay. They said they were going to try to get me out of there and I said, "Just get me a grenade or somebody who can throw a grenade." They brought up a grenade and said, "Tell us where the guy is." I said, "Just give me the grenade. I'll throw it. I know exactly where he is."

I was shot in the right shoulder, the arm I throw with, but I do everything else left-handed. I write left-handed and I shoot left-handed. But either way, all I had to do was pull the pin and toss the grenade over my head to get him. He was only about five to ten meters away. The enemy knew he was pretty much done because he grabbed ahold of that trigger and he didn't let go until the grenade went off.

Everybody rushed to me to see if I was okay, and that was the point when the pain really kicked in. I was definitely not feeling good. It felt like my shoulder was on fire. They gave me some morphine and I was doing pretty well. I got some water in me because I was dehydrated. Then they cut off all my clothes and I was naked except for my boots and my boxer shorts. The medevac helicopter was en route. I was in the battlefield with just my boots and boxers on. I was feeling kind of vulnerable but I was drugged up so I didn't really care.

They put me on a stretcher and loaded me right up on the bird. The morphine was kicking in and I was flying high. I was the only American on board other than the flight crew. They were loading all these foreign fighters onto this helicopter. One of them was sitting right across from me. I had my hand on the stretcher in front of me because it helped with the pain. He looked at me, leaned over, and put his hand on top of mine. I just lost it. I threw my Kevlar and I think I hit him in the head. One of the crew members came over and asked what was going on. I said, "Tell that guy to never touch me again. I will kill him right on this bird." The crew member said, "Okay, okay, just calm down." They moved him away from me.

I was really dehydrated. I probably hadn't had more than a canteen of water in the past three or four days. I asked one of the crew members if they had any water because I was dying of thirst. He brought out this big water jug and said he'd keep pouring it in me as long as I kept drinking it. That water tasted so good.

When I was on the bird, they treated me a little bit. I didn't have any of those crazy wounds like you see in the movies, where there's blood spurting everywhere. The bullet hit me in a really meaty part of my arm so I wasn't bleeding badly. It didn't puncture a lung. I could breathe just fine. I wasn't going into shock. I was stable. It just hurt a lot because of the nature of the wound. Once I got to southern Iraq, all the doctors came in to see me and the care improved. At that point, I was probably one of their earliest casualties. Next they sent me to Kuwait and then to Spain, where I stayed about a week. Then I was sent back to the States.

I came home but my whole regiment was still in Iraq. My life at Camp Pendleton was pretty sad. I was going crazy because there wasn't anything to do, and I'm the type of person who needs to do something. For about a month and a half I was on leave. Then they were going to send replacements over for marines who had gotten wounded and I said, "Get me on that bird."

I linked up with my old platoon and they were all excited to see me. It was good to see the guys and acknowledge what we'd been through and the sacrifices we'd made. The day I got my award, it was just for doing my job, trying to stay alive. That's all it is. I received the award for my entire unit. I mean I'm happy to get the Navy Cross, but we did it all together. It represents the brotherhood that I made there. That day we got close and we're still close. Those are the things that happen whenever you're under fire.

Joseph Perez has returned to Iraq three times. He has reenlisted for another four years, and after that, his approach is to take it "one enlistment at a time." He plans to return to school to get his BA in math.

WORKING THROUGH IT

★

Patrick Quinn, Master Sergeant, U.S. Army

Cromwell, Connecticut

SILVER STAR; IRAQ; 5 APRIL 2003

Master Sergeant Patrick M. Quinn was awarded the Silver Star for leading his Special Forces team and a group of Kurdish militia during a battle against an Iraqi armored unit in April 2003. During the eleven-day battle, Quinn's actions resulted in the destruction of two tanks and four Armored Personnel Carriers, thirty dead Iraqi soldiers, and the seizure of thirty kilometers of ground.

PATRICK QUINN

I joined the army because I wanted to do my patriotic duty and to see the world. I didn't have the money or the grades to go to college. I lived in Germany for six years, spent rotations in Bosnia and Kosovo, and went to places I never want to see again, like West Africa. I was an infantry team leader with the Eighty-second Airborne Division in 1991, and that was the first time I went to Iraq. During that first tour there was nothing too intense. We mostly performed security details and took prisoners. I joined the army when I was seventeen years old, so I'd already been in the service three or four years at that point. It didn't seem crazy being just twenty years old and taking enemy prisoners, but when I talked to my wife about it, she said, "When I was twenty, I was in college and I could barely take care of myself." I went into Special Forces right after Desert Storm.

The second time I went to Iraq was in 2003. I was under the command of Major Eric Howard. I loved him. He was very straightforward. I could always speak my mind with him. I could present a plan to him, and if he liked it, he'd give the go-ahead. We had a very good working relationship. We had everything we needed to do our job, except certain gear that was just sitting at the port in Turkey. But we still had a timeline to meet. Special Forces are unique in that we can adapt and it's a team effort. I may be in charge, but there are so many people around with experience that any one of us might have the right solution.

My team was just awesome, probably the best team I've ever been a part of. Even before our time in Iraq, I would say, "If I ever have to go to war, these are the guys I want to go with." Every guy was supercompetent. Most of them had experience. They were motivated. We had a good mix of personalities. I always like to take suggestions from my guys and I tell them, "If you've got a suggestion, voice it." Whenever you give people a vested interest, and they feel and know they're doing something they thought of, they're more apt to go into it wholeheartedly. From the outside, I guess people would say we were a bunch of smart-asses. But we could back it up. We got the job done. The first time we were in a firefight, we moved out just like we did when we trained. It just happened. We reacted instantly and everybody did what he had to do. This was the result of training, muscle memory, and knowing each other. We could communicate without saying a word, just by our actions.

We were doing a reconnaissance with the Kurds. I dressed up as a Kurd, with no body armor, and took a civilian car up to the front line. I picked Sergeant Singer to go along with me. It was an isolated area and we had to go across a pontoon bridge. Once I crossed it, I realized the enemy was pulling back to the top of this ridge, and our orders were to maintain contact with them. I took half of our team forward with about ten Kurds and we maintained "eyes on the target." The following morning, the rest of our team came up to join us, and we cleared a minefield.

The Kurds sensed that the enemy had withdrawn so I called my higher-ups and asked them what to do. They told us to gain as much ground as we feasibly could. One of the Kurdish generals came up to me and we talked through an interpreter. He sent his guys ahead and we moved down the road. We called it our "Million Man March to Mosul." It was surreal. I looked at the map and I said that either the enemy was going to do nothing or they were going to fall back to the ridges and defend them, because that was the last piece of defendable terrain. We knew it would be dangerous.

When we got to that ridge, the whole place just erupted with enemy artillery, mortar fire, and machine-gun fire. Our people were diving everywhere. It was total chaos. We advanced to try to get a better view of the enemy but we were pinned down. There were thousands of enemy soldiers. We could see them operating all their mortars and machine guns. Their trucks were coming our way.

What flashed through my mind was that we needed aircraft. It was a perilous situation. Mortar fire was hitting right next to us. Each detonating round lifted us into the air and dropped us back down in the same spot. The earth was shaking us like one of those vibrating beds, but magnified fifty times. Artillery. Mortar rounds. RPGs. It was a bad spot. We knew we had to return fire. Sergeant Gillett was our air force combat controller. He and Sergeant McGowan stayed out in the open because he didn't want to lose communications with the aircraft. They were receiving intense fire. He was only about twenty-one or twenty-two years old. The rest of the guys and I would pick targets, feed him the coordinates, and he would direct the bombing operations. He was amazing. He'd have ten to twelve airplanes stacked up in order—basically he was like an air traffic controller—and he was directing all the air firepower. Total craziness was going on and he kept his cool. He talked to the pilots, giving them instructions, and I was listening in. We have a saying that calmness breeds calmness. He just stayed calm because he didn't want the pilots to know the peril we were in, because then they'd amp up and make mistakes. When he was off the mike, he'd be agitated, but then he'd get back on the mike with the aircraft and he'd say something like, "Roger that," cool as a cucumber. I put him in for the Silver Star.

The aircraft had an amazing effect. With that, our machine-gun fire, and the Kurds, we kept the enemy in check. Without aircraft support, there was no way we could have controlled them. We'd have been overrun.

For three or four hours we were in direct fire with a ton of Iraqi soldiers. Then later that afternoon the rest of the team with Captain

Carver came up. We consolidated our position. The enemy tried to outflank us, but fortunately Major Howard was monitoring the radio. He knew about our predicament, so he came up with a Quick Reaction Force (QRF) to help us. Major Howard and the QRF stayed right with my team that night, along with a whole bunch of Kurds. It was getting dark and we didn't want to fight at night with the Kurds because we hadn't trained with them. We said, "Okay, we'll quit for the night and bed down and form a plan in the morning."

The Kurds are incredible. They aren't on par with a Western military force, but they demonstrated command and control and they knew tactics. We actually trained with them a little bit on the fly. They picked up everything fast. They followed orders. We had one group that was like the Kurd Special Forces, and they stayed with us the whole time. Later in the week, there were a couple of Kurds wounded and killed. Their morale dipped a little bit. One of the Kurd leaders came up and told them, "This is war. That happens." The Kurds were very dedicated. They listened to us.

The next day we saw the enemy was dug in at the ridgeline. They had been hitting us hard with artillery throughout the night. They were firing tank rounds into our positions nonstop. It just rained 120mm and 155mm rounds, pretty heavy-duty stuff. Our plan was to shock them with B-52s, to basically walk them down this ridge, bombing as they went. Systematically, our aircraft bombed their heavy artillery along the ridge. We would pick targets, give Sergeant Gillett the coordinates, and he'd be on the radio to the aircraft. There was the large village of Khazir next to where we were bombing, so we had to be very careful. Our goal was to move out and get to a key bridge before the enemy blew it up. If we did that, we could take Mosul the next day. It was that close.

Once the B-52s did their bombing run, we started moving forward. There was an enemy trench network on the other side. We worked through that problem. We pushed forward toward the bridge and a lot of the Kurds made it across. Suddenly the Kurds came running back down the road screaming what sounded like "Dababa." Major Howard and the rest of us asked, "What the hell are they saying?" They were saying "Tanks!"

We could hear them coming at us—a deafening, grinding roar. We started to fall back. We weren't equipped and we weren't in a good spot. We were in low ground and had no defendable terrain. My big concern was defending the road. We dug in. If we were going to get overrun, we were going to fire everything we had at them. The Kurds had AK-47s and some RPGs, and that's no match for a tank. We had five Javelin missiles and five AT-4 rocket launchers. We got the aircraft back online but the enemy was using smoke generators. They were driving up and down with trucks, kicking up dust, so our aircraft couldn't see the tanks to bomb them.

Artillery was raining down on us. The enemy was putting up a hell of a fight. We didn't know it at the time, but we were up against a regular Iraqi infantry brigade, a battalion of armored Republican Guard and their fedayeen battalion commanders. This was the very best the enemy had to send into war.

We were pinned down and we formulated a plan. We would get the enemy vehicles that were within three thousand to thirty-five hundred meters with our Javelins. Once they ran out, we'd go to our AT-4s and RPGs. Then we'd take it from there. We were going to throw our heavy stuff at them first and hope for reinforcements or an opportunity to attack them from the air. The process took all day.

It started to get dark and their tanks came over the ridge onto the bridge. We couldn't see them, but they were firing into our position and artillery was just raining from the sky. We just waited. My whole team did what they were trained to do. It's not a natural thing—tanks were bearing down on us, and we just stayed there. We figured they'd attack at dawn, and in the meantime they'd refit, get ammunition and fuel, and get ready to overrun us.

Long story short, by the end of the night either navy or air force aircraft picked up their tanks on radar and decimated them. But the enemy had hidden a couple of tanks in the village buildings, so for the next five or six days, we just got pounded by those tanks. With artillery, you can hear it coming, but with tank rounds, once you hear the explosion, the tank round is already hitting your position.

For the better part of a week, it was back and forth. Every time we didn't have aircraft, they'd assault our positions. We would hit them with aircraft and seize some ground, but we couldn't hold it and we'd get pushed back. There were over six thousand enemy soldiers. They'd come with a bucket loader to take the dead bodies away. Then we'd see buses come in with fresh troops and they'd go right into their fighting positions.

One day a small group of us were assaulted by some infantry and we were going to get overrun. Captain Carver and Sergeant Perez and fifty Kurds fought their way up the side of the road to relieve us. They saved us. Another time, one of the Kurds was hit, so I jumped in a truck and weaved my way through artillery rounds, stopped, and scooped him up. I put him in the truck and drove back to our firebase. I'm sorry to say that he was dead at that point.

There were so many instances over that eleven-day period when there were bullets flying right by our ears. Or we could feel the heat of a tank round that skipped six inches over our heads. There are countless scenes. I was concerned about the welfare of my guys. We were very close. We'd been on the same team for a long time. Being a leader . . . sometimes I fought myself for being too close to my men. I did a lot of stuff myself because I live by the philosophy of "Follow me." I don't ask somebody to do something if I'm not willing to do it myself.

The battle continued for approximately eleven days straight, twenty-four hours a day. It was frustrating because their artillery was constantly pounding us. The air force and navy pilots of the aircraft carrier *Teddy Roosevelt* were awesome. At one point we were pinned down and about to get overrun. We needed help and the navy pilots were out of bombs. They came down pretty low and they used their machine guns and cannons to strafe the enemy. They stayed on position for us longer than they had to. They knew if the enemy heard their jets, they wouldn't attack us. There were times when they would tell us they were almost out of fuel and we wouldn't be getting aircraft for a couple of hours. I told the air force guys that if we lived through this, I'd wear my air force T-shirt to the next Army versus Air Force football game. That's exactly what I did, because my men and I wouldn't be here if it weren't for the U.S. Air Force.

The first couple of days were really intense and then we fell into a rhythm. Neither side wanted to fight at night. We'd fight hard all day; we'd fight a little bit in the evening. They'd shoot artillery at us throughout the night, so we'd call in aircraft to try to knock out their artillery. We had a guard shift so the rest of us could try to catch some sleep. But we didn't sleep because we were waiting for an artillery shell to land on us. We grabbed food when we could. We ate with the Kurds and ate whatever they ate, mostly beans and rice.

We needed cannons because we didn't have any connected with our team. The Kurds brought up these old World War II cannons left over from the British, the kind of old cannon pulled behind a truck. Sergeant Frazier and I went and laid them all out. We used the GPS and a map to locate our targets, and we coordinated a fire mission with these sixty-year-old cannons. We were going to use these cannons to support our next assault to try to take the bridge. We started with a bombing run by our B-52s, and then we planned to go to our cannons before taking the bridges. That was our plan. The morning we were going to do that, the enemy blew up the bridge and retreated. Then one of the most amazing things I've ever seen happened.

The Kurdish commander asked us what we were going to do. I called Major Howard for orders and he said, "If you make the bridge crossable in a couple of hours, use that bridge to go to Mosul." I relayed that to the Kurdish commander and also sent a reconnaissance team out to see if there was another way to get across the river. The Kurdish commander was very disturbed when I told him that if we couldn't get across this bridge in a couple of hours, we would have to part company. Immediately he had thousands of Kurds—I mean they came out of the woodwork—driving trucks into the river and pushing blown-up Iraqi vehicles in. They got rocks and dirt and rubble and junked cars—whatever they could find—to fill in the big chunk of a hole that was blown off the bridge. They worked with shovels and bulldozers and picks, and they were amazing. It wasn't pretty but it was passable. As I drove across this makeshift bridge, the song from *A Bridge Too Far* played in my head.

The next town we went into was a Christian village and the people lined the streets cheering. From there we went straight to Mosul, and our guys did great things in Mosul, especially with the small number of people we had.

I didn't put myself up for the Silver Star. Honestly, I was just doing my job. Getting medals isn't what I'm all about. When I went and got my award, I represented my whole team. The medal is a tribute to everything that my attachment did during our fighting in Iraq. As I wear it the rest of my life, I'll always think of the guys I was with, not what I did personally. There are amazing soldiers in the army and they're doing amazing things every day. And a lot of that story's not getting out.

★

Patrick Quinn is currently on active duty in the U.S. Army serving as an ROTC instructor at the University of Connecticut.

THAT A MAN LAY DOWN HIS LIFE FOR HIS FRIENDS

★

Scott Montoya, U.S. Marine Corps

Scout Sniper with the Second Battalion, Twenty-third Marines

Orange County, California

NAVY CROSS; IRAQ; 8 APRIL 2003

On the outskirts of Baghdad on April 8, 2003, Scott Montoya, the thirty-year-old marine they called "Grandpa," was bringing mail and cigarettes to his fellow marines when the scene erupted in a firefight that would last thirty hours. One after another, Scott carried four injured, dazed, or unconscious marines to safety while under enemy fire. When civilians were trapped in a disabled car in the middle of the road, in the thick of the fight, he hustled them to safety. "What I did," says Montoya, "was an action of love. This award is for all the marines that came before me and those that will come after me."

SCOTT MONTOYA

I was introduced to the martial arts when I was fourteen. When I first attended a class, I saw these guys doing things with their bodies that I couldn't imagine. As time went by, I looked at them and thought, *Hey, I can do that.* At first, I took general classes and devoted Tuesday and Thursday nights to it. The next year, it was Monday, Tuesday, Wednesday, and Friday. The studio was six miles from my house, and I would walk, run, or ride my skateboard. On school nights, my instructor, Paul Dye, would give me a ride home. He was an exceptional human being. I was what you'd call a young tiger, very quick to anger and very slow to forgive, and he was very, very patient with me. He showed me that the best thing in life is to be selfless, not selfish, to think of somebody else before yourself, and ultimately by helping others you help yourself. I've been in training at the same place for twenty-four years and Paul is like my surrogate father. He gave my life structure and that was good for me.

My home life was kind of chaotic. I had an older brother and sister, and a younger brother and sister. My father died when I was really young. Sometimes I got huge amounts of discipline and sometimes I didn't get any at all. The first time I put on my uniform, I knew that this was something special, something great. I behaved and got good grades because of martial arts and because Paul was the kind of guy who said, "If you can't respect your mom or you can't do well in school, you can't come here." To me, that would have been heartbreaking.

I took the Sheriff's Department test to become an employee and passed it. In the Sheriff's Department, there was a group of deputies who had a special bond with each other. It didn't matter if they knew each other; they just shared this special bond. They'd meet each other and greet each other in their own unique way, using words like

"Devil Dog" and "Leatherneck." What they had in common was that they'd been marines. That drove me crazy. I wondered, *What's so special about the Marine Corps?* I wanted that brotherhood. I wanted to become something greater than what I was. I wanted to be a part of that special brotherhood. I didn't want to join the military. I wanted to be a marine. I don't know how to explain it except to say that when you see something special in your life, you want to grab on to it.

I saved up all the money I could. I sold my car, computer, motorcycle, and stereo. I sold everything and put all my money—$6,000—in the bank, and then I joined the Marine Corps. I was twenty-five years old, and in boot camp they called me the "grand old man." Most of the guys were eighteen or nineteen. My drill instructors were around twenty-five. Week eight of boot camp was the hardest for me. I had to ask my friends and family for money to pay my house payment because I didn't want to lose it. I missed my girlfriend, who I loved very much. I missed my dogs. I missed my family and friends and I was thinking, *I'm really far away from home.* But I always knew I was going to make it. That wasn't even a question. Martial arts helped me with so many aspects: discipline, mental health, and physical strength. Obviously I could have run more. That's what everybody says. I ran so much in boot camp that it forced me into shape. I wasn't a spoiled kid growing up, so between that and my martial arts training, I excelled in the marines right away. I was the number-one guy from the first week.

When the Marines Corps evaluates you, they test you for maturity, leadership, physical fitness, stuff like that. Here I was twenty-five years old, I'd been a black belt since I was nineteen, and I'd been to college and gotten a degree. I'd already done a lot. All I wanted to do was be a marine. But I wanted to be what you call a "grunt," the infantry. It's the hardest job in the military and I wanted to do the hardest job. It means you hump a pack, you stay in the field, you're cold at night, you starve, they treat you like crap, but you also have the most exciting and most adventurous job in the Marine Corps. You're the first one to go to war. You get the best training. After basic training, I went to the School of Infantry to learn how to be a rifleman. They only make marines in South Carolina and San Diego. You're either a sand flea marine or a Hollywood marine. I was a Hollywood marine.

The training I took for the Sheriff's Department was simulated. In the Marine Corps, it's real. We threw real grenades. We blew up real mines and shot real weapons. I excelled in that too. When you grow up in a large family like I did—we had aunts and uncles and tons of us in that house—you become either selfish or selfless. You think either, *I want to get mine*, or you are into sharing. My mother taught me about sharing. If it looked like somebody was getting more McDonald's French fries than somebody else, she'd literally divide them out and make sure everybody got the exact same number. She'd level off the Cokes. She taught me that sense of fairness and I'm eternally grateful to her for that. That philosophy carried me through college, through the marines, and through Iraq. To me it didn't matter if you were the commandant of the Marine Corps or a PFC. What's right is right and what's wrong is wrong, no matter who you are or how long you've been doing it.

As a leader, I'm not a screamer. I'm not a dictator. To my marines I said, "I'm going to show you what I expect of you, exactly what to do and how to do it." I was really good at it. I would tell them to do something and they would move heaven and earth to do it. I know that the word "leadership" is not a noun, it's a verb. You have to stand up, make decisions, get dirty. You say, "Let's do it together." My guys always responded to that. They'd say, "Hey, Scotty can do it and he's not an exceptional athlete, he's not exceptionally smart or big or tough, but you know what, everything he asks us to do he does."

Leadership in the Marine Corps starts with knowing your marines. It goes like this: judgment, justice, decisiveness, integrity, dependability, tact, initiative, enthusiasm, bearing, unselfishness, courage, knowledge, loyalty, and endurance. Those are the benchmarks on which Marine Corps leadership is based, along with our values: honor, courage, commitment. These are the principles that accomplish the mission and ultimately take care of the troops. In the Marine Corps, you accomplish the mission first, then you take care of your troops. Mission first, but then you're thinking of somebody else before yourself.

When a lot of guys were called to go to Iraq, many said, "Yeah, I want to go and kick some butt." I wasn't like that. I was very intrigued by the chance to go there, but I was not looking forward to it and I was a little bit scared. I know this isn't the manly thing to say, but I was scared because if I died, I felt that my family would be very upset with me. I was supposed to get out of the Marine Corps, but I reenlisted and I didn't tell them. I extended to go to war. My mom and brothers and sisters aren't military people. It was hard for them to grasp that sense of loyalty to your country I had or the sense of loyalty to your brothers in the Marine Corps, the band of brothers.

I had been in the Marine Corps for nine years and I'd been to the School of Infantry, Scout Sniper School, Combat Man Tracking School, M.O.U.T. training, Martial Arts Instructor School, Survival Evasion Resistance and Escape, all of these special schools to make me into a well-rounded marine. Add to that thousands and thousands of hours of going to shoot houses and grenade houses and learning how to enter buildings and precision shooting from long distance on selected targets. I had extensive training. And all of a sudden, here comes the Super Bowl of it all. I wasn't scared for myself, but I was scared that if I died my family couldn't justify why I would do something like that.

My other side was telling me to do my job professionally and compassionately. I understood that I was going to somebody else's country. My country was calling me, but there are people in Iraq who have chosen not to fight and have laid down their arms. My job was not to kill them, raid them, pillage them, or steal a single thing. I did not take one thing that did not belong to me. Do not take one thing that doesn't belong to you. When I was in combat, I would go into a house where everyone was dead and everything from money to jewelry was around. I never took a thing. I would never allow anybody that I was with to take a thing, ever. The marines I was with would never think of doing that. It wasn't even an option. If we found gold bullion or a million dinars, we wouldn't have taken a thing. We would count it, bag it, and call and tell somebody to pick it up. We weren't there for that.

Sniper training is very individualized, a very specialized skill. When you're a Scout Sniper, it's very demanding. I would always think of this Psalm: "Blessed be the Lord who trains our hands for war, our fingers for battle, our loving God and our fortress, our stronghold and our deliverer, the one in whom we take refuge, the one who subdues people under us." That is how I would train. That was in my mind. I went to church before I left for war. My pastor would read Psalm 91 to me and tell me that I was protected by the shield of God's armor. I read this book before I left for Iraq titled *No Greater Love*. In the epilogue it reads, "Greater love hath no man than this, that a man lay down his life for his friends." I took that to heart. It was just a little paperback book, but it served the purpose of letting me know once again, service before self.

A lot of people ask me about April 8, 2003. And the long and the short of it is, there was nothing spectacular, nothing award-winning about it. I did the average things that average marines do. On that day we had gotten mail and mail is extremely morale raising. You pick a marine to write to and he'll be so happy. I can't explain it, just a letter from home, even if he doesn't know the guy. Even from a stranger. Especially if you don't get mail, it's huge, huge, huge! We separated the mail and went to deliver it to the other snipers who were assigned to Fox Company. We looked up their grid and drove out to their location. Someone, I can't remember who, asked us, "Do you mind going on patrol with us?" We replied, "Sure."

As we went on patrol with them, we ran into a firefight. We were on the outskirts of Baghdad, the little city called Saddam City. It was the most populated part of Iraq that I'd ever seen. There were buildings and small stores. There weren't cows or sheep or anything. It was more of an urban-type place. The other marines and I were basically shooting at everybody. Shop owners might come out and look to see what was going on, but they weren't fighting and we didn't engage them. If they were shooting at us, I shot back.

*Then it happened. We were on this block, sitting down and getting some rest, passing out the last of the water to Fox Company and our snipers. We stayed there for about an hour. We kept hearing rifle fire to our north but we thought one platoon from Fox Company must have made contact with the enemy. We were searching for any of Saddam's army. The fighting and the rifle fire started to increase. I had an uneasy feeling like you get before the shooting starts. I had already been in a couple of good firefights and I could tell this was going to be a good one. We were separated from the other platoon and we had no mortars or tanks for support. There was a lot of confusion because we didn't know what direction the bad guys were coming from. We changed directions two or three times. We were walking down the street indiscriminately, almost like guys walking through a village. We weren't sure what was going on. The small-arms fire was moving closer to our position.

We patrolled to another part of the city and met up with the other platoon. Now First, Second, and Third platoons were together. We were in a little part of the city where there were a lot of closed shops, kind of like a garment district in Los Angeles, although much smaller and the

---

*This excerpt comes from Scott Montoya's personal journal.

shops were closer together. We started to take small-arms fire, but then an explosion filled the area. Across the intersection we saw automatic and small-arms fire coming at us from all directions. An RPG hit right next to me. The fragments hit two marines who were standing next to me and they both went down. They were bleeding from the head and arm. The corpsman treated them and requested on the radio if we could medevac them to friendly lines. We had the only vehicle there, so we loaded the two marines up and Doc gave them some medical aid for their bleeding.

It was now clear the moment of passage had come. We were in one of the heaviest firefights that our company had ever seen. We were pinned down in all directions and we already had two hurt marines. We'd barely been in the fight for five minutes. The fighting started getting worse and we worried that the armed vehicle would drive at us. And then another explosion hit right next to me and broke a window on the wall. I had small pieces of shrapnel in my forearm and I was unsure if I was hurt. It was crazy. It was chaos. There was smoke everywhere. There were firefights going on indiscriminately around us. The platoon seemed to get down into a low position and started to spread out. I wanted to check out the area.

When I went to the other side of the building, just past where the two marines had been hit, I heard someone calling for a medic. I ran there and saw a white vehicle shot up. There were five people in it. There was a baby inside the vehicle along with other adults. I was not sure who shot the vehicle, but later I found out that it was us, because it wouldn't stop. A bunch of marines, maybe eight to twelve, moved across the street to the building that was open. Most of the snipers had already taken high ground and went to the top of the building. But something told me to stay down on the ground where the fighting was. I could do more damage if I was there. I could help people if I was there and I could find out where my fellow marines were laying down fire.

I saw a squad of marines making its way to the vehicle, and I guess I would have to say that I was a little bit scared but I knew that these were civilians and not Iraqi soldiers. They had just been caught up in a cross fire and they were sitting in the middle of the street bleeding to death. Three females and two males were inside the vehicle. We had to get them out of there. Two marines ran up to the vehicle with me and we tried to pull the driver out. The man was crying and shaking. He was talking in Arabic and seemed to be slipping into shock, when suddenly the Iraqis started shooting at us. He had a big gaping hole where his shin used to be and he was slipping in and out of consciousness. I pulled him around the corner, where the other docs were working on another woman. I asked what I could do to help. I noticed one of the women was screaming in Arabic and the other kept asking, "Why did you shoot us? Why did you shoot us?" I couldn't believe she spoke English. I asked her her name. She kept yelling, "I am dying, I am dying." She eventually told me her name was Anna and her sister was Nora.

There were explosions all around us and I knew we had to get off the street. We were being shot at from the mosque behind us, and I couldn't believe that they would actually shoot at us from a holy place. All the Iraqi civilians ran for cover. There were marines yelling and the bullets were striking the ground next to me. Nora was bleeding from her stomach. She was in great pain and it was horrible to hear her scream. We moved from that position and another position and more marines got hurt. The docs rendered some aid. I wasn't sure what was going on but I knew that we were deep into the fight. I knew this would be the test of all tests.

I ran across the street and saw a marine had been hit by an explosion, and I ran over there to pick him up and help him to safety. Everything started to break loose. We were in the middle of the fight and I could see rounds going down the street. I was leaning against the wall thinking that I was never going to make it to this marine. The other marines had left him lying in the middle of the street, and I knew if he stayed there he would surely be caught or taken prisoner. I knew I couldn't leave him there. I ran across the street, hoping to God that I wouldn't be shot.

Another marine helped me pull off what gear he was wearing. I attempted to pick him up twice but I couldn't lift him because he was too heavy. I had a bunch of adrenaline but I wasn't strong enough to lift him. I guess I was just weak. I came back to the section, picked the marine up, put him on my shoulders, and ran him about five hundred yards with rounds going by me striking the ground. Never was hit once. I couldn't believe it. The firefight continued. But I am tired now and I will write more later.

Saving marines didn't seem like a thing to document. I was just doing my duty. I never met those marines before that day. I didn't write about the marines; I was writing more about civilians. These people were caught up in a firefight in the middle of the street, where their car was shot up. The driver was dead. The passenger had a gaping wound in his leg. The only thing that was holding on from the knee down was just his calf muscle. He was screaming, going in and out of consciousness. Nora was hit in the belly and bleeding. The other woman had been shot in the finger and it had been knocked off. The grandmother was screaming in Arabic. There were bombs and explosions going around, RPGs were landing. And incredibly the baby was untouched.

You know the docs were trying to hold their composure, but I could see all their medical gear left on the street. I ran back and forth, risking getting shot, trying to get it all back. In the Marine Corps they teach you to develop what they call a casualty collection point, where all the resources of the docs go to one place instead of being spread out. If this doc doesn't have a needle, if that doc doesn't have a bandage, they can share supplies while they're working on these people.

Pretty soon, I was bringing marines back in—one, two, three marines—while this firefight went on. They were making fun of me: "That's number three, that's number four, that's number five." They were joking about it. I was running out, grabbing people, and bringing them in. I didn't log that in my journal because I didn't think it was particularly important or anything.

The Marine Corps is rich with warrior culture. The Marine Corps proudly calls itself a band of brothers. As a marine sergeant, I can tell you firsthand that the spirit is alive and well. We marines also believe that marines don't abandon their fellow marines. As a marine, you instinctively know that you're never alone and you will never be left behind, just as you do not leave others behind. Marines are acutely aware of their duty to preserve the warrior legacy handed down to them. Amen, brother.

When I was getting my medal, I remember this one marine was a Navy Cross recipient from the Korean War. They took a picture of us and he was hugging me, saying thank you. I looked at that picture later. If you look at his hands, he's missing two fingers. He had been in Korea and it was so cold his hand got frostbite and his fingers fused together and he lost them. His fingers almost looked webbed because he's missing his index finger. You could tell where the surgeons fused what was left of the meat of his hand together, and he is hugging me and you can see his hand on my back. It's amazing. Absolutely one of the best hugs I've ever had in my life. When marines like that come up to me and say, "Hey, thank you for carrying on my legacy," that's the greatest honor you can possibly have.

The medal is cool, don't get me wrong. There are a lot of people who said, "Oh, wow, this is great, Sergeant Montoya." They see the award and not the man. But the marine hugged me for being a man.

★

Scott Montoya is back home in California, living in Montclair and working full-time as a patrol deputy for the Orange County Sheriff's Department in the city of Stanton, California.

IT FELT WRONG NOT TO PULL THE TRIGGER

★

Thomas Adametz, Lance Corporal, U.S. Marine Corps

Winslow, Maine

SILVER STAR; IRAQ; 26 APRIL 2004

"I saw this crazy maniac firing away so all the marines could come back alive." That's how Lance Corporal Carlos Gomez-Perez described his brother marine's actions on April 26, 2004, in an alley in the northwest section of Fallujah. It was a five-hour firefight for Echo Company, Second Battalion, First Marines. Pinned down, surrounded, outnumbered, and with half the squad wounded, Lance Corporal

THOMAS ADAMETZ

Thomas Adametz took a stand in an exposed courtyard and grabbed a machine gun to fight off the advancing enemy only ten to twenty meters away. He saved his fellow marines from certain death. With Adametz providing covering fire, three trips were made to the medevac vehicle to load the wounded. One observer recalled: "Each trip was a religious experience with the closeness and number of enemy. One trip, Lance Corporal Tom Adametz was so close to us, protecting the wounded, that the noise from his SAW [squad automatic weapon] deafened me and the brass rained down on me." Adametz earned our nation's Silver Star for combat bravery.

My dad was with the navy for twenty years. He met my mom at Subic Bay in the Philippines. My brother and sister and I were all born in the Philippines. We moved to the States when I was a year old. My dad was stationed all up and down the East Coast, so every four years he'd reenlist and we'd move. I've lived everywhere from Georgia to Canada. I must have gone to seven different schools, maybe more. His last duty station was the Naval Air Station in Willow Grove, Pennsylvania. Then he retired and we moved to Maine. I finished high school in Winslow.

I kind of got scared before graduation. The guidance counselor was getting together information for a flyer with every graduate's name and what they were planning to do next. I didn't know. I remember one buddy of mine, his name was Maxwell, said, "Man, if I could, I'd go right into the marines." I looked at him and said, "Yeah, you know, Max, that's not a bad idea." Most people going into the marines jump right into it. Other people sit around and think about it. I'm one of those who jumped right into it.

Basic training was on Parris Island, South Carolina. I really didn't know what to expect. We were finally introduced to our four drill instructors, and our senior drill instructor said, "You're on my time now." Pretty much all hell broke loose. Basic training was real hard physically, and mentally, too. The yelling was constant. These were kids, teens taking it to heart, and they were crying a lot. I told them, "You know, these guys don't know you. Just have a thick skin. If the drill instructor says, 'Hey, are you an idiot?' just tell them what they want to hear and they'll leave you alone." Really, any Joe on the street could complete it, no problem, as long as he could stick it out mentally.

After I left basic training, I had ten days of leave before reporting to Camp Lejeune, North Carolina, for all my infantry training. This was going to be my job for four years. When I was talking to my buddy, I said, "If I'm going to be in the marines, I'm not going into anything else but the infantry." I wanted to do the hardest job. I wanted to be on the front line.

I reported to California for a six- or seven-month training cycle. We started hearing rumors about making our way to the Middle East. I said to myself, *Well, this is what we get paid to do.*

I'd say I was 90 percent scared and 10 percent excited. Or it may have been 90 percent excited and 10 percent scared. By that time I'd been in the marines for barely over a year, but I felt I was trained and ready to go. I was over in Iraq for Operation Iraqi Freedom twice.

The first time we pushed through from Kuwait to Iraq we were riding in assault vehicles. There were a bunch of reporters with us. Most of the time the Iraqi forces really didn't put up a fight. We would point a weapon at them; they'd throw down their weapons and throw up their hands. They had been out of food and water for a couple of weeks. We captured quite a few, well over four hundred prisoners, on the first day. We treated them fine. We kept pushing forward to the city of An Nasiriyah, and believe it or not, I still hadn't fired my weapon once. The enemy didn't want to fight.

We were the reaction force. Wherever the military wanted us, that was where we went. We didn't get a whole lot of resistance. I think the Iraqi soldiers were happy to surrender because they knew we were going to give them food and water if we captured them.

My best memory from that tour was of this elderly man walking with his son over to us. The son was translating what his father was saying: "Thank you. I've been waiting seventy years to be free and now I'm free."

We got the order that they didn't need us anymore so we hopped on a C-130 cargo plane. We were back in the States for eight months and then we were called back overseas again.

We got our orders to go to Fallujah next. I did my research, and it was described as hell on earth. The soldiers in the 101st Airborne were saying that it wasn't a matter of *if* you'd get a Purple Heart, it was a matter of *when*. I'd torn the ACL [anterior cruciate ligament] in my right leg and had reconstructive surgery, so I didn't have to go to Fallujah. In fact, the doctor on the transport ship recommended that I not go. On my own wishes, I went back into battle. The doctor made me sign a waiver. That pretty much set the tone for everybody else: I hurt my leg and I'm fighting. The message was: you guys need to suck it up.

We had a tight-knit unit, a bunch of comedians. We were like brothers. If I've got five bucks in my pocket, you've got five bucks in your pocket. I'd give you the shirt off my back and you'd do the same for me. Carlos Gomez-Perez was a rifleman in our group. He was originally from Mexico City, Mexico, and now he's from El Cajon, California. He's a natural born leader. He's an animal. He's so smart and he knows so much and then he puts it to use.

We were all sitting around in Kuwait for a week and then we started to convoy up. It took us about thirteen hours to get from the border of Kuwait to Fallujah. We were lucky because we didn't see one roadside bomb the whole way. Then we reached Camp Fallujah. I remember guys from the 101st Airborne telling us that if we did foot patrols in Fallujah, we were crazy. It was something that had always been done on mounted patrol. When we finally took over for them, we didn't know what to expect. I remember hearing these *thud, thud, thud*s, and I thought, *What the hell is that?* We were getting mortared and rocketed every single day. For the first three days, we were running around, grabbing our helmets and body armor, but the army guys were doing nothing. They told us, "Don't worry, you'll get used to it."

We started out doing mounted patrols in Fallujah, just getting situated. The next thing we knew, a roadside bomb blew up and marines died. Colonel Olsen said that we weren't going to have that, and that we should get ourselves ready to go into the city. This was the first foot patrol ever done by the military in Fallujah. At the time we got our orders, we were watching the story of the three American contractors who were captured inside the city and were burned and hanged from the bridge.

The first day we patrolled for eight hours and we ran out of water by the end of the day. We were all dehydrated because the temperature was pushing ninety-five degrees. We received a couple of potshots, RPGs, and there was a car bomb detonated near one of the other platoons. We returned to the observation post and let the people who lived in Fallujah know that we were coming into the city and that they should leave. We got our orders to push into the city. You could see this fairly intense firefight going on. We were driving in our Humvee getting shot at by snipers, and mortar rounds were impacting next to us. I was thinking, *This ain't good.*

We had orders to link up with the rest of the company. Our first mission was to take this old schoolhouse, a big two-story building with an open courtyard. We took a lot of casualties, men I've known since I checked into the unit. I thought, *Wow, this is war.*

We didn't want to keep our platoon there so we ended up changing places with the Third Platoon on the ring, the outskirts of the city. We were in a house near a cemetery and the mosque. We were receiving potshots and mortar rounds but nothing too intense. We stood on the roof and could see the insurgents running around the streets, darting from house to house and hugging the eight-foot walls that surrounded every home.

I remember being on watch with Lance Corporal Sanchez from Inglewood, California. I said, "Hey, I got a bad feeling." Everybody else had that same feeling. About four thirty a.m., it was still dark out and we really couldn't see, so we were all wearing night-vision goggles. We got tapped to go to a house on the north side of a T intersection. We patrolled the nearby cemetery and then scaled the wall with a makeshift ladder. We moved through so quietly you couldn't tell we were there. There was no activity whatsoever.

I was on the downstairs floor just waiting, watching for anything going on. Our mission was to locate the enemy and take them out. At eight a.m. one of the other teams took a mortar round to the house they were in. No one was hurt, but the enemy knew we were there. We got orders to leave half of our squad inside the house and the other half would go and clear out this big mosque. It was eight stories, straight up in the air. We cleared it out and didn't find anything. We pushed back to our friendly lines and rested for twenty minutes.

Then we heard six or seven loud explosions on top of our roof. We had been so worried about looking down the street and trying to find sniper positions that we forgot about the houses right next to us. There were insurgents on the roof of the house next door launching grenades. The next thing I knew, Lance Corporal Fincannon ran down the stairs missing half his left arm. The insurgents had thrown a grenade and Fincannon was trying to use his body to protect his machine gun. He's a machine gunner and he didn't want anything to happen to his weapon.

Corporal Gomez ran upstairs to help bring the wounded down. We got on the handset and told them we needed medevacs. Instantly, we ran outside. I was shooting my M16 through a window right across from where I was standing. About the closest target was fifteen meters away. I was shooting fast and burned through two magazines like they were nothing. I saw insurgents with turbans, beards, and AK-47s running back and forth. I was just amazed; they were in the building right next to us. If I had wanted to, I could have jumped from one rooftop to the next where they were. We fought and fought, and then I went back in to reload a magazine into my M16. A grenade went off in the courtyard. Lance Corporal Valencia took shrapnel to the left leg. Our assault gunner fell to the ground, too. A machine-gun crew picked up his machine gun. I went out there shooting my M16. We had some impressive fire going on. While this was happening in the courtyard, there was still this crazy battle going on upstairs on the roof.

Gomez was readying to go back up on the rooftop because we had to retrieve Buchanan's M240G machine gun. Gomez looked at me and said, "Hey, you got grenades?" I took out my two grenades and gave them to Gomez, one of which he then gave to Austin. They went to the third-floor roof for the machine gun, a radio, and a sniper rifle. As soon as they got up there, they were just blasting away from the rooftop. Austin took his grenade out, pulled the pin, and threw. As he did, he got hit. The shot spun him around 360 degrees. The bullet came right inside his body armor where there is no plate and came out his back. Gomez threw his grenade onto the enemy's rooftop and grabbed Austin. As he was pulling him to safety his body armor got caught. Gomez got shot in the left shoulder. If he had been a normal person, like myself, the bullet would've ripped his arm clear off. But Gomez, he's a beast. The exit wound was the size of my fist, but Gomez kept going, doing CPR on Austin, beating on his chest, trying to get a heartbeat out of him. They took him downstairs, where the medic, Dan, gave him a tracheotomy to get him breathing again.

I was trying to provide suppressive fire with my M16, which wasn't working at all. I picked up the machine gun and ran outside and started blasting away. When I first got the machine gun, my adrenaline was pumping. For some reason the gun wasn't firing, so I grabbed the barrel, which was red hot, just glowing and melting. I burnt my hand instantly, third-degree burns before I had even started shooting. I emptied a whole drum of two hundred rounds. I went back in for more ammo. The only way I could effectively engage the enemy was from a totally exposed area. Lance Corporal Bell did the same thing. Bell had an M203, a rifle with a grenade launcher underneath it. He fired a grenade right through the window, and when he did, this face popped up, an insurgent. We were ten to fifteen meters away from this house. All I remember was Bell hitting the trigger and then hearing this little *blink* sound as the grenade launched and then the explosion when it hit. The grenade armed itself and blew up in this guy's face. We said, "Whoa, yeah!" Everyone was getting pumped up.

I was firing from an exposed position in the courtyard. I was shooting so much that the barrel seized up on me. I got that barrel off and threw another one on. A Humvee pulled up with Sergeant Major Skiles, who was trying to assess the situation and get the wounded out. They were going to need cover fire. I said, "I got it." I was out there shooting away into these windows. Insurgents were running by the house shooting back at us. Cruz was out there with the machine gun and he saw this object get thrown over his left shoulder. I remember because it was like slow motion: I looked at the object and then back at Cruz, and we looked at each other at the same time and yelled, "Grenade!" It was like an old World War II pineapple grenade with red striping on it, sitting right there on the ground. We tried to run back into the house where everybody else was, but it was just a regular-sized doorway. Cruz and I managed to barge in and we heard the grenade go off. Lance Corporal Bell was the only one hit because he couldn't get through the door fast enough. He got a dime-sized fragment in his hip. He walked in the house and saw that there were some hurt worse than he was, so he said, "Well, I'd better go back."

The whole time I was shooting, I noticed this tree sticking out. I remember thinking as I was firing, *Why are all these leaves falling to the ground?* They were just falling and falling. Little did I know that we were taking sniper fire from the mosque that we'd cleared out. I fired and fired. It felt wrong not to pull the trigger. If I didn't pull the trigger, the insurgents were going to overwhelm us. The after-action report stated that they had 360 degrees on us. We were being attacked by fifty insurgents who were being reinforced by 150 more. These guys were coming up the street in a regular public transportation bus, just like they were going to work. It was crazy. Their reinforcements were never-ending.

At one point I remember this petty officer running along a wall near me. I could see the impact of the bullets chasing him. It looked like every bullet was getting closer. Every step was just a little bit faster than the bullet impacts. He slid into the house. I was providing cover fire for everybody. I had tunnel vision. My adrenaline was pumping. I didn't think twice about getting hit by a bullet. I thought, *I'm not going to die in this country.*

I was the only cover for the people getting the wounded out of there. It was me. Otherwise they had no cover whatsoever. They were all saying thank you, even the wounded. I didn't realize how many people were going past to get to the Humvee. I think we had eight major casualties that day. There might have been ten minor ones. Just my hands were hurt. I started to blister up from burning them. I looked like the Stay Puft Marshmallow Man.

I remember saying, "We gotta get out of here, there's an air strike coming." We were the last to go, myself and Corporal Gomez. This kid was so hard-core he was trying to change magazines with one hand. I told him his arm wound was huge and he said, "Really?" We were the last ones to leave. I said, "Gomez, I'll pop out and shoot and you go," and he said, "No way." We were arguing back and forth about who was going to go first. Finally, I said, "Shut up and go," and he did. We made it back to safety. We got there and they called in an air strike on our two buildings. That ended the firefight. The first sergeant told me afterward that the enemy had been so close there was an empty magazine from an AK on top of the hood of our Humvee.

A couple of days afterward, I picked up a machine gun like the one I used. It had a full drum of ammo on it and I put it to my shoulder. I thought, *There's no way, this thing is way too heavy to be firing from my shoulder.* The gun weighs something like twenty-three pounds. I had been shooting a twenty-three-pound machine gun from my shoulder and hip. Everybody was cheering me on and calling me a crazy man. I was going completely nuts. The adrenaline was kicking so much that it didn't even faze me. Sometimes I look back and think that there's no way I could've done it. No way it's true. When it was all happening, it was like a bad nightmare.

People tell me, "Wow, that's impressive what you've done." I was just doing my job. The United States asked us to be there and to help the Iraqi people. That's what we're there to do. I don't think we're going to leave until the job is done. Maybe there are a lot of sacrifices that people have to make so other people can have a better life. I know that when a soldier, a sailor, an airman, or a marine goes overseas, they're going to do the best job they can to help those people. And they're going to get it done.

When I first got my Silver Star, I gave it to my parents. I figured it was more for them than for me.

★

Tom Adametz has left the United States Marine Corps and attends college in Pittsburgh, Pennsylvania.

BALANCING ACT

★

Leandro Baptista, Sergeant, U.S. Marine Corps

Bravo Company, Second Platoon, First Reconnaissance Battalion

Born Rio de Janeiro, Brazil; hometown: Miami, Florida

SILVER STAR; FALLUJAH, IRAQ; 7 APRIL 2004

Sixty fortified insurgents ambushed a convoy south of Fallujah on April 7, 2004, and Sergeant Baptista led the counterattack and turned the tide. He sprinted across a shallow canal, climbed a ten-foot berm, and charged the enemy. Under fire, he knocked out one machine-gun nest, disarmed an improvised bomb, and led the attack against eleven insurgents from two angles. Baptista killed at least four insurgents at close range.

LEANDRO BAPTISTA

I grew up in Rio de Janeiro. It was great and I have only good memories of my childhood. There is a lot of contrast between rich and poor and there is a history of violence, but apart from that it is generally great people and a great place.

Ever since I was young, I always liked the military. It was one of my dreams to be a soldier. My philosophy was, If I'm going do something, I might as well go all the way. I looked around and I saw that the best military was the United States'. I went to the U.S. embassy, I got a book about the Naval Academy, and there was a picture of a marine. I moved to the United States by myself when I was fourteen, to get a head start. I lived with a guardian I didn't even know, a friend of a friend of my dad's. It was my first time living away from home, so all I could do was go to school, study, and learn the language.

I'd taken English courses in Brazil for a few years but it was one of those one-hour-a-day, twice-a-week deals. I wasn't prepared for a full conversation at all. Math was the only class that I had a good time in. In Miami, they speak a lot of Spanish, too, so it was hard. It took me a while but I eventually caught on.

I joined the marines in 2000, when I was twenty years old. I always looked at it as the elite military unit in the United States. I didn't want to settle for less. I was hard-core; I really liked the warrior spirit. I enlisted as an infantry marine. Basic training was at Parris Island, South Carolina, and it was an interesting experience. It was a real awakening into military life and its discipline. I can't say that it was what I expected or that I enjoyed it. Shooting a rifle is a great thing. They put all that stress on us because in combat there's going to be a lot of stress. At the beginning of boot camp, it was like I was breaking my crust, adapting to the whole military life. I can say basic training made me a stronger leader. My confidence level shot up sky-high. I thought I could do anything I wanted. My English got a lot better. We talked to each other as men. The brotherhood, that's where it all started, in boot camp. It's lasted all the way from boot camp till now and it's going to last all my life.

I was happy to know we were going to Iraq. In the military we do a lot of hard-core training. There are those who have been in the military for twenty years but have never had the chance to use what they learned and practiced for, like training for a football game and never getting to play. I was feeling happy because we'd just gone through training and now I would have a chance to utilize all the skills I had just learned. I was happy and it was scary at the same time. I was young and thought I was invincible.

Training can take you only so far, and then you've got to fill in the rest yourself. During my first and second tours to Iraq, after making my transition to the recon community, I was with Bravo Company, Second Platoon, First Recon Battalion, First Marine Division, and these guys are real characters to start with. It was a tight group. They all had this warrior mentality times three. There were a lot of big egos and strong personalities. Very smart marines. They had all excelled in some area of their life and they were put together into this one tight unit. It was just a recipe for success.

I actually haven't told the story of what happened on April 7, 2004, so I might be a little shaky on the details, but I'll tell you as much as I remember. It was my second time in Iraq; we were moving from Base Camp Fallujah and we really weren't on a mission yet. We were going through a main supply route that was well known for the heavy presence of improvised explosive devices. We were going down this road across the Euphrates, a two-lane road with a gas station to our right. We stopped for a security patrol, which was part of our standard operation procedures. We got out of our vehicles and conducted a 360-degree search and checked spots around our vehicles for IEDs. We felt things weren't right. There was a crowd of people gathered at the gas station, like they were waiting for a show to happen. A lot of kids, who are usually running around, they weren't running around.

On down the road, past the gas station, things just felt out of place. We took this as a sign of potential contact with the enemy. Even though we knew that it was there, we weren't going to turn away. We just kept pushing through. I got this eerie feeling something bad was going to happen. We kept pushing down the road. There were four vehicles in front of ours; we were in the fifth and final vehicle. Each vehicle carried a five-man team except vehicle four, which had four marines. Behind us were a couple of supply vehicles, but they weren't fighting units. Of course, everybody in the Marine Corps is a rifleman, but they were quite a far distance away from us.

All hell broke loose. The enemy started the ambush with machine-gun fire and incoming mortars. We didn't know where it all was coming from at first. Everybody was speeding, racing down the road, and we saw that the first three vehicles were in the kill zone right away. Mortar rounds landed everywhere around us. We could see the machine-gun fire kicking up asphalt. Dust clouds formed everywhere around us.

We trained for an ambush and we executed our training. The vehicle in front of ours turned hard right—a ninety-degree right—and we went down a dirt road that led us across a canal through a small concrete bridge. We crossed this bridge with the fourth vehicle, which was now in the lead. As soon as we had turned, the machine-gun fire focused on us, because they saw we were trying to flank them. They didn't like that at all.

Immediately, I told my gunner to engage with the .50-cal on our turret. The vehicle in front of ours had a Mark 19 and they started engaging, too. As soon as we stopped, we got off our vehicles while the gunners maintained suppressive fire. In the meantime, vehicles one, two, and three were still drawing heavy fire on the road and an RPG hit vehicle number one. Half of their team got knocked out. The team leader sitting in the front right seat got shot through the right arm. The guy in the turret got shot in the leg. Their radio operator suffered the worst, losing both arms as the RPG seared through the right side of the vehicle and out the back. They were trying to push through the kill zone. The team leader started shooting with his left hand because he had a golf ball–size wound in his right arm. Vehicles two and three were staggered in the kill zone, but still using their vehicles and whatever terrain was available to get some cover and keep engaging the enemy. During this initial engagement, the platoon commander was fatally shot during a blunt counterattack, after having crossed the canal while going over the berm on foot. Vehicles one, two, and three were still getting lit up. We were, too, but we were in a better position to do something about it. A couple of us had sniper rifles, so we engaged the enemy with those. The ambush was about a whole kilometer long.

If you can picture it, a canal ran parallel to the right of the road all the way down; next to the canal, on the far side, was a berm. A few small concrete bridges crossed the canal. Secondary canals ran perpendicular to the main canal, past the berm, every four hundred meters or so. On the other side of the berm, there were about fifteen enemy machine-gun positions, each with two or three enemies with RPGs and AKs. We didn't know that at the time of the attack. Initially, after making the hard right crossing the concrete bridge and the berm, we ended up along a secondary canal separating us from the enemy to our left. From this location, we only had contact with the four closest enemy positions. We continued engaging with our sniper rifles and went over this waist-deep canal on foot toward the enemy, and set up positions on the other side. We were trying to get closer to the kill zone to help out the first three vehicles, but Murphy's Law was in effect and it was a mess. We started taking fire from almost every side. It was just everywhere.

After suppressing some of the enemy, we got back in our vehicles and got back on the road. We moved a few yards closer to the kill zone, and I dismounted with about four marines. We bounded laterally across the canal and the berm once again. We'd cover and then we'd charge, cover and charge. We pinned down the enemy, didn't give them much of a chance to fight back, and we killed them. We killed four guys and collected their weapons and put them in the vehicles. At that point, the medevac arrived, but we had no idea who was injured and who wasn't. We just had to take care of business. Our guys were in an ambush. We got back in our vehicles and got back on the road and moved forward.

We saw vehicles that we thought were vehicles one, two, and three and we moved up, and then stopped. In order to get in a better position to support the rest of the element, my vehicle went off the road to the right, leaving vehicle four still on the road. As I went off road, my gunner told me he saw a wire stretching all the way from the berm to the road. I told my driver to halt the vehicle just past another small concrete bridge just short of the berm. I got off and, concerned with the possibility of enemies nearby, told two of my guys to start clearing to the right. I followed the cable along toward the road, and it turned out to be an IED. I yelled for the vehicles to push farther down the road, and I waved the Quick Reaction Force that had just arrived away from the bombs. I followed the cable back to its point of origin and disengaged the IED myself. I didn't want to wait for anybody. I figured it was a pretty simple setup, so I supposed that I could do it myself. There were no booby traps or anything, just a cable, positive and negative through a semi-full circuit. I just broke that circuit before it could become a full circuit, and that deactivated the IED.

When I was walking back to my vehicle, there was a big explosion and I dove for cover. I thought it was an incoming mortar that had hit right next to us, but actually an enemy guy had popped a grenade and he was trying to kill himself and my two guys who were clearing to the right. He wasn't able to kill our guys. In an instant, my gunner whispered to me that there were bad guys to the left of our vehicle, so I started to engage them and I took three of them down.

I kept moving along the berm and saw more and more of the enemy. I was clearing all by myself with my gunner shooting over my right shoulder with a 240G machine gun (our secondary turret gun, since the .50-cal was down due to a malfunction). I saw another guy farther down. I engaged that one, took him down, and kept moving. There was a fifth guy I took down and a sixth that I am not sure remained alive, because I could not pinpoint his location. I wasn't sure because at that point I had a little bit of tunnel vision. I was reloading on the move, dropping mags, reloading, shooting, you know, dodging for cover.

My driver and gunner took the initiative to drive up to where I was. They caught up to me to give support because I was all by myself up there. We all started to link up as a team. A senior enlisted caught up to my position and told me the colonel wanted the ambush area evacuated right away because of all the casualties we had taken. I was a little pissed off about that because we had turned the ambush around. We had them on the run. All we had to do was clean up that area now. We still had sporadic fire but it was no big deal. I had to follow orders. I said, "Sir, roger that."

I told my driver to back up. We fired suppressive fire from the hood. We saw machine-gun positions every five meters or so. The enemy seemed to be on some kind of drug. There were sacks of a substance that appeared to be hashish, but I am not sure; I'm not an expert, so don't take my word for it. They had water jugs filled with fluid to sustain themselves. It was actually a very well-set-up ambush. They had the higher ground. They had IEDs on the road. They were waiting for us and they had all kinds of weaponry. I guess they didn't know the unit they were messing with. They thought they were going to shoot up a convoy, and a lot of convoys that get fire just try to barge through because they don't have the firepower or the mind-set to fight back. We were ready for a fight.

One marine was killed and six or seven were wounded out of a platoon of twenty-four. I might have lost some hearing for a while but that was about it. As far as coping with the death and casualties, we did it as well as a family could. We went back to the barracks, but we didn't have as much of a break as you'd think. I don't think they wanted to give us time to think about things and get depressed. They figured if we had another mission to think about, that would help us in the coping process.

I was in Iraq another six months and then I came home. It was time for me to go. My enlistment was up. I loved what I did, I enjoyed reconnaissance, I enjoyed the whole experience. A lot of good things, a couple of bad things. I'd seen most of it, or at least some of it, and I decided it was time for me to get out. There was a girl I had a crush on. You know, it's always a girl.

As far as the stories I heard and the things I saw, for me, that was enough justification for going in there. I didn't need any weapons of mass destruction. We found piles of bodies, not just men, but women and children too, piled up in some underground chambers because they spoke their minds or they didn't feel right about the government at the time. Iraq could be a great country. It's a beautiful area. It really is.

I was never one of those guys who came home after the war and used it as an excuse. Everything is normal for me. I've still got my fighting spirit, my warrior spirit. My life is all about going back to the action and making my wife happy. My life is that balancing act between my warrior side and her. As far as earning the Silver Star goes, what happened happened because I was in a position to take charge and do something about the ambush. I didn't do it because I'm some super-warrior. I was just in the position to do it and I had the training and the mind-set to do it. I'm just a regular guy like everybody else, just doing my job. I believe everybody in the platoon there in the ambush deserves some kind of award, because in the end, what counts is teamwork. My Silver Star is in the garage. It's not hidden or anything; it's there with my Marine Corps stuff.

It is not easy to stand aside and watch others do the fighting for me.

Sergeant Baptista has recently reenlisted with the USMC, having reported to First Force Recon on August 2, 2006.

LAY THE HAMMER DOWN

★

Neil Prakash, First Lieutenant, U.S. Army

Second Battalion, Sixty-third Armor Regiment, First Infantry Division

Born in India; hometown: Syracuse, New York

SILVER STAR; BAQOUBA, IRAQ; 24 JUNE 2004

With Baqouba under siege, Avenger Company, 2-63 AR BN, headed into the city just north of Baghdad with Prakash's First Platoon in the lead. In an hour-long battle spread out over one kilometer, well-trained insurgents poured RPG and machine-gun fire onto the tanks and unleashed an onslaught of IEDs. Prakash is credited with eliminating eight enemy positions, an enemy resupply vehicle, and several insurgents during the battle. He earned the Silver Star.

NEIL PRAKASH

My parents moved to America before I was born, but my mom went back to India, to a smaller city near Bangalore called Chikmagalur, to have me. She was more comfortable giving birth to me in India, where all her family lived. Both my parents were raised and educated in India; my mother is a dentist and my father is an orthodontist. As a kid, I had a straight-up, normal American childhood. My parents encouraged me to play the piano and my older brother to play the violin. I didn't like the piano and my brother didn't like the violin. He pushed for guitar, and by the fifth grade I was playing the drums. They tried to get us to play tennis but my brother loved football, and he was my hero so I played football, too. We had a very good childhood. My brother and I have always done very, very well in school.

When I was fourteen I had really bad back pain after the football season was over. My mom took me to a spine specialist and they did an MRI. It turns out I had a congenitally narrow spinal canal, bulging discs in my lower back, pinched nerves, and that's what caused a lot of numbness in my legs. The doctor told me I'd be in a wheelchair by the time I was twenty-one. I cried because I couldn't play football anymore. One of my friends wanted me to try out for cross-country. I said, "Dude, I'm 185 pounds and a center on the football team." But he convinced me and I started running and I had a really good time with it.

I wanted to go to West Point and I got the congressional nomination to go. I never told them about my back problems, but when they looked at my medical records, they found out.

I applied to Johns Hopkins as my backup but I was die-hard about going to West Point. On June 11, 1998, I got the letter saying they were sorry to inform me but my medical waiver was denied. I was brokenhearted but I went to Johns Hopkins University. My second or third week there, I saw my first ROTC cadet. I loved the uniforms and I said to myself, *I've got to do this.* It turns out Johns Hopkins has one of the oldest and best ROTC programs in the country. I joined and I fell in love with it. I did Ranger Challenge, which is the ROTC version of Ranger training. I went to Air Assault School, where we rappelled from a Black Hawk helicopter. I was close to being kicked out of ROTC because of my back but finally I got a family friend, Dr. Ravi Shah, to give me a medical waiver. I got a two-year scholarship.

At the end of my junior year, I saw my first tank at Fort Lewis and I knew that was what I wanted to do. My parents were hoping that I'd go to medical school but they saw how happy I was in the military; they got excited right along with me. They were 100 percent supportive. I graduated from Johns Hopkins, got commissioned, attended Armor Officer Basic Training in Fort Knox, Kentucky, finished that, competed to go to Ranger School, got a slot, went to Ranger School, proposed to my girlfriend, and went off to Germany.

Ranger School was way harder than anything in Iraq. Way harder. Physically and mentally. Ranger School is like this: They take away a person's food and their sleep for sixty days. They put him through the worst physical conditions and roughest terrain, and they make him lead his peers. They determine what his threshold of pain is and how far he can push other people. I had a gimpy back but I knew I could do it. I didn't quit. There wasn't too much you could apply from Ranger School to actual combat as far as skills. But I'll tell you, on June 24, when I got in that ambush and my soldiers were saying that they were going to pass out, I told them, "No, you're not. Suck it up. I've been through hotter and sweatier and more dehydrated situations than this. You can do it."

I was excited to be in Iraq and I was eager to prove myself. When

I was home on R and R, my dad asked me how I felt about going to war. I told him that I'm not a warmonger but I love my job. I said, "Imagine going to medical school and never practicing on a patient." He understood. What people have to understand is that those of us in the military love the mission and we want to see it through. That's not a political statement; it's just a testament to how great and disciplined our military is and how awesome our sense of integrity and security is. We don't decide policy. We execute the military side of it.

It all began on June 23. We were setting up what we call OPs, Observation Posts. My wingman and I went out in our tanks and sat with other tanks on a path of road in front of FOB Scunion and FOB Warhorse. The first patrol was from three a.m. to six a.m. Pretty boring; not much happened. When we came in at six o'clock, we heard all this gunfire. While we refueled, we heard big explosions. It was the air force dropping bombs. The 1-6 Field Artillery Battalion was in heavy fire so I knew we had a mission coming up, even though tanks don't usually go into the city. We went back out; we were monitoring the net and we knew something was going down. Keep in mind we'd been up since midnight so we were exhausted. We heard a crazy amount of gunfire. I called in and they told me to be on the lookout for about twenty-five armed insurgents carrying RPGs, coming our way. We saw nothing.

About ten a.m. they called us in and we reported to our company commander. Our whole company geared up and was doing weapons checks and loading up ammunition. My commander told me the enemy had taken control of the city. They were sending in our tank company to lay the hammer down. First Platoon would be in the lead. I was fired up. I hadn't seen any combat action yet. We were all lined up, waiting for the green light. On the battalion net I heard, "Avenger Six, this is Lion Three." He was about to give my boss a situation report. He said we were going to face two hundred armed, well-trained insurgents who intended to stand and fight. They weren't going to run. They were on the rooftops in groups of four using RPGs and RPG-7s. They said the attack would start from our left and then come from all sides. I wondered how the hell they knew all this. We'd never had that kind of intelligence before. I found out later that there was an unmanned drone circling above, looking at the insurgents.

We got ready to push off and I thought, *Damn, I forgot my chewing tobacco.* My gunner, SGT Pritsolas, offered me a smoke. I don't know how to smoke and it's not permitted in the tank, but I did it anyway. The sergeant major stood outside my tank, ready to wave us through, and he just shook his head at me. I smiled at him. I was fired up but I was nervous.

We got the green light and we filed out in a single line. We got to the perimeter of the city and were about to pass over a footbridge when we spotted a five-gallon water can on the ground. It didn't look American, kind of suspicious. I thought, *What if that blows up?* It was quiet. No people. No one walking around. All of a sudden, an RPG came flying out from the left, one hundred meters away, and blasted the left side of my tank. I told my gunner, "Left." He took the gun left and blasted this house. I was pretty confident we'd taken out any enemy who were in that house.

The entire median of the road erupted. Later we counted twenty-three craters, IEDs buried in the median. The whole left side of our column just exploded. Then all hell broke loose. They shot at us from every side. Of the four-man enemy teams on the rooftops, one detonated the IED, a second fired the RPG, a third sprang up with a machine gun, and a fourth tried to lob grenades into our tanks. We pulled the hatches down. My gunner was looking for targets all over the street but he had tunnel vision. Tanks were designed to engage from one to four kilometers away. The enemy was just thirty meters away, and my gunner was yelling, "Where are they?" I was seeing everybody because I was on the outside of the tank, totally exposed. I grabbed the override and I held down the machine gun trigger, just spraying bullets. I got the .50-cal on top of my tank and I was hitting guys on rooftops.

Guys were running in front of us, red and green scarves wrapped around their faces, so I could only see their eyes. They would just stand, square their shoulders, put their RPGs to their shoulders, and shoot at us. When an RPG comes at you, it looks like a baseball. It comes at you swirling, not straight at you, and when it explodes, it's not the fireball you see in the movies. It's fast enough that you can't do anything about it but slow enough that you can see it coming. I can't describe it. It would explode right in front of my face. My ballistic eyewear was getting peppered with the explosive. I could taste it, metallic and gritty. The RPGs were hitting our hatch and my driver was screaming, "I just got hit in the hatch with an RPG!" I said, "Are you okay?" And he said, "Yeah, I'm okay," and we just kept rolling along at five miles per hour.

My commander asked where the enemy was and I told him they were everywhere. Rooftops. Second floors. In windows. On the ground. In Dumpsters. I was everyone's target. Everyone had RPGs or AK-47s or grenades. Our tank kept getting hit and I thought, *Oh my God, they're gonna hit the rear sprocket, the tank's gonna stop, and we're just gonna be a giant target.* Somehow we kept rolling. We were halfway through a one-kilometer stretch. The attack had lasted one hour. It seemed like ten minutes. All of a sudden my gunner said, "Sir, the turret's got a malfunction." I thought the hydraulic had gone out and I could switch over to manual. I could still use the machine gun on top but I knew we had to give up the lead. We were no good up here. We were still getting peppered. An RPG blew up my navigation system so I pulled out a map, because I had to let base camp know where we were. I used to have a nice computerized map and now I had a paper one. And then, *blam!* An RPG hit the left side and went into our air filtration system. The alarm was screeching in the tank. I tried to hit the alarm mute. Then an RPG blew up a storage box that contained all our rifles and manuals. The rifles were blown sky-high out of the tank and landed on the turret. All the manuals, all the books were now on fire. I was still trying to turn the tank around and we were getting calls: "Red Six, your tank's on fire." I responded, "No, it's just the manuals." I was riding out of there with huge flames coming out of my tank, M16 rifles all cockeyed on the roof of our tank. We pulled back. Circling the wagons. We found a downed tank and towed it back to base camp. Next, we pulled back out of base camp to the outskirts of Baqouba and set up a blocking position.

My commander radioed me that we had to go back into the city. He said, "Red Six, do you want to take the lead or do you want Red Seven to do it?" I said I'd take it. It had nothing to do with heroism. The choice was to send someone else or to do it ourselves. We sent ourselves. After what we'd just been through, I thought it was easier for me to be out front again. It was where I belonged. We took the lead back into the city again. Fortunately, there wasn't very much heavy contact. The only thing we ran into were these little pickup trucks with RPGs in the back driving through the side streets. We saw the tail end of one truck trying to get the hell out of Dodge. We blasted that one with the main gun. Other than that, no real contact.

That first hour when we were in the ambush, I had no idea how bad it really was, how thick the fighting was. Fifteen RPGs were fired at my tank and seven of them hit. We went in expecting contact but nothing like that. Later on, my commander said that nobody in the First Infantry Division had seen this much contact since World War

II. But nobody was killed in our company and nobody was wounded in our tank, so there were a lot of high-fives and laughter when it was all said and done. There were RPGs that hit us that were one-in-a-million shots. RPGs should have penetrated certain spots but they didn't. A lot of luck was involved. Plus, the insurgents weren't expecting tanks. Anything besides tanks would have gotten shredded. Only tanks could have survived that.

If you read my Silver Star citation, they give me a lot of credit for destroying so many enemy positions. In the army, you have to look at command responsibilities and, yeah, I did that. But my gunner was the one pulling the trigger on the main gun. My driver was down there and he's more out front than I am. My loader, he's exposed like I am. I wish every kid could get recognition or the Silver Star. Other guys deserve it more than I do.

★

Upon completion of his mission in Iraq, Neil redeployed to Germany in early 2005 with the First Infantry Division. In late 2005 Neil returned to the United States, married his fiancée, and deployed to Iraq six months later with the Fourth Infantry Division.

WHEN YOU GET YOUR CALL

★

Jeremy Church, PFC, U.S. Army Reserves
724th Transportation Company
Hudson, Illinois
SILVER STAR; IRAQ; 9 APRIL 2004

On April 9, 2004, at eleven a.m., more than 150 insurgents ambushed a twenty-six-vehicle convoy taking fuel to Baghdad International Airport. After an improvised explosive device blasted a tire, Church found himself driving on three tires and a bare rim, firing his M16 at the enemy and rendering first aid to his injured lieutenant. Once Church made it through the four-mile kill zone to safety, he gathered troops to go back for the wounded soldiers and civilians in a disabled vehicle. While under intense and constant enemy fire, he

administered emergency first aid, carried ten seriously wounded U.S. soldiers and contractors, scoured the scene for sensitive items, and, because of capacity problems, stayed at the disabled vehicle with his gun blazing while the others were evacuated. Jeremy Church earned the nation's third-highest medal, the Silver Star, and was promoted to specialist.

I've spent half my life in Missouri and the other half in Illinois. My dad is a chiropractor, and at the clinic he's Dr. Church and he's all business. When he's off the job and we hang out together, he makes me laugh so hard I cry. We're more like best friends than father and son. My first job was at the ice cream station at the local Steak 'n Shake. I think I earned about $5.15 an hour. When it was time to learn to drive, my dad was busy in Springfield, Illinois, and my mom was working someplace else, so they didn't have time to take me out. I "acquired" a car and taught myself how to drive.

Ever since I was a little boy, I wanted to be in the military or a cop. I did them both by becoming a military policeman. My recruiter's name was Casey and he told me the truth. He said when I first got into the army I was going to hate him, but when I got out I'd know why I did it. He said, "You'll know who you are when you get out of the army and you'll know why you did the things you did." He was right.

I took my basic training at Fort Leonard Wood, Missouri, and our unit was segregated from the regular soldiers. Then it was a straight shot from there to active duty.

When I got my orders to go to Iraq, I was all for it. If I had wanted a regular job, I'd have joined the regular army and served my hitch. When I joined the Army Reserves, it was a calling. When you get your call, you know the army truly needs you. A soldier doesn't have the luxury of being selfish.

When I got to the Middle East, I didn't know what to expect. It's best not to arrive with any preconceived notions or expectations. You've got to be adjustable, flexible, and roll with the punches. You have to stay focused and keep your military bearing. You have to adapt, because if you're rigid you're not going to have a very good time over there.

Everything the army needs to run requires fuel. We were on the road every single day, working on four or five hours' sleep, getting up, getting there, and delivering fuel. We did that for a straight month and then we got leave. We were running gun trucks. The night before we pushed out, I didn't sleep well at all. I picked up First Lieutenant Matt Brown and we thought we were going to Al Asad, but then the mission changed. I said, "Sir, I've got a bad feeling about today." He said, "You know, I've got that same feeling, too." All of us had bad feelings.

As soon as we hit Baghdad, we were ambushed and it was pretty intense. There were enemy soldiers everywhere. Bullets were flying through the front window. RPGs were hitting. IEDs were going off. Thirteen IEDs went off and the fourteenth hit us. It blasted our tire and we drove on three tires and a rim. There was so much fire we couldn't even hear the radios.

One of our men was sticking out of the top of the Humvee firing. Another gunner was firing from the other side. Lieutenant Brown was firing out one window and I was firing out the other. We had trained to drive and fire simultaneously. Things were getting worse and worse and Lieutenant Brown said, "Hey, let's get out of here." I said, "The accelerator's on the floor, sir."

I started to fire out the window again, and as I turned something hit the side of my face. It jerked my head back. It was the window glass that had been shattered by a bullet. I got hit by the glass. Lieutenant Brown got hit by the bullet. I looked over at Lieutenant Brown and he was holding his face, blood everywhere. To tell you the truth, my one concern was to get him out of there. This was my lieutenant. As I popped my head out the window, two more IEDs went off. I gave Lieutenant Brown a muscle patch to control the bleeding, and at the same time I talked with Kellogg, Brown, and Root, the guys who were in our convoy behind us. They were screaming for help. The only thing I could say to them was, "Keep your wits about you. You're doing a great job, keep pushing forward. If you break down, there's a gun truck behind you and we will stop for you." I said, "Keep following me. I'm the one who knows the path and we're going to get there."

Just when I thought the attack had quit, it would start back up again. I knew that a cavalry unit had been overrun by insurgents only six hours before. There was still fighting at the front gate when we got there. Once we got to safety, we knew that there was a downed Humvee full of wounded, so we went out again. At first I was going to go alone, but then another Humvee and a Bradley went with us. When we got to the Humvee, so many rounds had torn through the engine block that it was disabled. I peered in and the first two sets of guys were covered in blood. I asked, "Are you guys dead?" One smiled, "Nah, we're just playing." I said, "Wanna get out of here?" "Yeah, hell yes," came the answer. I grabbed both of them and picked them up. They'd been shot in the legs. I put them in the Humvee. A couple of the other guys had bled to death. The insurgents were still coming at us, right out of the woodwork. We had space problems so I waited in the disabled Humvee until they could deliver the wounded and come back for me. That's what happened.

I slept like a baby the first couple of nights after April 9. I was exhausted. I was so tired from carrying everybody out and my emotions were so high, I just crashed. Then I'd wake up and crash again. The next night, we had another mission. We ended up getting into another firefight, but this one was mild by comparison. It lasted just forty-five minutes.

I went back home in February 2005. What I went through was traumatic. It does something to you. You shut things out. But it made me appreciate life a lot more. I've carried dead friends out. I was working with a guy who died in my arms. Most people don't experience that jolt of reality. Afterward, you see through the stupid stuff. It's pointless to fight a belligerent drunk in a bar. You blow it off. You learn to deal with situations better. You come back and you see through all the masks and shadows. You see through people's pretenses. You discover what is important. You make better decisions. As far as the medal goes, I don't think I earned it. I'm just glad I didn't get shot.

I'm going back to Iraq. My captain, who is now a major, and Lieutenant Brown, who lost an eye, are going back, too. The two squads that make up our team, six or seven of us, we all volunteered to go back to Iraq. I'm a soldier. The mission comes first. I'm doing it and it is something I believe in.

★

PFC Church has since returned to active duty and redeployed to Iraq.

WERE IT NOT FOR HIS ACTIONS

★

Jason Dunham, Corporal, U.S. Marine Corps

Third Battalion, Seventh Marine Regiment, First Marine Division,

First Marine Expeditionary Force

Scio, New York

Died on April 22, 2004, from injuries received on April 14,

near the Iraqi and Syrian borders

POSTHUMOUSLY AWARDED THE MEDAL OF HONOR

*Jason L. Dunham was manning a vehicle checkpoint near Husay-bah after a convoy was ambushed on April 14. He observed a car pull up and a man jump from the vehicle, sprinting away. Dunham—in full combat gear—chased the man down, tackling him to the ground.

DEB DUNHAM

---

*Excerpted from an article in the April 29, 2004, *Marine Corps News.*

Other marines came to assist in the apprehension, when the terrorist pulled a pin from a hand grenade. Dunham dove onto the grenade, taking the blast into his own body, saving the lives of his marines. Dunham suffered serious wounds, along with two other marines. But were it not for his actions, all three might have died.

"He knew what he was doing," said Lance Corporal Jason A. Sanders, twenty-one, from McAllester, Oklahoma, and a mortarman with Company K. "He wanted to save marines' lives from that grenade."

Another mortarman with the company, Lance Corporal Mark E. Dean, twenty-two, from Owasso, Oklahoma, described Dunham as an unselfish marine. Dunham's enlistment was to end in June, but he voluntarily extended his contract to join his marines.

"We told him he was crazy for coming out here," Dean explained. "He decided to come out here and fight with us. All he wanted was to make sure his boys made it back home."

"The only way to honor him is in his own way," said Captain Trent A. Gibson, commanding officer for Company K. "We must continue to do our duty, take care of our marines, lead by example and take the fight to the enemy."

Dunham dreamed of joining the Los Angeles Police Department after his tour.

He was born November 10, 1981, and joined the Marine Corps July 31, 2000. The marine completed recruit training at Marine Corps Recruit Depot Parris Island, South Carolina. He joined Third Battalion, Seventh Marine Regiment in September 2003, serving with Fourth Platoon as a machine gunner.

Dunham had survived his wounds for eight days when his parents, Daniel K. Dunham and Natalie J. Sherwood, made the decision to end life support for the marine. Commandant of the Marine Corps General Michael W. Hagee and Sergeant Major of the Marine

Corps, Sergeant Major John L. Estrada, were at Dunham's bedside with his parents at Bethesda Naval Hospital in Maryland when he died, according to Sergeant Major Wayne R. Bell, First Marine Division's sergeant major.

"That in itself speaks volumes, knowing that no matter who it is—general officer or a corporal—his act alone warrants a visit from the commandant," Bell said. "I know that the marines who are alive today, because of what Corporal Dunham did, will never forget that marine as long as they live.

"Corporal Dunham is everybody's hero," Bell added. "He sacrificed his life so his marines could continue the mission."

"God made something special when he made Jason," Dean said. "It was a privilege and honor to know him. It's sad he is gone but he is living it up in heaven and I'm happy for that."

Jason Dunham's Stepmother, Deb Dunham:

Jason came into my life when he was five years old. I never saw a kid who could get up in the morning and hit the floor smiling. He was good-hearted, willing to help, and he liked to please. Jason was fun and people gravitated to him. You couldn't help but love him.

As far as discipline goes, all we had to do was talk with Jason and he was good. I can still remember one time he said, "Couldn't you just spank me? You guys just talk but I think it'd be over quicker if you spank me." We didn't have to do that with him.

Jason didn't have a temper but he had a strong sense of right and wrong, even as a kid. I know one time he came home and he said, "Mom, I was in a fight." He told me he was defending a friend who couldn't defend himself. By the time the boys got to the principal's office, they were all friends again.

As a student, Jason worked hard and had to study for what he got. If a subject didn't appeal to his interests, he had to work at it. He did well enough in school because he had to in order to be on the sports teams. I remember he retook a math class because he didn't like his grade. He repeated it as a junior.

I wouldn't call him a perfectionist so much as someone who loved a challenge. Jason wanted to go to college but he knew it would mean a lot of student loans. For him, the GI Bill was the right idea. At first he was hell-bent on being a Navy SEAL, but the summer before his senior year he met a marine recruiter. I don't know what he said to Jason, but after that all Jason thought about was joining the marines. He wanted to work with the best, train with the best, and be the best. If Marine Corps training was the toughest, that's where he wanted to be. He didn't go around with his chest puffed out, but he was very proud of being a marine. If someone called him a Devil Dog, he'd just turn around and smile and say, "You bet your ass I am."

At one point during boot camp Jason developed an infection on his heel that grew worse until he ended up in the hospital for three days. The marines were going to make him stay an extra week but Jason wanted to graduate with his class. He said he'd do whatever it took to finish. And he did. He graduated with the group he entered with. There wasn't a school the Marine Corps offered him that he didn't take. He wanted to make himself a better marine. When I looked through his marine records, he had a perfect PT score.

Jason learned his work ethic from his father. He learned that when you have a job, you do it to the best of your ability. We found an English paper that Jason had written about his dad being his hero and the person he admired most. Those are things that guys don't say to one another, but they just kind of took it for granted. From our family Jason learned that you can be angry and still love people. He learned that when somebody had an argument, people don't walk away.

Jason was taking college courses in California when he was with the marines, and he wrote an essay about leadership for one of his classes. I happened to have a rough draft of it. He believed in leading by example. He didn't tell anybody to do something he wasn't willing to do. I understand that when they first went to Iraq one of the things they had to do was shore up some of the walls with sandbags. He did it right alongside his men in the broiling sun. That was an assignment he could have given to the younger recruits or the guys of lower rank. But he worked right beside them.

While in college, every time he called he had a different career in mind. He was going to be an engineer or he was going to do this or that. I said, "Jason, I thought you always wanted to be a police officer or a state trooper, you know, to serve and protect." He shot back, "Mom, do you know what the starting salaries are for some of these other professions?" I told him that I chose to teach in Scio, New York, because I like my job and I'm happy here. I said, "You have to go to bed and you have to like yourself in the morning. You have to look in the mirror and like the guy who's looking back at you."

He called home one night and I could tell by the tone in his voice that he'd had a bad day. I said, "Jason, are you okay?" and he said, "Yeah, I'm fine." I said, "Jason, this is your mother." He said, "I had a bad day." He had been out on the rifle range when he heard a shot followed by screams. Jason ran over because he thought it was his best friend who'd had an accident. But it was another guy, who'd shot himself on purpose. He shot himself under the chin. Everybody was just standing there so Jason put his thumb up under his chin and his other thumb where the bullet had exited out the side of his temple. Two doctors arrived, an older one and a younger one. The younger one was doing this and doing that, taking out bone and teeth and tissue and trying to clear an airway. The older doctor was trying to explain to the younger one that the boy was gone.

I told Jason it sounded like he'd done the right thing. In the next breath he asked me if I could get him an application for the New York State Troopers. I said, "I thought you wanted to be an engineer or something?" He explained that he'd been worried he wouldn't be able to do the job of a state trooper. Now he knew he could.

When Jason was mortally wounded in Iraq, our neighbors in Scio knew that he'd been hurt, but they didn't know that he'd died. When Dan and I got back into town, American flags lined the street. Every tree on the school property where I work had a yellow ribbon.

The person I turn to is my husband. I don't think Dan let go of my hand for three months after we lost Jason. When we went out anywhere, he'd have ahold of my hand because he knew I needed that connection. Dan and I are closer now than we've ever been. I was scared to death that not only would I lose my son, but that I'd lose my husband, too, because these things can really affect a marriage. When I conveyed that to him, Dan just looked at me and said, "No, that is not going to happen."

I get to make new memories with my other children, Katie, Kyle, and Justin. I get to go to their weddings and see their kids. But I don't get to make any new memories with Jason. What I've learned from this tragedy is that if something gets broken, it's no big deal. It's only money, it's only something material. We know what's important. Sometimes when I hear parents screaming at their kids I want to say to them, "This is a picture of my son Jason. I can't scream at him anymore. I can't hold him. I can't kiss him. This is a boy who had three tattoos, and as his mom I wasn't really fond of them. But he could have three more if I could still have him back. I would take him to the tattoo parlor." Our family values one another more and the time we have with each other. We've learned to be nicer to ourselves.

I know there are people who don't have faith or who have never been in this position so they don't really understand it. But God provides things that we didn't know we needed until they were there. Dan and I have always believed in heaven and hell and a Christ who saved us. But our faith became stronger. We're not the type to sit in a pew on Sunday. Our lives have always been busy and Sunday has always been family time. I'm more adamant in my knowledge that there is a Lord and that I'm going to see Jason again. I know Jason was a gift. I feel cheated. I know when I see God I'm going to ask that question: "You gave Jason to me and then you took him away. Why?" Dan says, "Isn't it an honor to know that God needed Jason for something higher and he chose to have our son with him in heaven?" Yes,

I'm really proud that he took our Jason, but I could have been proud a little later.

★

Jason Dunham is buried in Scio, New York. On Tuesday, March 14, 2006, the president signed into law S. 4515, which designates the facility of the United States Postal Service located in Scio, New York, as the Corporal Jason L. Dunham Post Office.

WILLPOWER

★

Raymond Bittinger, Staff Sergeant, U.S. Army

Second Battalion, Second Infantry Regiment, First Infantry Division

Chicago, Illinois

Silver Star; Buhritz, Iraq; 9 April 2004

In April of 2004, Staff Sergeant Ray Bittinger's Bradley unit was in the small Iraqi town of Buhritz. When his first squad of dismounts was pinned down by insurgent fire, Bittinger placed his Bradley in the line of fire to save his soldiers. In the sixth hour of an intense firefight, the order came to break contact. His wingman's 25mm gun jammed, so Bittinger once again moved his Bradley around to cover his withdrawal. With small-arms, machine-gun, and RPG fire intensifying, Bittinger's gunner was killed and Bittinger was hurt and disoriented. He took charge of the gun, evacuated his gunner, and fought on.

I grew up in Chicago, went to Wilbur Wright Community College for two years after high school, and then joined the army. I thought I'd do my little four-year stint and that would be it. I never thought I'd still be in the army thirteen years later, but it kept getting more and more fun. I thought, *Okay, I'm going to stay.*

I got selected to be an instructor on a Bradley Fighting Vehicle and now I'm in Germany. I'm teaching young soldiers for three weeks and then they move on and I get a new bunch to train. We train in combat arms, combat service support, and night vision. I teach them how to "safe target" and how to set up a good tactical range. I'd like to go back to Iraq or Afghanistan but the army thinks I'm needed more here, training soldiers. That could change anytime and hopefully it will.

It's hard to put into words how I felt when I got the call to go to Iraq. I'd been in Kosovo twice and I wanted a drastic change from that. In Kosovo, we were on the Serbian border. It took us two hours to get up those icy hills, where we sat in a Bradley watching the Albanian rebels train. The second time we were there, we were watching for smugglers and then reporting to the Kosovo police. Those were pretty boring assignments. At first, it sounded like that was the kind of thing we were going to be doing in Iraq, providing a safe and secure environment for the Iraqis, providing the basic necessities. Every third world country has the same problems and needs: food, water, clothing, and jobs. It's those four things everywhere you go in the world.

We got to Iraq in March of 2004. We were doing a lot of patrols and nothing much was happening. Then April kicked off and I don't know what happened but it was crazy. On April 7, one of our helicopters was shot down and we went to secure the crash site. That same night, we were back on patrol and we got ambushed. My Bradley had broken down so I was in a Humvee. We were driving along and we suspected something was going on, because we started hearing these *booms* everywhere. We wondered, *Whoa, what was that?* Then we eventually learned the enemy was shooting RPGs and small arms and they had a signal guy up on the roof with tracers. That started our first firefight. The problem was, the enemy was all over the place, so it was hard to catch them. We had three Bradleys, two dismount squads, and one Humvee. I couldn't divide up the squad four different ways because I'd lose command and control. We just sat there, and the dismount units tried to cover from one end to the other. That was an interesting night and then everything was calm.

Then on April 8, we got the report that there were a bunch of insurgents in Buhritz and they had RPGs. We were ordered down there. As soon as we rolled in, we saw that there were two narrow roads on each side of the creek. As we passed the police station, we started getting hit with RPGs. We were fighting there for six hours. We'd move back and forth, from one side of the creek to the other. Our Bradleys couldn't get into the heart of this little city because the streets were too narrow. We were very concerned about collateral damage. We were careful what we did. There were a lot of kids watching in the middle of the town; don't ask me why. The insurgents were using those kids as guards and shields. They'd shoot at us with an RPG and then run in front of the kids, and we wouldn't shoot because the kids were in the background. The brigade commander sent in tanks, but they didn't have firing pins for their cannons so all they had was 7.62- and .50-cal.

I was the platoon leader's wingman and we were in a Humvee. The platoon sergeant was in the rear of the battle in case anybody needed to be medevaced out. We were shooting, trying to destroy the insurgents, when my platoon leader's gun went down. We were told to fall back. I stayed with my crew to provide support fire and we got barraged with RPGs. I got knocked out and everybody thought I was dead. Everything happened so quick. It was just a second. One RPG exploded right on top of me and another one hit to the left side. My driver was really messed up and my gunner was, too. I didn't know what hit us or from where. I thought an electrical cable had fallen on us because everything was all smoky and just crazy. An RPG had bounced off the tow launcher and gone down the hole between the hull and the turret. There was smoke and a concussion from the grenade. It was the strangest thing I'd ever seen, just a lucky shot. I immediately went to our left and started laying down suppressive fire. It didn't make sense to give first aid there because we would have all been killed. Once we got to a safe environment, I told the platoon sergeant that we had a man down.

I provided first aid on the way back, and then when we got to camp we pulled my gunner out very carefully because I didn't know what had happened. They told me at the aid station that he died. This was unbelievable. We waited around there for two hours, and then we got the call that Baquabah was under siege by insurgents. Our orders were to guard two bridges and not to let anyone cross. I asked if anyone wanted to volunteer; everybody did.

My driver became my gunner. I gave him a crash course in how to control the Bradley turret, weapons systems, how to arm, what to use, and how to use the thermals. Thank God he's pretty smart and he knew what he was doing. We linked up with the tanks from another base across the street and we rolled out. It was some fierce fighting, probably some of the worst I'd ever seen. But we made it to the bridge and stood guard there from midnight till seven a.m. Then we headed down to An Najaf.

Our training helped us survive, but more than that it was the willpower to get the job done. As far as the Silver Star goes, I was just doing my job. I was just wondering why my gunner got the Bronze Star with the "V" for Valor and not the Silver Star. He's the one who made the ultimate sacrifice, because he didn't stop pulling the trigger until that RPG hit us. It's not like he stopped or choked or panicked or did something wrong. He kept pulling the trigger and they got a lucky flank shot on us. That was my reaction to getting the Silver Star. I still wonder that to this day, why didn't he get the Silver Star instead of me?

★

Staff Sergeant Bittinger and his family currently live in Germany, where he continues serving on active duty, training soldiers on the Bradley Fighting Vehicle.

I DON'T QUESTION IT

★

William Thomas Payne, Staff Sergeant, U.S. Army

Alpha Company, First Battalion, Ninth Cavalry Regiment

Shawnee, Oklahoma

SILVER STAR; HAIFA STREET, BAGHDAD, IRAQ; 12 SEPTEMBER 2004

When a vehicle-borne IED slammed into a thirty-three-ton Bradley Fighting Vehicle, its upper cargo hatch was blown off and the rear cargo ramp was engulfed in flames. Under intense enemy fire, Sergeant Will Payne and Specialist Chase Ash rescued the soldiers from the disabled Bradley and got them to safety.

WILLIAM THOMAS PAYNE

Both my dad and my stepmother were in the military and we moved around a lot. I went to six or seven elementary and middle schools and five high schools in four years. We often moved in the middle of the year, and I had a lot of acquaintances but not many friends. That's true today. I was very athletic. I played baseball, soccer, and football. My dad is a very intelligent man. If you ask him a question about anything, 95 percent of the time he has the answer and the rest of the time he'll get the answer. I've always admired him and wanted what he had. I've seen my dad cry three times in his life: once when his mother died, another time when I went off to join the military, and then when I was deployed. All I can say is, I hope I'm like him.

I'm a pretty big old boy, six feet five inches and 320 pounds. I like to think I'm a good soldier, but people tell me I'm better than what I say I am. You'll have to forgive my language but I think my soldiers would say that I'm the hardest person to work with, but when the shit is hitting the fan, they know they can count on me. It may take a while for me to run my big old ass over there, but I'll be there. I don't get to know a lot of people because people have to earn my trust. I trusted my squad 100 percent. There wasn't any doubt in my mind that I could leave one member by himself for twelve hours on watch and he wouldn't fall asleep. I wanted their respect; I didn't expect to be their friend. I couldn't care less whether I'm popular but I'll be there when you need me, thick or thin. That's the way I was raised. That's the kind of person Dad is, too.

It was September 12 on Haifa Street in Baghdad—September 11 back in the States. We dropped off some Navy SEALs who were setting up an observation post on top of one of the tallest buildings in

Baghdad. It was an apartment building and we were going to leave them there for twenty-four hours. It was a battalion-sized mission with twenty to twenty-five Bradleys but no tanks. Our unit was fourth from the last. We hadn't gone but three miles when they started to get shot up. We got our orders to turn around and pick up the Navy SEALs. The caravan moved like it did the first time through, only in reverse. Same mission, except this time we were picking up instead of dropping off.

My squad dismounted and moved to the left, to the west. We had to climb over an eight-foot wall. Like I said, I'm a big boy, so I threw my guys over the wall and then it took four of them to haul me over. We were about forty meters from the Bradley. We couldn't see it but we could hear it running. We were within hollering distance. All of a sudden, we heard gunfire but couldn't tell where it was coming from. I pushed two of our guys out about hundred meters to the west on Haifa Street, and then all of a sudden we heard tires squealing. An old Chevy Caprice ran into the right rear end of Alpha 5-0, the executive officers' vehicle. The blast picked me up and pushed me back three feet in the air. It was a pretty good old concussion and it threw all my squad to the ground. All we could see was a weird mushroom cloud, and as soon as that happened I started running toward the exploding vehicle, right through a metal gate, so I could see what was happening. When I glanced over my shoulder, my whole squad was behind me. Once I got through that gate, I was twenty-five meters from the vehicle, so nobody had better eyes-on than I did. The right rear vehicle was on fire. Though we didn't know it at the time, a vehicle-borne suicide bomber had run into the Bradley. The Chevy Caprice was so destroyed you couldn't even tell it was a car. No frame. No tires. Nothing but a big black smudge on the ground.

The Bradley was about twenty to thirty feet from the building, so we thought a bunch of RPGs or about twenty grenades had come from inside the building. All my guys lay down on the far west side and started scanning the area. When people stuck their heads out, they fired. We figured if they were poking their heads out, they were up to no good. I ran to the Bradley's driver's hatch and it was already open. I could hear rounds, like little firecrackers, a twirling noise, as they spun past me. I heard that continuously as I ran to the driver's side and looked in the Bradley. The driver wasn't there. I didn't have time to think and figured they'd gotten up to leave. I tried to call, but there was so much traffic on the radio I was constantly getting cut off. I just had to make my own decision. I climbed up onto the vehicle.

The smoke was so bad I don't know how the occupants lasted as long as they did. Specialist Ash ran to the driver's hatch and he noticed the Bradley's engine was in the driver's seat. It was pushed up against the driver, and if it had moved another inch, it would have crushed him. Then Ash stayed on the ground and I got on the Bradley. I threw my M4 down so I could get up there. I guess I wasn't thinking straight. Then I straddled over the cargo hatch, and I was pulling soldiers up, handing them to Ash, and he hustled them across the street to safety. There were four that we took care of. There was a lot of gunfire going on. One guy didn't have his Kevlar helmet so I put him in a headlock to protect him.

We got everybody back to the west side of Haifa Street and set up behind a three-foot wall. At that point, we still didn't know that it was a vehicle-borne IED. Finally, I got the call through and they told us what had happened. Our guys calmed down, knowing that information. A Bradley came back and we got all the occupants of the disabled one and half of my squad in it. The medic was administering first aid to one of the injured soldiers who'd busted his nose. Four of us were left behind. There was not the slightest doubt in my mind that the A team was my best and I wanted them by my side. I chose them to stay there with me. It was kind of lonely because we could only watch for enemy in a few directions. That's when the rounds in the disabled Bradley started cooking off. M16s and 25mm. It was crazy. I called up and explained that nobody was firing, it was the rounds in our Bradley.

About that time, we started getting hit by grenades. They were just dropping out of the sky. Luckily, none of them landed near enough to hurt us. I knew we needed to move and the nearest Bradley was 150 meters away. The Bradley lowered its ramp and we started our run toward it. I jumped over that three-foot wall, and as soon as I did a grenade hit about ten feet in front of me. It scared the shit out of me, so I jumped back over the wall for protection and I told my men, "Let's wait."

I started shooting toward the guy who had fired that grenade. I covered while my guys took off running for the Bradley. I was right behind them. Two more grenades went off behind us as we were running. We got loaded up. We were all fine. We were all good. We got back to our forward operating base, and then it hit us what had just happened. I broke down and cried; I can't lie about that. Then I had to do my debriefing.

The whole ordeal lasted thirty minutes. The extraction of the wounded from the disabled Bradley took five minutes. That was the first time we'd ever lost a Bradley in combat but nobody died. Not a single American was killed. The insurgents had that Bradley picked out for some reason, but they picked the wrong one because it was one tough vehicle. The gunner who was looking through the periscope when the suicide bomber hit busted his nose. That was the worst casualty. An RPG hit the Bradley when I was on it and Ash was on the ground, but it didn't blow up. It didn't detonate. Don't ask me how that happened. I don't know why I'm alive but I don't really question it. I'll just leave it at that. I'm more quiet now. It gives me a more realistic look at life and a greater appreciation for all that I have. Everything I have here I worked hard for and I need to appreciate it and not waste it. I'm not someone who brags. All I can say is that I earned my pay that day. I owe everything to my squad. If my squad wasn't there I couldn't have completed that mission. My squad was there for me—that's what it comes down to.

Specialist Ash stepped up and did a leader's job. He did the job of a noncommissioned officer. He's one smart kid. You could talk to him about anything, from Egyptian times, John Wayne movies, Elvis Presley, social problems, anything. He's got two loving, awesome parents. He got his Silver Star in June of '05 and now he's going to college in California.

I was stationed in Korea when the Iraq war broke out. I reenlisted with First Cavalry so I could go to Iraq. I asked to be there, so I can't complain. I learned a lot and I want to go back. That's what I came into the army for. It took me twelve years to do that and I don't want it to be another twelve.

What I learned about myself is that I can do anything if it needs to be done. I can be counted on.

★

Will Payne's Silver Star was pinned on his chest by his father, Carl Payne. He is currently serving with the HHC 1-8 CAV in Sadr City, Iraq.

THERE'S NOTHING LIKE BEING ALIVE

★

Josh Ryan Szott, Sergeant and Forward Observer, U.S. Army
First Brigade Combat Team Reconnaissance Troop,
Fourth Infantry Division
Sacramento, California
SILVER STAR; IRAQ; 18 SEPTEMBER 2003

On September 18, while conducting combat patrols east of Tikrit, Josh Szott and his men came under heavy mortar and machine-gun fire. It was the first coordinated ambush of the war. Specialist Wright, Sergeant Thompson, and Specialist Arriaga were killed. Szott took a bullet to his left leg and a hunk of shrapnel to his right leg. Driving and firing to flee the ambush to get medical help, Szott saw that the other vehicle failed to follow. He went back into the kill zone to load fallen soldiers.

JOSH RYAN SZOTT

I was born in Chicago and lived there until I was three, and then we moved to Sacramento, California. I moved out when I was sixteen and got a job, trying to put myself through community college. I was digging pools for a company that built outlandish pools that ran $50,000, $60,000 or $70,000 apiece. Money was just pouring in and I was working six days a week. I said to the boss, "Hey, I'm thinking about taking weekend classes. Is there any way I can get Saturdays off?" He said, "Yeah, you can have Saturday, Monday, Tuesday, Wednesday, Thursday, and Friday off, too, because you won't be working here anymore." They needed guys, and if I wasn't going to do it, then someone else would.

The funny thing is, all the time before that I was convinced I wasn't going to join the military. I thought they messed with your head. But I was sitting around, going through a rough time because I couldn't go to school, when my roommate and I saw this commercial for the army. I said, "You know, that's not a bad idea." I was thinking about it really strongly, about the benefits and all the things I could do. I went down to the recruiter and I told them that I didn't want an office job; I wanted to be in the infantry, go airborne with Ranger School and get over to Special Forces. They told me that I couldn't be in the infantry because the infantry was full but that I could be a forward observer. I asked, "What's a forward observer?" They explained it to me and said I'd be walking around with the infantry but I'd be doing cooler jobs. I said, "All right, let's do it."

In fact, I actually went down and talked to the recruiters on May 16, but that was two days before I was old enough, so they said, "Come back in two days." I left for basic training on June 18. I enlisted on my birthday.

Basic training was not a pleasant experience. The Oklahoma weather was a shock. I was used to California, with 10 percent humidity, and I went straight to 100 percent humidity and ninety degrees. I thought I was going to die. It was bad. I was there for seventeen weeks, four days, and four and a half hours.

I trained to be a forward observer and it's the best. We really are the castoffs. We call ourselves the bastard children of the army. We're the eyes, the radio, and the spotters, but we don't really fit in with the guns. We don't have a home. There are just three forward observers for an entire troop. But when you get in the heat of everything, then everyone's your friend. The brotherhood is really tight.

I served in Iraq for eleven months and three weeks. Anybody who says they're not scared is lying. I was real nervous going in. My stomach was messed up. When we drove in, we had a lot of potshots taken at us and there were some mines on the side of the road. For somebody who has never been to a third world country, it's a real eye-opener. I wondered how these people were able to live in these conditions. They didn't have running water. In the rural areas especially, they didn't have much of anything.

I stayed in a couple of Saddam Hussein's palaces and visited a third one. Even the small house that we had in Tikrit, which was right next to Saddam's wife's house, had marble bathrooms, amazing handcrafted tapestries on the ceiling, everything hand-painted. There were bronze statues of Saddam that weighed hundreds of thousands of pounds. In the United States, these things would have been worth millions because the labor costs would have been so high.

Soldiers get extremely acclimated to the noise, almost to the point where we can sleep through anything, anything that's not a threat. If there is stuff blowing up in the distance, that doesn't bother us much. I mean, we don't even jump. About six months into my tour of duty in Iraq, I was asked if I wanted to go on mid-tour leave and go home.

I turned it down. There were a few guys in my unit who had families they needed to see. I gave one guy my spot and he actually got home in time to see his kid born. He made it by a couple of hours. I didn't need to go home.

On September 18, I was on night patrol. I was just filling in as a gunner-driver and Sergeant Thompson was in charge. I'm a good shot and they usually put me on the gun. Specialist Wright said, "Hey, Szott, can you please drive for me tonight because my sinuses are killing me." We switched and we said that later on we could switch back if he got tired of being on the gun or I got tired of driving. There were some explosions over the riverbank, and they wanted us to check them out since we were in the area.

We went out that night and it seemed like any other routine patrol. It was kind of an eerie feeling. The ride was really smooth. We slowed down for a second, a flare popped up, gunfire opened up on us, and we were in the kill zone. We were drawing fire from multiple positions, including one on a distant hill. It was literally a barrage of bullets and RPGs. I've been told the gunfight lasted just a couple of minutes but it felt like forever. Things happened in slow motion. We didn't have time to think; we just reverted to our training, total reaction. Even when I came up on guys who were injured, I did everything textbook style. I didn't even think about it.

We got initial contact and I returned fire. Mine was the first vehicle and it just got riddled with bullet holes and RPG shrapnel. You know the cartoons where they shoot an outline all around the person? There were close to twenty bullet holes like a cookie cutter around me in the Humvee. I heard bullets lodging in our vehicle and whizzing overhead. I saw bullets inches from my face. I could feel the heat of the bullet and the spiral of the spin all around my face. I continued to fire back. I finished my first magazine, switched mags, and attempted to step out of the vehicle. A strong force and vibration hit my leg, leaving it very numb. The force pushed me back in the vehicle and I continued returning fire. I glanced back at my team and saw Sergeant Ray engaging the enemy in a fighting position five feet off the road, standing toe-to-toe. We all fired back for the protection of one another. We pulled out of the area, trying to get away from the ambush site. I'd been shot in one leg and took shrapnel in the other. I honestly didn't feel it.

I did not see Specialist Wright standing in the gunner's hatch. Then I saw him in Specialist Flores's arms and Wright was bleeding badly. It was too dark to see where he was bleeding from. Flores attempted to get a conscious response from him but he did not reply. Flores continued to hold him and return fire. Still returning fire, I attempted to step out of the vehicle again. I got one foot out and heard the spin of an RPG that flew under our vehicle and detonated. I saw shrapnel blow through the seat and my right hamstring became very hot. Sergeant Ray had been standing on the right side of the vehicle and shrapnel came through the bottom and hit him in the lower back and buttocks. At around the same time, a bullet struck Sergeant Ray's hand and weapon. His left hand was shredded and his weapon was rendered inoperable. He jumped into the vehicle and said that his weapon was jammed. Sergeant Flores returned to the vehicle and said, "Specialist Wright is hit, let's go!"

I started to pull out slowly. The gunfire had stopped. I reached down my leg to feel for the severity of the wound and my seat was soaked in blood. I located a perfect 7.62mm hole on the outside of my leg. Then I located the exit wound, which was the size of a quarter, on the inside of my leg and it was bleeding badly. My first thought was that it had hit an artery and I wasn't going to last long. Then I reached down to my right hamstring, located a tear in my pants, and removed a very hot piece of shrapnel from my leg.

Our vehicle had been hit. Sergeant Ray tried to get the radio working but his hand was failing him due to his injury. I reached over, connected the hand mike, switched radio frequencies, and handed it to Flores. He said, "We've got a man down."

We'd moved about two hundred meters from the kill zone. I glanced back, and our other vehicle, G31, was not behind us. We had to go back and get the other team. I turned the vehicle around; Sergeant Ray jumped behind the M-249 and Flores jumped into the TC [Truck Commander] seat. I said to myself as we drove back, "This is it. This is where I die. This is the final showdown."

We returned to the kill zone to see G31 nose-down off the side of the road in a ditch, and two soldiers were in the middle of the road. Both Flores and I ran to the two as Sergeant Ray pulled security. I ran to Sergeant Thompson and Specialist Flores ran to Specialist Arriaga. I checked Thompson's vitals. He wasn't breathing and I couldn't feel a pulse. I kept talking to him and I tried to get him breathing again. His eyes were open and staring right back at me, his face expressionless. I didn't want to believe it, so I was just convinced he was all right. I grabbed Thompson. He's a decently big guy, 220 pounds, about the same as me. I got him in my arms and tried to stand, but my leg just collapsed underneath me.

I thought I might be able to get Arriaga because he was considerably smaller. He was just five feet away. I squatted down to check his vitals, and he wasn't breathing and had no pulse either. Arriaga gave me the same look back that Thompson did. I attempted to pick him up, got him all the way up, and then my leg buckled. About that time another truck showed up. Another guy got out and we both carried Arriaga to the truck. Two other guys grabbed Sergeant Thompson.

I asked all four, "Where's Cross?" They replied that he was MIA. My heart just dropped. I couldn't believe it and I immediately jumped off the ledge and ran over to the vehicle, looking underneath the Humvee that was in the ditch. I started yelling and looking for him. We called out his name and he responded, "I'm right here, Sergeant. Hey, I'm okay. Let's get out of here." We loaded up all the vehicles and conducted our evacuation.

I was worried about my leg, so I had the other guy drive and I jumped in the passenger seat. I got the radio back up again and called the commander. We evaced out to the aid station. Then we got trucked into north Tikrit. That was about a fifteen-minute drive and we were buck-naked, underneath a thermal blanket, which is just two pieces of foil slapped together.

Sergeant Ray was hurt. Wright was unconscious so we didn't know what his injuries were. It turned out he'd taken a round into his jugular. He actually bled to death on my shoulder while I was driving off.

A lot of the guys in the fight I'd known for three years. We'd done everything together. Specialist Arriaga was just a little guy and I'd taken him under my wing when he got to the unit. I kind of saw him as a younger brother. He'd been hit by an RPG. That was a big blow when he was killed because we'd gotten pretty close. The bullet I took missed my femoral artery by an inch.

The next day when I was in the hospital, they sent an entire battalion of infantry guys into the area. They locked down a village and brought everybody out and lined them up. They finally found one guy who was all proud and he said, "I was involved. I was there." They convinced him to show them everybody else who was involved and he went down the line and he said, "This guy had RPGs. This guy had an AK-47. This guy had this and this guy had that." They got them all. We actually knew the guy who had funded them but we didn't catch him until a month later. He was a major in the fedayeen.

He'd taken a bunch of poor farmers, trained them and funded them. It was the first coordinated attack they had seen in Iraq.

Josh Szott refused to be evacuated out of the country to recover from his wounds. He went back to his unit. Upon completion of his tour he returned to the United States and has since redeployed to Iraq.

—— AFTERWORD ——

WE ASK OUR BEST AMERICANS among us to fight in Iraq and Afghanistan and I am grateful for their service and sacrifice. Every American is. These are men and women who put their mission first; their fellow soldiers are a close second, and their own self-interest is way down the list. These qualities come through loud and clear when we read the stories of the special men and women who have earned our nation's highest military honors.

They come from all branches of the service and all ranks. They come from all parts of the country and all walks of life. What unites them is that they are tough, brave, and very young. When every survival instinct they possess tells them to run, they rush headlong into danger. They make on-the-spot, split-second decisions to put their own lives on the line for their comrades. Their actions go far beyond the call of duty. They are the heroes of our time. We're proud of them and we owe them so much. Battlefield honors are hard-won, and these men and women deserve to be recognized, but the medals they earned are the last things on their minds.

Read their firsthand stories and you will see that they talk about their service without exaggeration or embellishment. Their humility makes them all the more admirable. They are deeply committed, fiercely determined, and unfailingly loyal to their battle buddies. They're proud and confident, humble, direct, down-to-earth, and decent. They're also very smart and highly trained. Their service to our country and the unbreakable bonds they've forged with their comrades give their lives meaning. To them, who they are is more important than what they did. As long as they live, they will always be warriors.

I learned a long time ago that there are some very special people who don't like to talk about themselves or their accomplishments, but they are who we need to hear. If you can get them to talk, you'd be smart to listen to what they have to say because it's going to be wise and true. The surest way to draw them out is to ask them about their fellow brothers in arms. Invariably they'll shrug off what they themselves did and extol the bravery and virtues of the guys fighting next to them. They trust their fellow patriots completely. They have to. I hope you draw strength and inspiration from that. I know I do. The next time you see a man or woman wearing a military uniform, go over and say thank you for serving our great and good nation. That's all they want. That's all they care about.

—Senator John McCain

Dear reader,

I thank you for your interest in the lives and experiences of the great Americans featured in this book. The idea behind the creation of *Heroes Among Us* was my desire to share the inspiration, gratitude, and humility I felt after serving with our troops and hearing their stories during my time in Iraq. The process of creating this book broadened my understanding of this war and those fighting it. I hope this has been your experience as well.

I have the greatest respect for the men in this book. I would be happy to continue the discussion beyond the last page by making myself available to groups or book clubs who have questions or comments to which I am able to contribute. Please contact me if you would like to learn more about the Americans profiled in these pages, as well as the challenges and triumphs they have encountered since the completion of this book. I can be reached at HeroesAmongUs@gmail.com.

Again, thank you for your interest.

Sincerely,
Chuck Larson

Major Chuck Larson served for a year with the U.S. Army in Iraq during Operation Iraqi Freedom and was awarded the Bronze Star for meritorious service in combat. He is a graduate of the University of Iowa and its college of law, and he served in the Iowa Legislature for fourteen years. He is currently a partner with the public affairs firm Lincoln Strategies Group. Chuck, his wife, and their two sons live in Des Moines, Iowa.